Ethnic American Cooking

Ethnic American Cooking

Recipes for Living in a New World

Edited by
Lucy M. Long

ROWMAN & LITTLEFIELD
Lanham • Boulder • New York • London

Published by Rowman & Littlefield
A wholly owned subsidary of The Rowman & Littlefield Publishing Group, Inc.
4501 Forbes Boulevard, Suite 200, Lanham, Maryland 20706
www.rowman.com

Unit A, Whitacre Mews, 26-34 Stannary Street, London SE11 4AB

British Library Cataloguing in Publication Information Available

Library of Congress Cataloging-in-Publication Data
Names: Long, Lucy M., 1956- author.
Title: Ethnic American cooking : recipes for living in a new world / Lucy M. Long.
Description: Lanham : Rowman & Littlefield Publishing Group, Inc., [2016] | Includes bibliographical references and index.
Identifiers: LCCN 2016006179 (print) | LCCN 2016013468 (ebook) | ISBN 9781442267336 (cloth : alk. paper) | ISBN 9781442267343 (Electronic)
Subjects: LCSH: International cooking. | Cooking--United States. | Ethnicity. | LCGFT: Cookbooks.
Classification: LCC TX725.A1 L646 2016 (print) | LCC TX725.A1 (ebook) | DDC 641.50973—dc23
LC record available at http://lccn.loc.gov/2016006179

♾TM The paper used in this publication meets the minimum requirements of American National Standard for Information Sciences—Permanence of Paper for Printed Library Materials, ANSI/NISO Z39.48-1992.

Printed in the United States of America

Contents

v

Acknowledgments

A project like this always requires people working behind the scenes, helping with tasks that are largely administrative and tedious. Holly Howard and Tavia Rowan have provided that support, and I could not have done this without them. Others stepped forward in gathering, revising, and testing recipes. First and foremost among these is Karin Vaneker, but I also want to thank Sue Eleuterio, Christine Haar, Charlie McNabb, and Sarah Tekle.

Introduction
Lucy M. Long

This is not an ordinary cookbook. It is meant to be cooked from, but it is much more. The recipes offer a taste of the multitude of ethnicities making up contemporary American culinary culture. They are "tidbits" of that richness, windows into the complexities and nuances of those cuisines, and mirrors on our own gustatory experiences, tastes, and assumptions. They illustrate how food cultures are fluid and dynamic, adapting to new circumstances and offering new ways for individuals and groups to express their identities, values, histories, and personalities. They also demonstrate that many individuals use food to find or maintain a sense of heritage, create communities around that heritage, and strengthen family relationships as well as the more pragmatic activities of filling one's stomach or making a living and securing financial stability. These recipes show that food nurtures in many ways—physically, socially, emotionally—and that taste can be a personal aesthetic pleasure as well as a reflection of cultural histories.

This is asking a lot from a recipe! Not all of that information is obvious in each one here—we sometimes have to learn how to "read" food—but brief introductions suggest ways in which a recipe represents either the culinary culture of an ethnicity or some of the processes seen in adapting foods to a host country. Ultimately, we hope that this cookbook makes us all more aware of the connections that food offers.

Many of the recipes are reprinted from the two-volume *Ethnic American Food Today: A Cultural Encyclopedia*, published in 2015 by Rowman & Littlefield and also edited by Lucy Long. Additional recipes are given for ethnic groups that did not include one in the encyclopedia, and, in some cases, alternative recipes are given. The *Encyclopedia* was organized by country of origin, and this cookbook does the same. This means that some ethnicities cross over national boundaries or that names of nations have changed, but ethnic identifiers have remained the same, so it is important to look at geographic regions as a whole. These are stated after the country, along with the name used by the group itself. Brief introductions to the recipes are provided, but readers are encouraged to turn to the *Encyclopedia* for comprehensive background on the foodways of immigrants to the United States as well as on the place of that food within American food culture.

Contributors of the recipes come from a range of backgrounds, including culinary historians, food studies scholars, professional chefs, cookbook writers, and home cooks. Many draw from their own experiences and family traditions, while others worked with community scholars or ethnographic data. Many recipes have been "translated" from oral tradition in an attempt to put on paper aspects of cooking done by taste and feel. Also, the recipes have been tested for use in American kitchens with ingredients available in American supermarkets. Some original ingredients are simply not found in the United States, and substitutions are suggested when possible, although, in some cases, it is actually easier to acquire certain ingredients here than in their home countries. Also, some ethnic groups that have been in the United States for extended periods have held on to recipes that are no longer in use in the country of origin or have added ingredients that are unheard of in that country.

Some definitions are helpful here. *Ethnicity* refers to "groupings that were culturally distinguishable from a larger social system of which they formed some part."[1] An important point here is that ethnicity exists within another culture, which in turn partly defines it and shapes the ways in which individuals within that group act out that identity. It is also a perception and emotional sense of belonging to that group. Individuals might have a particular ancestry but not recognize it as part of their personal history or identity—or, ideally, can recognize it and use it as a cultural and aesthetic resource according to different situations. Food is one way in which individuals and groups acknowledge, perform, and negotiate their ethnicity. It is used to define that ethnicity as well as to shape relationships to it.

In this sense, ethnic food plays a significant role in how people live in today's multicultural world. It can help individuals find a place in the present while also maintaining a sense of connection to their past and forging new futures. It can also, though, be turned against them, to pigeonhole them and keep them as outsiders, or to emphasize difference as something negative. Understanding the complexity of ethnic food can help us understand the subtle and not-so-subtle ways in which such divisions are created. While appreciating someone else's food does not automatically lead to appreciation for their culture, it can be a step in that direction. *Ethnic American Cooking* offers these recipes partly with that goal in mind. It also offers them for the aesthetic and sensory pleasures these dishes can give, pleasures that speak to our common humanity. Through preparing and tasting them, we can better see the similarities between cuisines—and individuals—as well as their uniqueness.

Further Reading on Food and Ethnicity in the United States (General Concepts)

Anderson, Lynne Christy. *Breaking Bread: Recipes and Stories from Immigrant Kitchens.* Berkeley: University of California Press, 2010.

Belasco, Warren James, and Philip Scranton. *Food Nations: Selling Taste in Consumer Societies.* New York: Routledge, 2002.

Brown, Linda Keller, and Kay Mussell. *Ethnic and Regional Foodways in the United States: The Performance of Group Identity.* Knoxville: University of Tennessee, 1984.

Denker, Joel. *The World on a Plate: A Tour through the History of America's Ethnic Cuisines.* Boulder, CO: Westview, 2003.

Diner, Hasia R. *Hungering for America: Italian, Irish, and Jewish Foodways in the Age of Migration.* Cambridge, MA: Harvard University Press, 2001.

Gabaccia, Donna R. *We Are What We Eat: Ethnic Food and the Making of Americans.* Cambridge, MA: Harvard University Press, 1998.

Inness, Sherrie A., ed. *Pilaf, Pozole, and Pad Thai: American Women and Ethnic Food.* Amherst: University of Massachusetts, 2001.

Levenstein, Harvey A. *Paradox of Plenty: A Social History of Eating in Modern America.* New York: Oxford University Press, 1993.

Lockwood, William G. "United States: Ethnic Cuisines." In *Encyclopedia of Food and Culture*, volume 3, ed. Solomon H. Katz and William Woys Weaver, 442–46. New York: Charles Scribner's Sons, 2003.

Long, Lucy M., ed. *Culinary Tourism.* Lexington: University of Kentucky Press, 2004.

Long, Lucy M., ed. *The Food and Folklore Reader.* New York: Bloomsbury, 2015.

Oring, Elliott. "Ethnic Groups and Ethnic Folklore." In *Folk Groups and Folklore Genres: An Introduction*, ed. Elliott Oring, 23–44. Logan, UT: Utah State University Press, 1986.

Pillsbury, Richard. *No Foreign Food: The American Diet in Time and Place.* Boulder, CO: Westview, 1998.

Ray, Krishnendu. *The Ethnic Restaurateur.* New York: Bloomsbury, 2016.

Royce, Anya Peterson. *Ethnic Identity: Strategies of Diversity.* Bloomington: Indiana University Press, 1982.

Spivey, Diane M. *The Peppers, Cracklings, and Knots of Wool Cookbook: The Global Migration of African Cuisine.* New York: State University of New York, 1999.

Stern, Stephen, and John Allan Cicala, eds. *Creative Ethnicity: Symbols and Strategies of Contemporary Ethnic Life*. Logan, UT: Utah State University Press, 1991.

Sutton, David. E. *Remembrance of Repasts: An Anthropology of Food and Memory*. Oxford; New York: Berg. 2001.

Wallach, Jennifer Jensen. *How America Eats: A Social History of U.S. Food and Culture*. Lanham, MD: Rowman & Littlefield, 2013.

Zanger, Mark H. *The American Ethnic Cookbook for Students*. Phoenix, AZ: Oryx, 2001.

Encyclopedias and Reference Works

Albala, Ken, ed. *Food Cultures of the World Encyclopedia, Volume 2: Americas*. Westport, CT: Greenwood Press, 2008.

Katz, Solomon H., and William Woys Weaver, eds. *Encyclopedia of Food and Culture*, 3 volumes. New York: Charles Scribner's Sons, 2003.

Long, Lucy M., ed. *Ethnic American Food Today: A Cultural Encyclopedia*, 2 volumes. Lanham, MD: Rowman & Littlefield, 2015.

Smith, Andrew F., ed. *The Oxford Encyclopedia of Food and Drink in America*, 2 volumes. Oxford: Oxford University Press, 2004.

Lucy M. Long, Editor

Note

1. As defined by the Oxford Dictionary, quoted by Elliott Oring, "Ethnic Groups and Ethnic Folklore," in *Folk Groups and Folklore Genres: An Introduction* (Logan: University of Utah Press, 1986), 24.

Maps

Political Map of the World

Africa

North and South America

Central America and the Caribbean

Asia

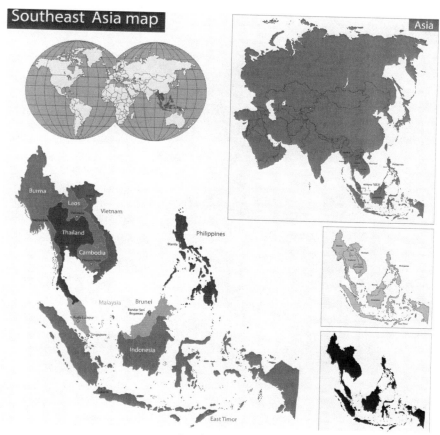

Southeast Asia

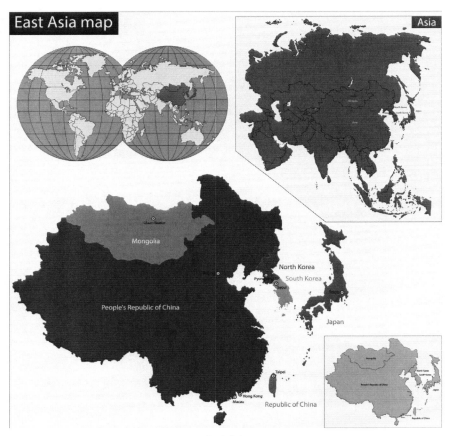

East Asia

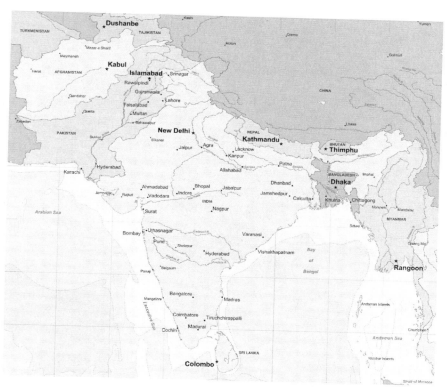

Indian Subcontinent

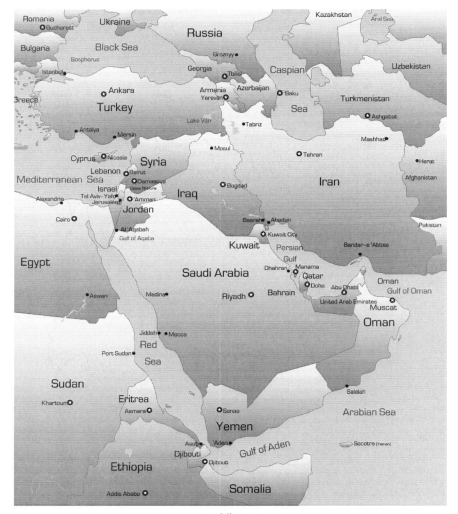

Middle East

Russia and Central Asia

Great Britain and Europe

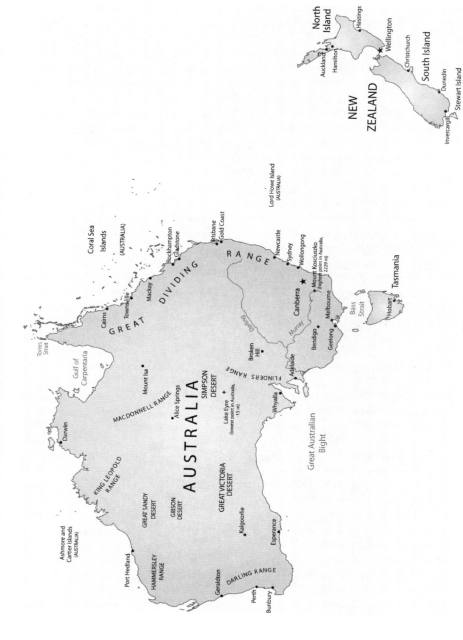

Oceania

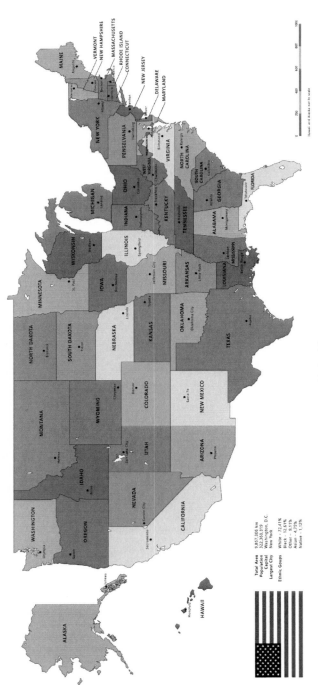

United States

A

Afghanistan (Southern Asia), Afghan American

Afghan food culture shares much in common with the surrounding cultures of Central Asia. Kebabs and other grilled meats and vegetables have a significant place in the diet, along with rice, bread, and yogurt. In the United States, Afghan Americans frequently find familiar ingredients and dishes in restaurants and groceries belonging to Pakistani and Indian Americans.

Roht is a thick and hearty cake that is often served with tea. This family recipe was brought to the United States in 1981 and evokes memories of the weekly Sunday ritual of the grandmother making these by hand while children played alongside her in the kitchen.

Roht (Hearty cake)

3 cups all-purpose flour
1 cup vegetable oil
2 eggs
3 tablespoons full-fat plain yogurt
1 cup sugar
½ cup of warm water
8 ounce packet of yeast
1 teaspoons cardamom

Thoroughly mix the flour, sugar, yeast, and cardamom together. (A food processor can be used, but it is traditionally mixed by hand.)

Gradually add yogurt, eggs, oil, and warm water to the mixture. Knead for about 15 to 20 minutes until a smooth dough forms. Shape the dough into a ball and place in a large bowl. Cover with a dishtowel and let rest for 2 hours until the dough has adequately risen.

Splitting the dough into two parts, roll out each section of the dough into an oblong shape with a thickness of about ½ inch.

Bake at 400°F for about 20 to 25 minutes until the *roht* achieves a golden color. Cool before cutting. Can be sprinkled with powdered sugar and served with tea.

Narwan Aimen
(See "Afghanistan," Narwan Aimen, *EAFT*, pp. 15–18.)

⁓

African American (North America), Soul Food, African American Food

African Americans are the descendants of (mostly) enslaved West, Central, and Southeast Africans brought to what is now the United States between the sixteenth and nineteenth centuries. The genetic and cultural base of African American history and culture is centered on interactions between Africans, Western Europeans, and Native Americans along the Eastern seaboard, and most pronounced in the colonial and antebellum South. The definition of who is African American includes those individuals grandfathered into this ethnic group by historical or family connection and by choice, often excluding self-identified African immigrants, Afro-Latinos, and West Indian or Afro-Caribbean, who are frequently misidentified as African Americans based on phenotype. Historically, African American cuisine was largely centered on West and Central African foodways—a large swath of the African coastline with a remarkably similar culinary pattern based on starches (yams, millet, bananas, plantains, *fonio*, sorghum, rice, and later cassava, corn, and sweet potatoes), and leafy greens, fresh fruit, soups, stews, and roasted or fried foods. Contemporary African American culinary culture has deep connections with southern "white" (British and German based), Creole, and Cajun cooking, but it has a reach beyond regions given the migratory patterns of African Americans in the late nineteenth through mid-twentieth centuries. The phrase *soul food* started being applied to it in the 1960s as a way to identify it as a distinctive cuisine with its own history and aesthetics. Today, the term is generally used to refer to African American food culture and is useful in distinguishing it from ethnic African cuisines being introduced into and adapted in the United States. Soul food now has numerous variations of its own, and recipes are adapted to fit any dietary need, as demonstrated in the recipe below.

Pan-Roasted Collard Sprouts

With permission from Michael Twitty, http://afroculinaria.com/2013/04/19/the-glory-of-spring-pan-roasted-collard-sprouts/.

"There's nothing really special about sautéed greens. It's a fact. It's a platitude of earthy, seasonal, farm-to-table cooking. It's a revelation to anyone who eats canned or frozen greens of any sort. It just is."

Fat element: choose according to taste and personal preference:
  4 slices country bacon cooked to render grease (drain it, cool it, chop it into little bits) or 4 slices beef, lamb, or duck bacon with a little oil added, cooked to render grease + 2 tablespoons of margarine or butter (drain it, cool it, chop it into little bits)
  or 3 tablespoons olive oil and 2 tablespoons of butter
  or 3–4 tablespoons olive oil
  or 2 tablespoons margarine
  or 4 tablespoons olive oil—no butter or margarine
  ½ pound of fresh, whole raw collard sprouts
  2 tablespoons minced shallot
  ¼ cup chopped white or yellow onion
  Kosher or sea salt and red or black pepper to taste

Put your choice of fat in the pan. Cook and render your meat fat or just put the olive oil and butter and margarine in the pan. Note: If using meat, render the grease first, then when the vegetables go in, add the margarine or butter.

Add the shallots and onion to the pan, and gently sauté. Keep the heat medium-low, cook the shallot and onion halfway, and then add the collard sprouts. Add the chopped bacon to the pan and toss around. Cook until glazey, gold on the edges and a little wilted or about 10 minutes total. Add salt and red or black pepper to taste.

Michael Twitty
(See "African American," Michael Twitty, *EAFT*, pp. 18–23.)

～

Albania (Eastern Europe), Albanian American Food

Albanian American foods tend to be similar to those found in the Mediterranean, especially the Levant region, with a heavy use of olive oil, tomatoes, cheese, and fresh herbs. They also share some ingredients and dishes with Greece, Turkey, Italy, and the Balkan countries. Albanians consume a wide variety of different meats. Lamb is a favorite but can be replaced with beef or goat. Pork is found but lacks prominence in the largely Muslim culture.

Stews such as the one created in this recipe are called *gjelle*. Albanian Americans would likely omit goat meat and, depending on the individual, use pork. The use of "low-salt" broth and redskin potatoes also reflects the use of ingredients more frequently found in American grocery stores than those in the Balkans.

Gjelle (Meat and potatoes in sauce)

1 pound beef or lamb
1 medium onion, chopped
1 green bell pepper, chopped
1 stalk celery, diced fine
6 garlic cloves, minced
¼ cup olive oil
¾ cup dry red wine
1 tablespoon tomato paste
¾ cup low-sodium beef or chicken broth
3 pounds redskin potatoes, cut into 1-inch cubes
2 tablespoons chopped parsley
Salt and black pepper to taste

Cut meat into large cubes and season with salt and pepper. Set aside in a small bowl. Sauté onion, bell pepper, and celery in oil until they begin to soften. Add garlic and continue to sauté until it begins to change color. Add meat and brown. Add tomato paste. Deglaze the pan with wine and add the parsley. Transfer ingredients to an ovenproof dish; cover and bake for 30 minutes at 325°F. Heat the broth and add it, along with the potatoes, to the dish. Season with salt and pepper and continue baking until potatoes are tender.

Charles Baker-Clark
(See "Albania," Charles Baker-Clark, *EAFT*, pp. 23–24.)

~

Algeria (North Africa), Algerian American Food

Algerian cuisine is an amalgam of Turkish, Berber, French, and Islamic influences and shares ingredients, dishes, and flavorings with Tunisia, Morocco, and Libya. As in Morocco, couscous (steamed crushed wheat) is the national dish. It is eaten every Friday, the day of the big family meal, and at any big celebration like weddings or funerals, but it is also a primary daily food item. *Mechoui*, roasted lamb, is just as important as couscous. The head is removed and the lamb is spiced and slow-roasted on a spit. The meat is then served with *harisa* (chili sauce), bread, fries, and salad, and occasionally with veggies and couscous. Stews, consisting of a vegetable sauce and usually lamb but occasionally chicken, are also a popular dish. Common vegetables include turnips, carrots, pumpkins, summer squash, tomatoes, and potatoes.

Algerian Americans continue to rely on couscous as a staple, but many use the preprocessed and packaged mixes available in most supermarkets since the traditional preparation of couscous takes several days of washing, cooking, and stirring the grains. Eggs also provide a quick protein source in place of lamb or beef and are a traditional part of breakfast. Beans (stewed or mashed) are commonly eaten at breakfast in Algeria, as they are throughout north African and west Asian cultures, and at least one Algerian American restaurant offers a "North African Breakfast," a traditional bowl of bean stew, topped with a fried egg and harisa sauce. In Algeria it is not uncommon to use more bell peppers than tomatoes, and to prepare *chakchouka* with eggplant and zucchini.

Chakchouka (Shakshouka) (Eggs in pepper and tomato sauce)
Recipe by Karin Vaneker

    1 medium onion, chopped
    2 garlic cloves, crushed
    1 teaspoon sweet (smoked) paprika powder
    1 red bell pepper, diced
    6 tomatoes, diced (canned tomatoes can be used)
    1 teaspoon salt
    ½ teaspoon black pepper, crushed
    4 tablespoon olive oil
    4 eggs

Heat the oil in a large skillet. Add the chopped onion and sauté for 3 to 5 minutes. Add the garlic, and stir in the salt and sweet paprika powder, and simmer for 1 minute. Put the bell pepper pieces in the skillet; stir and sauté for 2 to 3 minutes. Add the tomatoes, stir well, cover the skillet, and simmer over low heat for 15 to 30 minutes, stirring occasionally. Break the eggs over the tomato sauce, spaced well apart, then cover and simmer for 4 to 5 minutes. Season the eggs with salt and pepper and serve warm with crusty bread.

Emily Hilliard
(See "Algeria," Emily Hilliard, *EAFT*, pp. 24–27.)

Amish (North America), Amish

The Amish originated in Switzerland with roots in the Protestant Reformation in the Anabaptist movement that started in 1525. Differences in doctrine lead to a split in 1693 within the Swiss Anabaptists into Mennonite and the followers of Jacob Ammann, the Amish. Religious persecution caused the Amish to leave their homeland in Switzerland and the lower Rhine Valley and, eventually, Europe altogether. They came to North America in two waves, in the mid-1700s and again in the early 1800s. There are no longer any Amish in Europe, but there are Amish communities in twenty-eight states, primarily in Pennsylvania, Ohio, and Indiana, where they maintain traditional language, religious beliefs, and lifestyles. Their foodways have a reputation for simplicity and wholesomeness, and they are particularly well known for their pies and baked goods. Whoopie pies (not actually a pie, but two large cookies joined with a cream filling) and shoofly pies are distinctive to the Amish and have become iconic.

Shoofly Pie (also called "Wet Bottom" Shoofly Pie)

1 unbaked pie crust/pastry shell
¾ cup light molasses (you may substitute dark Karo syrup or King syrup in place of some or all of the molasses if you prefer)
¾ cup boiling water
1 egg yolk
1 teaspoon baking soda
For the crumbs:
1 ⅓ cup flour
⅔ cup brown sugar
1 teaspoon salt
½ teaspoon cinnamon (some older recipes don't call for any spices beyond the brown sugar, flour, and salt)

¼ teaspoon nutmeg
Pinch cloves
Pinch ginger
3 tablespoons shortening

Mix liquid ingredients together until one consistency (baking soda will foam). Crumbs: Mix dry ingredients together, then cut in shortening until shortening clumps are pea-sized and mixture is well blended. Reserve about half the crumb mixture.

Alternating liquid and crumb, layer in an unbaked piecrust, ending with the reserved crumbs on top. You might also experiment with the layering of the liquid and crumbs (all liquid poured in first, then all the crumbs on top, or layer crumbs first then liquid, etc.). However, crumbs should completely cover the liquid. Bake in a 400 degree oven for 10 minutes (or until pie crust begins to become golden), then reduce heat to 325°F and bake another 20 minutes or until firm. Pie should not jiggle when removed from oven. Allow to rest at least 5 minutes. Best served warm.

Sally Adair Van de Water
(See "Amish," Lucy M. Long, *EAFT*, pp. 28–30.)

∼

Andorra (Southern Europe), Andorran American Food

Andorra is a tiny country in the Pyrenees Mountains between Spain and France. Known for tourism, financial prosperity, and having the second highest life expectancy in the world, Andorrans have little reason to emigrate, and Americans are more likely to move there to join the vibrant ex-pat community. Andorran culture and food is traditionally Catalan, an ethnicity prevalent in northeastern Spain.

La Trucha à la Andorrana (Fried trout with dry-cured ham)

8 thin slices of dry-cured Spanish ham (Serrano)
4 trout, with head, cleaned (filets can be used, but whole fish is preferred)
4 tablespoons white (wheat) flour
2 teaspoons salt
¼ teaspoon pepper
Olive oil

Put 2 tablespoons of olive oil in an 11-inch skillet or frying pan and pan-fry the Spanish ham on medium-high heat until crisp on both sides.

Remove the ham and fat from the skillet and clean the skillet with a paper towel.

Mix the flour with the salt and pepper on a plate and pass the trout through the flour (shake off the excess but make sure the trout is covered with flour).

Heat 3 tablespoons of olive oil in the skillet, arrange the trout in the skillet, and cook until golden brown, about 5 to 6 minutes per side on medium-high heat.

Serve hot and arrange two slices of ham on each trout.

Lucy M. Long and Karin Vaneker
(See "Andorra," *EAFT*, pp. 30–31.)

〜

Angola (Middle Africa), Angolan American Food

Located in the southernwestern part of middle Africa, Angola became a center of the trans-Atlantic slave trade under Portuguese rule. Over five million Angolans are estimated to have been taken from there to North and South America, and it is a significant heritage for many African Americans. African culinary traditions brought to the United States by these individuals were incorporated into southern cooking, but the cultural identity of those traditions has been obscured and unrecognized. The peanut (also known as groundnut) is a significant food item throughout much of Sub-Saharan Africa. Originating in South America, it was probably first taken there by European explorers where it joined a repertoire of other legumes, and was then brought to North America, probably by slaves. Toward the end of the 1800s, a number of people, including Dr. John Harvey Kellogg (creator of Kellogg cereals), experimented with making a paste from peanuts, probably not recognizing similarities with the peanut paste used in much African cooking. It was a former slave, however, George Washington Carver, who, in the 1910s and 1920s, promoted peanut products, and he is popularly thought of as the inventor of peanut butter. Peanut butter frequently appears in the cooking of contemporary African immigrants to the United States.

Kizaca (or Quizaca) (Cassava leaves and peanut butter stew)

2 pounds cassava leaves (or spinach)
1 cup peanut butter
1 teaspoon salt

Palm oil

Chili pepper

½ lb. dried, smoked fish or dry prawns (optional)

Wash the fish, place in a bowl, cover with boiling water, and set aside for about 20 minutes. Drain, again cover with boiling water, and set aside for 60 minutes. Drain, cool, and by hand remove the bones from the fish, and break the meat into pieces.

Wash the cassava leaves and pat them dry. Chop or cut the leaves in small pieces. Put the leaves in a soup pot, cover with water, add salt, bring to a boil, and simmer for about 60 minutes, until the cassava is tender. Drain the leaves and put back in the pot. In a bowl, mix the peanut butter with 1 cup of lukewarm water, and add to the leaves. Season with salt, palm oil, and add the fish pieces, and cover with water and simmer until the water is almost reduced. Serve with rice, *funje* (cassava flour porridge), boiled plantains, or (boiled) cassava pieces.

Lucy M. Long and Karin Vaneker
(See "Angola," Lucy M. Long and Susan Eleuterio, *EAFT*, pp. 31–32.)

∼

Argentina (South America), Argentine American Food

Argentine cuisine is characterized by heavy beef consumption, and this carries over easily to an American setting. The five key spices are similarly familiar to Americans: nutmeg, bay leaf, oregano, paprika, and cayenne. *Empanadas*, half-moon-shaped hand-held pies typically filled with meat and vegetables, are a "signature" dish of Argentinian Americans, popular for everyday as well as celebratory meals. They also are popular snacks. Although meat pies are found throughout the world, hard-boiled eggs and green olives give these empanadas a distinctive taste.

Beef *Empanadas* (Meat pies)

750 grams (6 cups) all-purpose flour

1 cup beef fat or butter

Coarse salt

Boiling water

1.5 kilo (3.3 pounds) of a flesh-cut rump or sirloin ball

2 onions

3 cloves of garlic
1 handful of green onions
4 hard-boiled eggs
1½ cups green olives
Salt and pepper
Chili powder
Paprika
Cumin
2½ tablespoons olive oil
One egg yolk

Dough: Place flour on counter, make an indention in the middle. Prepare a brine of boiling water with 1 to 2 tablespoons of salt and let cool. Melt fat in a frying pan and let cool slightly (but not until it is solid). Pour fat and a few tablespoons of brine into the flour. Add brine as necessary until the flour is all worked in and you have a fairly stiff dough. Roll dough out with a rolling pin, and cut discs 4 inches in diameter. Allow dough to cool.

Filling: Dice meat and chop the onion, green onion, and garlic. Julienne the green olives. Sauté onion, garlic, and green onions in oil.

In a separate bowl, mix 1 teaspoon paprika, 1 teaspoon chili powder, 2½ tablespoons of cumin, and 3 tablespoons of cold water. Add spice paste to the sautéed onions.

Add meat and sauté, stirring occasionally. Remove from heat when the meat is cooked but still juicy. Add seasoning to taste. Let cool 2 hours in the refrigerator.

Fill empanada pastry circles with a heaping tablespoon of filling, an olive, and an ⅛ of an egg. Fold the pastry over and seal edges with a bit of water. At this point, either paint the pies with egg yolk and bake in a hot oven until golden brown or fry pies in a deep pan.

Eat empanadas hot with red wine.

Emily Ridout
(See "Argentina," Emily Ridout, *EAFT*, pp. 32–35.)

⌁

Armenia (Western Asia), Armenian American Food

This pilaf typically accompanies Armenian meat and vegetable dishes, but it can be used as a side dish for almost any occasion. The Golden Grain

Macaroni Company created the still-popular brand Rice-a-Roni in the 1940s based on a traditional pilaf recipe by Armenian American Pailadzo Captanian. The "San Francisco Treat" from an Italian American company is really an Armenian dish.

Pilaf (Rice)

4 ounces butter (2 ounces melted)
4 ounces thin spaghetti or vermicelli, broken into 1-inch lengths
1¼ cups long-grain white rice (Carolina brand, if possible)
1 quart (4 cups) chicken stock
Minced parsley
Nuts (pine nuts, walnuts, or almonds) for sprinkling (optional)

Melt half the butter over medium heat in a large pot. Add the pasta and brown, being careful not to burn. Add the rice and stir to coat, about one minute. Add the stock and bring to a boil. Adjust heat to very low. Cover and cook, checking for desired consistency after 20 minutes. Cook slightly longer uncovered if too soupy. Let sit five minutes, fluff with fork, and then turn out onto plate. Top with melted butter, parsley, and optional nuts, and then serve.

Arthur Lizie
(See "Armenia," Arthur Lizie, EAFT, pp. 35–37.)

～

Austria (Western Europe), Austrian American Food

Sachertorte and Wiener Schnitzel are well regarded as quintessential Austrian dishes, and Austrian restaurants on both sides of the Atlantic serve both items because of their instant name recognition. These foods are eaten all year round in Austria, although the Sachertorte is usually reserved for special occasions, or a trip to the Sacher Hotel. In the United States, however, there is less adherence to tradition. Some cooks opt to leave out the layer of apricot preserves from the center of the Sachertorte, and others might substitute chicken for the more expensive and controversial veal in Wiener Schnitzel. However, even with small alterations, these Austrian delicacies fill you up on a cold winter's day. Pair the Sachertorte with a strong cup of your favorite coffee and your Wiener Schnitzel with a nice cold glass of Grüner Veltliner (Austrian white wine).

Sachertorte (Cake)

Preheat oven to 325°F and have a 9-inch, ungreased, removable-rim (Springform) pan.

5 to 6 ounces semisweet chocolate, grated
½ cup sugar
½ cup butter
6 egg yolks
¾ cup dry breadcrumbs
¼ cup finely ground blanched almonds
¼ teaspoon salt
6 egg whites
Apricot preserves (optional)
Strong coffee

Cream granulated sugar with butter. Beat in egg yolks, one at a time, until the mixture is light and fluffy. Add grated chocolate to this mixture as well as dry breadcrumbs and almonds, along with ¼ teaspoon of salt. Beat until stiff, but not dry, and fold in 6 egg whites.

Pour into ungreased pan and bake for 50 minutes to an hour. When cool, slice the torte horizontally through the middle and place 1 cup apricot preserves in between the layers.

To make the glaze, melt 7 ounces of semisweet chocolate in a double boiler with 1 tablespoon of butter. Bring to a boil ¾ cup of sugar and ⅓ cup of water (3 tablespoons of which should be strong coffee), and then pour this syrup into the chocolate slowly while stirring constantly. Pour this mixture over the cake. Be careful to pour the glaze all at once as it hardens immediately. Serve cake slices with whipped cream.

Wiener Schnitzel (Viennese cutlet)

6 to 8 ounce pieces of veal, pork, or chicken
Salt and pepper
Flour for dusting
2 eggs, plus 2 tablespoons milk, beaten, for egg wash
Matzo Meal or breadcrumbs
Lard, butter, or olive oil for frying
Parsley (optional)

Take veal pieces and pound with a meat cleaver until they are as thin as possible without tearing. Season them with salt and pepper. Lay flat on both sides in the flour. Dip in egg wash and coat with breadcrumbs. Using a 9-inch skillet, deep fry in lard, or a combination of butter and olive oil. Cook until golden brown on both sides and cooked all the way through (approximately 3–4 minutes per side). Transfer to paper towels to blot for excess grease. Garnish with lemon wedges and parsley.

Anne Flannery
(See "Austria," Anne Flannery, *EAFT*, pp. 41–44.)

～

Azerbaijan (Western Asia), Azerbaijani American Food

Although technically part of western Asia, Azerbaijan shares little in common with the cultures of the Arabian Peninsula. It is part of the Caucasus region bordered by Armenia, Georgia, Iran, and Russia, with an extensive coast on the Caspian Sea. As such, Azerbaijani Americans identify more with those cultures than with cultures typically thought of in the United States as typical Middle Eastern ones. The languages spoken also indicate cultural affiliations: American English, Azerbaijani, Russian, Persian, and Turkish.

The Azerbaijani diet traditionally emphasizes meats, including lamb, mutton, beef, and poultry. Vegetables include roots such as potatoes as well as cabbage and beets. Bread is a staple part of the daily diet. Rice is also popular and is frequently prepared as a pilaf and served fried with various meats.

Chyghyrtma (The name means "crying," the sound of frying chicken)

1 whole frying chicken
Cold water as needed
1 tablespoon peppercorns
2 yellow onions, medium size
Juice of one lemon
2 eggs, large
4 tablespoons whole milk
2 tablespoons butter
2 tablespoons olive oil, extra virgin
Salt and pepper to taste

Place whole chicken in a large saucepan and cover with cold water. Add peppercorns. Poach the chicken in the water until nearly done. Remove from heat and permit chicken to cool. When the chicken has cooled, cut it into quarters, pat dry with a paper towel, and set aside. Reserve the cooking liquid. In a medium-sized bowl, lightly beat the eggs and mix in the milk. Peel and slice the onions. Heat butter and olive oil in a large skillet. When butter and oil begin to sizzle, add the sliced onions a handful at a time. As the onions begin to change color, add the chicken pieces and brown on all sides. Sprinkle the chicken with lemon juice. Pour the egg and milk mixture over the chicken and onion and add ½ cup of the reserved poaching liquid. Continue to sauté until the eggs are finished to desired consistency, stirring as needed.

The leftover broth can be used as soup.

Serve with warm bread, such as Turkish *Pide*, and roasted potatoes.

Charles Baker-Clark
(See "Azerbaijan," Charles Baker-Clark, *EAFT*, pp. 44–46.)

B

Bahamas (Americas-Caribbean), Bahamian American Food

Bahamian cuisine is perhaps most famous for its preparations of conch, a large mollusk with a spiral shell. The variety consumed in the Bahamas is the Queen Conch, and it must be tenderized or "cracked" before consuming by pounding it. The two favorite preparations are conch fritters, in which the meat is finely diced and mixed into a seasoned batter with onions and herbs before being fried in small balls, and conch salad, in which it is chopped and mixed with citrus juice and chopped vegetables. Conch also features in stews, soups, and a popular chowder. Grouper is the most popular fish and can be served fried or grilled, although it is most popular boiled and served with grits as a breakfast dish. Also popular for breakfast is johnny cake, consisting of wheat flour, butter, milk, sugar, and baking powder baked in a large, round pan and sliced. Pork chops, oxtails, and goat also make appearances on the Bahamian table. Popular side dishes include a mayonnaise-based potato salad, baked macaroni and cheese, and fried sweet plantains.

Conch Salad

1 pound raw conch meat, chopped
1 cup white onion, chopped
1 cup green bell pepper, chopped
½ cup celery, chopped
½ cup tomato, peeled and chopped

½ cup lime juice
¼ cup olive oil (optional)
1 tablespoon Worcestershire sauce
Salt, pepper, hot sauce to taste

Combine all ingredients in a large bowl. Let marinade for at least 3 hours, but preferably overnight. This keeps in the refrigerator for 4–5 days.

Carlos C. Olaechea
(See "Bahamas," Carlos C. Olaechea, *EAFT*, pp. 47–50.)

⁓

Bangladesh (Southern Asia), Bangladeshi American, Bengali American Food

Bangladesh, the country of the Bengali language, has a rich culinary culture that it shares with the state of West Bengal in India. Bengali food is an important aspect of the Bengali identity both among Bangladeshi Muslims and their Hindu neighbors in India. The importance of fish defines the Bengali diet, and the availability of traditional fish is one of the striking features that distinguish Bangladeshi ethnic stores from Indian ones in the United States. The former always have large refrigerators filled with frozen fish lining a large portion of the store. Traditionally, Bengali food is cooked in mustard oil, however, in the United States, vegetable or olive oil is commonly used. Fish, usually cooked in a gravy sauce called *jhol* or *jhaal* (if spicy hot), is the staple dish of Bangladesh, and Bangladeshi and Indian Bengali immigrants have continued that tradition. Tilapia is one of the most popular fish used, although it would be prepared whole. Bengalis like their fish "boney," but fish in the United States is more often sold as fillets. Also, Bengali children raised in the United States are not used to eating boney fish, nor have they mastered the techniques for eating it, so many Bengali families have adapted to using fillets. The following recipe is adapted from Nasrin Banu, a Bangladeshi woman who lives in Central New Jersey.

Fish *Jhol* (Fish in sauce)
4 servings

Any large whole fish or fillets (tipalia, catfish, or salmon)
1 onion
4 tomatoes

½ teaspoon ginger, powdered (fresh is preferred)
½ teaspoon *haldi* (turmeric powder)
½ teaspoon red chili powder
½ teaspoon *jeera* (cumin)
¼ cup fresh cilantro
¼ teaspoon *mirchi* (green pepper)
Oil, vegetable or olive

Take any big fish and cut it into 1-inch pieces. Marinate it with *haldi*, red chili powder, and salt. Then shallow-fry it in oil, remove, and keep aside. For the *jhol* (curry), cut and fry pieces of onions in the pan. Add red chili powder, *haldi*, ginger, and *jeera*. When onion gets fried a bit, add pieces of tomatoes. Stir for a few minutes, then add the 1-inch pieces of the fried fish. Add some water. Lower the heat and let it simmer for a bit. Before taking the pan off the heat, add some freshly cut cilantro and pieces of *mirchi* (green pepper). Serve hot with rice.

Puja Sahney
(See "Bangladesh," Puja Sahney, *EAFT*, pp. 50–55.)

⁓

Barbados (Caribbean Americas), Barbadian or Bajan American

One of the most popular dishes in Barbados is Cou Cou served with flying fish, which is native to the island and usually prepared by frying. Cou Cou is a type of polenta (cooked cornmeal), which has popular variations throughout the Caribbean. In the United States, those from Barbados as well as other Caribbean islands enjoy cooking and eating Cou Cou for the power of its flavors to transport them back to the native aromas of their country. In the United States, cornmeal is used along with other ingredients that are easily available.

Cou Cou (Polenta with okra)

2 cups of cornmeal
Water
1 cup okra, or frozen okra, sliced into rings after cutting the tops and bottoms off
1 onion, diced

4 tablespoons of butter
Salt and black pepper, to taste

Place all of the cornmeal in a bowl and fill with enough water to moisten it; cover it, slightly, with water. Stir and set aside. Place the sliced okra in a pan. Add 2 cups of water, chopped onion, and salt. Bring to a boil. When the water begins to boil, reduce the heat to medium and boil until the okra has softened (approximately 5 to 10 minutes). Strain the okra and set the strained liquid aside in a bowl. Add about ⅓ of the reserved liquid into the pan and add the now softened cornmeal. Whisk the *Cou Cou* until it is cooked through. Gradually add the rest of the remaining liquid. You will know the *Cou Cou* is cooked when it starts to lightly bubble on the top. Stir in the okra and butter with salt and pepper to taste. Remove from heat and serve.

Alexandria Ayala
(See "Barbados," Elinor Levy, *EAFT*, pp. 55–56.)

⁓

Basque (Southern Europe), Basque American Food

The autonomous Basque Country is nestled in the inner elbow between northeastern Spain and southwestern France. Politically a region in Spain, it has its own distinctive language, history, and culture. Basques have settled in the western part of the United States, particularly in Idaho, where they have continued traditions of sheep herding along with other cultural forms, including foodways. Many Basques believe that this simple garlic soup is a common cure for a head cold or the flu. Another highly recommended use is to relieve a hangover the morning after.

True codfish, or *bacalao*, inhabit the North Atlantic waters. Basque fishermen have caught, consumed, and sold this fish for centuries, and Basque cooks have a two-part preparation for this traditional main dish, reconstituting the dried, salted cod). The method may also be used with thawed, frozen cod.

In Spain an omelet is called a *tortilla*, with a rolled "r" pronunciation. The Mexican *tortilla* is pronounced flatly, and the two are very different dishes. In Mexico, the tortilla is a flatbread of cornmeal or flour. In Spain, the tortilla is varied, but a favorite is the potato omelet often served with slices of toasted baguette.

Bereakasopia (Garlic soup)

1 to 2 tablespoons mild vegetable or olive oil
1 or 2 cloves of garlic, chopped
¼ teaspoon ground chili pepper
2 to 3 cups water
2 to 3 slices dried bread
Optional *chorizo* sausage

Brown the chopped garlic in the hot oil. Add the bread and water; let it soak. Add chili pepper and stir gently. Serve hot. Chorizo may be added if desired.

Bacalao a la Viscaya (Cod in tomato sauce)

1 ½ pound dried, salted codfish
Mild olive oil
1 clove garlic, minced
1 large onion, sliced
Canned tomato sauce
Purchased hot or sweet pepper sauce

Desalt the codfish by soaking for 24 hours in water. Change the water as often as possible. Drain the cod and press firmly to remove the water. Brown the garlic and onion in oil, add the cod, and cook slowly. When the cod has cooked for about 10 minutes, serve with tomato sauce flavored with the red pepper seasoning.

Tortilla de Patatas (Potato omelette)

4 large or 5 small eggs
2 cups of diced or thinly sliced potatoes
Salt and pepper
½ onion, finely chopped
1 clove garlic, crushed
½ cup cooking oil

Prepare the potatoes, onion, and garlic and set aside. Heat oil in sauté or omelette pan. Cook at a medium heat. Add the potatoes and cook until partially soft, and then add onion and garlic. Salt to taste. Beat eggs well, add salt and pepper to taste, and add to the potato mixture. Continue to cook, jiggling the pan a little to make sure it is not sticking. When the bottom of the mixture is slightly browned, place a plate over the top of the pan and turn the tortilla onto the plate. Slide the upturned tortilla back into the pan and cook slowly until the vegetable and egg mixture is firm. Serves two.

Jaqueline Thursby
(See "Basque," Jaqueline Thursby, *EAFT*, pp. 56–61.)

⌢

Belarus (Eastern Europe), Belarusian American Food

While immigrants from Belarus have arrived in America since the colonial period, definitive numbers are difficult to track because Belarusians have often been identified with other cultures, particularly Russian. Waves of immigrants from this country arrived during the early twentieth century, before and after World War II, and following the collapse of the Soviet Union. Concentrations of Belarusian Americans have settled in areas around New York City and New Jersey as well as Detroit. A Belarusian American Association helps maintain social networks, and there is a Belarusian cultural center in Strongsville, Ohio.

The traditional foodways of Belarus strongly reflect the influence of the surrounding (and more powerful) cultures of Russia, Poland, and Lithuania. Potatoes, onions, cabbage, pulses (dried beans), grains, and sausages (*vereshchaka*) make up a large part of the diet. Belarusian Americans brought those culinary traditions with them. *Draniki* (potato pancakes) are part of their everyday diet. One aspect of this recipe that makes it unique to Belarus and other adjoining cultures is that the potatoes and onion are grated together.

Draniki (Potato pancakes)

6 potatoes, Russet or Idaho, medium size
1 yellow onion, medium
2 garlic cloves
Vegetable oil for frying
Salt and pepper to taste

Peel and grate potatoes and onions. Use a grater with small holes so that the product will be closer to a mush than shreds. Peel and mince garlic. Combine ingredients. Add salt and pepper to taste. Heat a small quantity of oil in a skillet. Place small quantities of the mixture on the skillet and shape into small pancakes. Fry until brown on one side and turn to brown the other, approximately 2 to 3 minutes per side. Adjust seasoning with salt and pepper as needed.

These may be served warm or included in other dishes such as meat stews.

Charles Baker-Clark
(See "Belarus," Charles Baker-Clark, *EAFT*, pp. 61–63.)

∼

Belgium (Western Europe), Belgian American Food

Belgium comprises three regions: Dutch-speaking Flanders to the north, French-speaking Wallonia to the south, and between them bilingual Brussels, the capital. There is also a small German-speaking community on the eastern border of the Walloon region. The regions share common foodways and embrace regional variations, reflecting centuries of inspiration and exchange with neighboring states. Belgium's foodways are linked to French and Dutch cuisine, with German influences, featuring meat, seafood, leeks, asparagus, potatoes, cheese, and beer as favorite ingredients, and waffles and chocolate are featured desserts. The food can be both hearty and delicate.

Belgian Americans, particularly those who live in rural enclaves, have maintained and modified their culinary traditions. Rural Belgian American foodways are seasonal and regional. Favorite meats are roast chicken, veal, sausages, and beef served as stew, meatloaf, or meatballs (*boulettes*); shellfish and fish such as smoked herring or fried perch, the latter with a sauce made of the fond (the pan remains); and vegetables that feature potatoes, root crops, leeks, and cabbage. Yeasted specialties include breads, pies, waffles, and beer. Fruits, such as apples and cherries, both locally grown in the Upper Midwest, are in pies and other cooked sweets. Urban Belgian American foodways emphasize mussels, *frites* (double-fried potatoes), and fine chocolate imported from Belgium.

Jut or Djote (Cabbage side dish)

1 medium savoy cabbage
3 strips bacon, diced
1 medium onion, diced (optional)
Salt and pepper to taste

Boil cabbage until tender but not limp. Cool. Drain all liquid. Sauté bacon and onion in skillet. Cut cabbage into thin slices. Sauté in pan with bacon. Season with salt and pepper.

A variant recipe, called *stoemp* in Flemish, combines the green vegetable with potatoes:

Stoemp (Cabbage with potatoes)

5 large potatoes, peeled and cut into chunks
1 medium cauliflower, broken into florets
1 medium head of cabbage (about 2 cups chopped cabbage)
1 medium fennel bulb, diced
3 medium leeks, cleaned and sliced into ½-inch rounds
4 tablespoons butter
¼ cup cream
½ cup vegetable broth
Salt and pepper to taste
Nutmeg to taste

Boil potatoes and cauliflower. When soft, drain and mash. Set aside. Sauté fennel bulb and leeks in butter for about 3 minutes. Add cabbage and sauté until soft and leek rings separate. Add vegetable broth. Add cream to taste. Simmer for about 10 minutes to reduce liquid. Add simmered vegetables and remaining liquid to potatoes and cauliflower. Mix. Add salt, pepper, and nutmeg to taste.

Anne Pryor
(See "Belgium," Anne Pryor, *EAFT*, pp. 63–66.)

⁓

Belize (Central America), Belizean American Food

Rice and beans are staples in Belizean cooking, and the first thing any visitor to Belize learns is that "beans and rice" and "rice and beans" are two different things. Beans and rice refers to plain white rice, preferably cooked with coconut milk, and stewed beans, which are dried beans, normally red kidney beans, but also black beans, black-eyed peas, or split peas cooked in a lot of water, with cumin, black pepper and fresh herbs, salted pig tail, and lots of garlic and onion until it forms a rich gravy. The rice is dished out, and the beans and their delicious gravy are typically spooned over the top. Rice and beans, on the other hand, is a dry mixture of rice and beans cooked together in the same pot. This dish is cooked in a number of countries, but this recipe is specific to Belize. Belizean Americans make this as an everyday dish, but also for celebration meals and as a comfort food that reminds them of home.

Rice and Beans

2 cups dry (uncooked) rice (white or brown)
About 4 cups of coconut milk
1 tablespoon coconut oil (optional)
About 1 cup of cooked, seasoned beans
Salt
Minced fresh oregano or cilantro (optional)

Making rice and beans is very similar to making plain rice. Put two cups of dry rice in a pot, run water over it and wash the rice, pouring out the water until the water runs clear instead of becoming cloudy with starch. Then put enough coconut milk (or water or broth if you don't want coconut rice) in the pot so that it reaches to the first joint on your index finger when the tip of your finger is touching the rice. I like a tablespoon of coconut oil added to the pot as well for extra coconut flavor. Add one cup of cooked beans to the pot as well. Just dump them in and gently stir them in before you even start the burner. Add salt to taste, remembering that if you seasoned your beans when you cooked them previously they may have some salt in them already. Put the pot over high heat with the lid off and let it come to a boil. When it has boiled until there is only a little liquid left over the top of the grains (which usually only takes a few minutes), turn the heat down to very low, add the minced herbs if you are using them, put the lid on, and let simmer for about 20 minutes (30 for brown rice) until the grains have absorbed all the liquid and are not tough or crunchy. Turn off the burner and let the rice and beans sit, covered, for a few minutes before you serve it.

Lyra Spang
(See "Belize," Susan Eleuterio, *EAFT*, pp. 66–68.)

⌒

Benin (Western Africa), Beninese American Food

Beninese American food shares much in common with other culinary cultures from western Africa, with the basic meals being a starch served with sauces and stews. There is also regional diversity within Benin. In the South, the primary staple is maize (corn) along with rice and manioc, eaten with peanut- or tomato-based sauces. Basic meats are chicken (grilled) and fish (smoked), but also beef, goat, and bush rat. Palm oil and peanut oil are used for cooking, as in fried plantains. Also significant are beans, usually cooked as a side dish, tomatoes, and fruit, such as oranges, bananas, kiwi, avocado, and pineapples.

In the North, yams are usually pounded into *fufu*, and millet and sorghum are the staple grains. Beef and pork are common meats, and a soft, mild cow's milk cheese (*wagasi*) is distinctive to the Fulani people who live there. Fruits include mangos, oranges, and avocados, and vegetables include okra, tomatoes, pumpkin seeds, peanuts, and eggplants. Chili peppers are also used and made into pastes and sauces.

Many of these ingredients can be purchased in the United States, although produce tends to have a slightly different taste. A ubiquitous ingredient throughout western Africa is Maggi bouillon cubes, introduced in 1908 by a Swiss entrepreneur and produced in Germany. The company merged with Nestle in 1947, and their products are now available in supermarkets in the United States, although they are frequently in international sections. *Piment* paste is also commercially produced but can be made at home by blending very hot chili peppers with onions, oil, vinegar, and fresh ginger.

Sauce d'Arachide (Peanut sauce with chilis)

3 tablespoons peanut oil
2 tablespoons tomato puree
2 teaspoons *piment* paste (chopped hot pepper can substitute, with the variety of pepper selected according to the spiciness desired)
½ teaspoon salt
1 beef Maggi bouillon cube
½ cup peanut butter (smooth, preferably homemade or natural)
⅓ cup minced onion
½ cup water

Heat oil to medium in a saucepan. Fry the onion and *piment* paste. When onion softens, add tomato puree and Maggi cube. Cook about 3 minutes, then add peanut butter and water. Whisk well and slowly bring to a boil. Reduce to a simmer and, stirring often, cook about 15 minutes or until the mixture thickens to coat the back of a spoon. (A food processor can be used to create a smooth consistency. Traditionally, some cooks would mash the ingredients in a mortar prior to cooking.)

Serve over *fufu* made from pounded yams (boiled then processed until smooth) or *ingame pile* (boiled and pounded malanga root).

Christine Haar
(See "Benin," Lucy M. Long, *EAFT*, pp. 68–69.)

⟅

Bermuda (Northern America), Bermudian American Food

Bermuda is often mistakenly associated with the Caribbean, but its food traditions reflects its status as a British Overseas Territory, the legacy of two hundred years of slavery, and the multiethnic population that has settled there. Imported salted codfish is one of their most common ingredients, featured in fish cakes and other dishes. It is fried up with potatoes for the traditional Sunday breakfast, a weekly occasion continued by Bermudian immigrants in the United States, and often served with hard-boiled eggs, bananas, onions, and avocado. Sherry pepper, a condiment made from hot peppers soaked in sherry, might also be served.

Cod Fish Cakes

1 pound frozen cod fillets
2 large potatoes, peeled and chopped
1 clove of garlic, crushed
1 tablespoon grated sweet onion
1 tablespoon butter
1 egg
1 teaspoon thyme
Pinch of seasoning salt
Pinch of black pepper
Flour (white or potato) for coating
Oil sufficient for pan frying

Boil the potatoes until soft. Thoroughly drain. Steam the cod with the onion and garlic until the cod becomes opaque and begins to flake apart. Mash or rice potatoes with egg, butter, and seasonings. Fold cod into the potato mixture. Chunks of cod should be visible throughout the mix. Chill the mixture in the refrigerator for an hour before handling. Form fish cakes and coat in flour. Pan fry in oil or bake at 400°F until golden brown.

Mathilde Frances Lind
(See "Bermuda," Mathilde Frances Lind, *EAFT*, pp. 69–71.)

⌒

Bhutan (Southern Asia), Bhutanese American Food

Bhutan's national dish, *ema datshi*, brings together two ingredients that are plentiful even at the high altitudes of the Himalayas—*sha ema* (chili peppers) and yak's cheese. Bhutanese *sha ema* are difficult to obtain in America. Some Bhutanese immigrants grow their own, but jalapeños and *serrano* peppers are commonly used as a substitute, as they fall within the lower Scoville range comparable to *sha ema*. Bhutanese farmer's cheese can be made of either cow's milk or yak milk, but both feta and *queso fresco* can be used to similar effect.

The following recipe for this simple Bhutanese stew serves two to four people.

Ema Datshi (Chilis with yak cheese)

8 ounces of Bhutanese *sha ema* peppers (substitute jalapeños)
1 onion, coarsely chopped
2 tomatoes, diced
8 ounces Bhutanese farmer's yak milk cheese (substitute feta or *queso fresco*)
4 cloves garlic, crushed
4 cilantro leaves
2 teaspoons vegetable oil

Slice the chilies into strips. Fill a saucepan with 12 ounces of water, and boil the chilies and onion until soft (10 minutes). Add the oil, onion, tomato, and garlic, and simmer for 2 minutes. Add cheese and cilantro, and allow to simmer for another 2 minutes. Serve with red rice.

Claire Y. van den Broek
(See "Bhutan," Claire Y. van den Broek, *EAFT*, pp. 71–73.)

Bolivia (South America), Bolivian American Food

Meat dishes are common in Bolivia and are usually eaten at the midday meal with corn and potatoes. With immigration to the United States, Bolivian Americans now eat their largest meal in the evening. These kinds of dishes are frequently offered in restaurants, often accompanied by a light salad of lettuce and tomato. Preferred meats include pork, particularly roast suckling pig, although chicken or turkey may be substituted for pork. An indigenous delicacy, *charque de llama*, or dried llama meat, is often fried by Bolivian cooks and served with stewed corn, hard-boiled eggs, and cheese. *Charque de llama* is much more difficult to locate in North American groceries, so pork is frequently substituted.

Fricassee (Pork stew)
Serves 8 as main dish

2 teaspoons oil
2½ pounds pork, cubed
1 cup white onion, cut into thin strips
2 teaspoons minced garlic (about 4 garlic cloves)
1 teaspoon cumin
½ teaspoon ground black pepper
1 teaspoon oregano (crushed)
1 tablespoon mint, finely chopped
½ cup cayenne pepper (¼ to ½ cup, extremely hot, use cayenne pepper to suit taste)
1 teaspoon salt
½ cup scallions, cut into thin strips
8 cups chicken or beef broth, boiling
½ cup breadcrumbs
4 cups cooked white corn (such as hominy)
8 potatoes, red or Yukon, peeled, cooked separately, and cut in big chunks

Heat oil in a large pot over medium heat. Add pork cubes and sauté until golden, about 10 minutes. Add onion strips, cumin, pepper, oregano, garlic, mint, salt, and scallions. Mix and sauté to blend flavors, about 2–3 minutes. Add cayenne paper (at level of heat preferred). Add 8 cups of boiling broth.

Cook over low heat for 2 hours, adding broth if needed. Meat should be tender and easily shredded. Add breadcrumbs to thicken. Serve in bowls, topped by pieces of cooked potato and corn.

Lois Stanford
(See "Bolivia," Lois Stanford, *EAFT*, pp. 73–76.)

～

Bosnia, Bosnia-Hercegovina (Eastern Europe), Bosnian American

Stuffing vegetables with a meat and grain mixture is common to most of the food cultures in Eastern Europe, with variations in spices, meats, and grains making the recipes distinctive. Although the dish has been adapted and incorporated into mainstream American cooking, it remains a significant one for many ethnic groups. This Bosnian recipe uses a specific type of pepper, fleshy round and oblong peppers called *Balkan* and *Romanian* in American markets. Bell peppers are considered tasteless and are never used. Paprika, the primary spice used by this group, should be from southeastern Europe. It is available in many markets servicing southern Europeans.

Punjene Paprike (Filled peppers)

> 6–8 green Balkan peppers (*not* bell peppers)
> 1 onion
> ¼ cup rice
> 1 pound ground beef (ground lamb would be even better)
> 1 egg
> 1 teaspoon Vegeta*
> Salt and pepper
> 1 large can tomatoes or 5–6 large, ripe, chopped tomatoes
> 3 tablespoons oil
> 3–4 tablespoons flour
> Sweet paprika (Balkan or Hungarian)
> Sour cream

Cut off stems of peppers, remove seeds, and rinse. Sauté finely chopped onion in 1 tablespoon oil until transparent. Add rice and sauté until rice is coated. Cool. Add meat, egg, Vegeta, and salt and pepper. Fill peppers.

Place in heavy pot with peppers upright. Add canned tomatoes with juice or ripe tomatoes with a little water to cover. Cover pot and gently simmer; add water if necessary. This is done when the peppers are tender, about an hour.

Make a *roux*: In a heavy skillet heat 2 tablespoons oil; add 3–4 tablespoons flour over a low heat. Stir the flour continually until golden brown. Add paprika. Add cold water slowly to bubbling flour mixture and cook for about 10–15 minutes. Stir continually or the flour will lump. The desired consistency is a thick but not stiff sauce. While stirring, slowly add some liquid from the pot of peppers to dilute it so that it can be poured back into the pepper pot. Shake the pot to distribute roux. Cook for another 10 minutes. Serve on a platter with the juice from the pan; pour sour cream over the peppers.

* Vegeta is a flavor enhancer consisting of dried ground vegetables, salt, and monosodium glutamate. It is available in markets catering to Bosnians.

William G. Lockwood and Yvonne R. Lockwood
(See "Bosnia, Bosnia-Hercegovina," William G. Lockwood and Yvonne R. Lockwood, *EAFT*, pp. 76–81.)

~

Botswana (Southern Africa), Botswanan American

Botswana is one of the most sparsely populated nations in the world. Once also one of the poorest countries in the world, the former British protectorate now enjoys relative prosperity. The country became known to many Western audiences through a popular series of novels by Scottish author Alexander McCall Smith, featuring Mma Precious Ramotswe, who runs the fictional "No. 1 Ladies' Detective Agency." The Botswanan national dish is a stew of shredded meat served with cornmeal. It can easily be prepared in the United States with American ingredients.

Seswaa or Chotlho (Pounded beef)

2 pounds beef shank on the bone (slow cooking beef, chicken, or goat can be used)
1 tablespoon olive oil
1 onion, peeled
3 bay leaves
Salt
Black pepper

Preheat the oven to 300°F. Cut the beef into about 4 large chunks. Heat the olive oil in a Dutch oven or crockpot and brown the beef on all sides. Put the onion and bay leaf in the pot and cover the meat with water. Bring to a boil; add pepper and salt. Cover the pot and place it on the middle rack of the oven, and cook for 4 hours or more, until the beef is tender. Use a slotted spoon to remove the onion and bay leaves. Heat the beef on the stove, bring to a boil to evaporate the cooking liquid, and "pound" the beef until it falls apart in shreds. If desired, remove the bone and brown the meat in a bit of olive oil. Serve hot with *pap* (cornmeal porridge), boiled green vegetables, or pumpkin.

Karin Vaneker
(See "Botswana," Betty J. Belanus, *EAFT*, pp. 81–82.)

⁓

Brazil (South America), Brazilian American Food

Brazilian food culture includes evidence of the country's colonial past as a Portuguese colony, but it also shows traces of various indigenous cultures and the nation's tropical climate. Commonly used ingredients include root vegetables (e.g., manioc, cassava, yams), tropical fruits (e.g., mango, guava, passion fruit), rice, beans, fish, beef, chicken, and pasta. Sausage is also prevalent, especially *linguiça*, a mild, cured pork sausage. Pastries and desserts, including *brigadeiro* (chocolate balls), are a perpetual favorite, and coffee is the national beverage. The national dish is *feijoada*, a type of meat stew with beans, and is usually served with a variety of side dishes that can include rice, sausages, polenta, and salad. Brazilian Americans, frequently mistakenly grouped with Hispanics or Latinos, continue making many of these traditional dishes.

Feijoada (Beef stew with beans)
8 servings

1 smoked ham hock or shank
½ pound thick-sliced bacon, diced
2 large yellow onions, chopped
½ cup green onions, chopped
2 cloves garlic, chopped
1 12-ounce package dry black beans, soaked in water overnight
1 pound boneless pork shoulder or boneless beef, any cut
Olive oil
2 bay leaves

Pinch of ground coriander
½ cup chopped fresh parsley
½ cup chopped fresh cilantro

Boil ham hock in salted water and bring to a simmer until the meat pulls away from the bone, approximately 1 hour. Meanwhile, in a pot or Dutch oven over medium-high heat, cook the bacon until crisp and the fat has rendered. Add the onions, green onions, and garlic, and cook until softened and barely translucent, approximately 4 minutes. Cut the pork or beef into 1- to 2-inch cubes and add to the onion mixture; cook on all sides until browned. Add the ham hock to the mixture, along with the beans, salt, pepper, coriander, and bay leaves, and cover with water. Simmer for 45 minutes to 1 hour, stirring often; if the mixture appears too thick, add additional water as needed. Add cilantro and parsley prior to serving.

Brigadeiro (Chocolate balls)
Makes two dozen small balls.

1 14-ounce can sweetened condensed milk
1 tablespoon unsalted butter
3–4 tablespoons cocoa powder
Variety of coatings of choice (chocolate sprinkles, coconut, crushed nuts, etc.)

Over medium heat, combine the condensed milk, butter, and cocoa powder; cook, stirring often, until the mixture thickens. Allow mixture to rest until cool. Form into balls, rolling in various coatings. Eat immediately or chill for a firmer texture.

Ryan S. Eanes
(See "Brazil," Ryan S. Eanes, *EAFT*, pp. 82–85.)

∽

Brunei Darussalam (Southeastern Asia), Bruneian American Food

With extensive oil and natural gas fields, Brunei is one of the richest nations in the world. Most Bruneians are Malay, and the official language is Malay, but many residents also speak English and Chinese. Although there are Christians and Buddhists, about 75 percent of the inhabitants are Muslim. Bruneians come to the United States primarily as students. Bruneian foodways are similar to those of Malaysia and Indonesia. Rice is the staple and commonly served with seafood, chicken, beef, lamb, and vegetables. Bruneian food is heavily spiced with chili peppers, ginger, garlic, turmeric, and curry.

Pais Daging (Grilled meat in banana leaves)

1 pound chopped or coarsely minced beef
4 spring onions, small rings
2 garlic cloves, minced
2–3 tablespoons chili paste (or 1 red chili pepper), adjust for spiciness desired
1 tablespoon cornstarch (flour)
1 teaspoon salt
¼ teaspoon pepper
¼ teaspoon castor sugar
1 tablespoon vegetable oil
Banana leaves, fresh (available frozen, thaw leaves for about ½ hour before using)
Toothpicks (wooden)
Aluminum foil

Heat oven to 300°F. Put beef in a bowl, sprinkle with cornstarch and mix with the spring onions, garlic, 2 tablespoons of chili paste, salt, pepper, sugar, and oil. Add a tablespoon of water. Mix well. Use scissors to cut out rectangles of the banana leaves of about 10 inches long and 6 inches wide. Rinse the rectangles under hot streaming water; pat dry. Put about 3 tablespoons of the meat mixture on a banana leaf and wrap it around the meat, leaving the top open. Use the toothpicks to close the top and bottom. Wrap a piece of aluminum foil around each package, put the packages on an oven rack, place the rack in the middle of the oven, and bake for about 30 to 40 minutes.

Karin Vaneker
(See "Brunei Darussalam," Lucy M. Long, *EAFT*, p. 86.)

⌒

Bulgaria (Eastern Europe), Bulgarian American

Tarator is found throughout the Balkan Peninsula—including Albania, Greece, Macedonia, and Serbia—but Bulgarians and Bulgarian Americans often claim it as a national dish. Milk and dairy products are important elements in Bulgarian cuisine, particularly a type of fermented milk known in Bulgarian as *kiselo mlyako* (literally, sour milk), but much better known worldwide as *yogurt*, its name in Turkish. *Kiselo mlyako* is made thanks to *Lactobacillus bulgaricus*, a bacterium first identified in 1905 by the Bulgarian doctor Stamen Grigorov. It is the primary ingredient in *tarator*, which is especially popular in summer, accompanied by a *shopska* salad—a combination of chopped cucumbers, onions, peppers, and tomatoes sprinkled with Bulgarian white cheese.

Tarator (Cucumber-yogurt soup)

1 pound of cucumbers
2 or 3 cloves of garlic
3 cups of yogurt
2 tablespoons of sunflower or olive oil
Salt and chopped dill to taste

Peel and chop the cucumbers into small cubes. Mince or press the cloves of garlic. Dilute the yogurt with one cup of water. Combine all ingredients and stir well. Cool in refrigerator for 30 minutes before serving.

James I. Deustch
(See "Bulgaria," James Deustch, *EAFT*, pp. 88–86.)

～

Burkina Faso (Western Africa), Burkinabe American Food

Poverty has driven emigration from the nation of Burkina Faso, and the United States now hosts approximately five thousand to six thousand Burkinabe Americans. Most of their traditional staples are available in American supermarkets, but some, such as sorghum and millet, are more likely to be found in health food stores or ethnic groceries.

Burkinabe food is typical of other West African cuisines with yams, sorghum, millet, rice, and corn being the basic staples accompanied by potatoes, beans, tomatoes, peppers, and okra. Protein is primarily from beans, chicken meat, eggs, and freshwater fish. Goat and mutton is also consumed. Palm sap is fermented into wine (*banji*). *Fufu* is the common basis of a meal, with various sauces accompanying it. European, particularly French, influence is seen in some of the cooking, such as green beans, *poulet bicyclette* (a grilled chicken dish popular throughout West Africa), and *ragout*. Okra is common in the cooking of both western Africa and the American South, and it is a central ingredient in Louisiana gumbo.

Maan Nezim Nzedo (Fish stew with okra)

1½ pounds freshwater fish, cut into pieces
3 tablespoons peanut oil
1 onion, sliced
3 carrots, sliced
8 okra pods
½ teaspoon chili or cayenne pepper
1 cup tomato paste
1 cup spinach
⅔ cup green string or runner beans
1 cup rice (uncooked)
2 cups stock, vegetable or fish
Salt

Slice the okra lengthwise in half. Heat the oil in a Dutch oven and add the onion, carrots, okra, chili pepper, salt, and tomato paste. Stir, bring to a boil, and simmer for about 10 minutes. Put in the fish pieces, spinach, beans, and a little bit of water. Simmer for 5 minutes and add the rice and stock. Cook for 20 minutes, until the rice is done, and add more stock or water if necessary.

Karin Vaneker
(See "Burkina Faso," Lucy Long, EAFT, pp. 88–89.)

～

Burma, Burmese American. See Myanmar.

～

Burundi (Eastern Africa), Burundian American Food

Burundi American food is typical of that of other central African cultures in the United States, but it differs in its Catholic affiliations as well as its history of being a German colony, which did not seem to actively influence the food culture. It also shares some ethnic food culture in the United States with other Francophone African nations.

Burundi Americans celebrate Christian holidays—Easter, All Saint's Day, Christmas, and other Roman Catholic holy days—and participate in mainstream American foodways traditions associated with them, but they also use them as times to gather with each other and share their traditional ethnic foods.

A special dish is red kidney beans with fried onions and bananas, and a banana wine (*urwarwa*) is used for special occasions.

Red Kidney Beans with Onions and Bananas

2 cans or 3 cups of red kidney beans (if using dried, prepare according to directions: soak and simmer, prior to adding to recipe)

2 tablespoons oil (preferably palm oil, but coconut, peanut, or other vegetable oil is acceptable)

1 onion, sliced thinly (red seems to be preferred)

2 plantains, peeled and chopped (green bananas can substitute)

¼ to ½ teaspoon salt

1 teaspoon chili powder or hot pepper sauce

2 cups water

In a large pot, cook onions in oil until soft.

Add beans, plantains, salt, and chili powder. Mix and cook another minute. Add water and simmer 30–45 minutes until plantains are soft and liquid has been reduced to just cover the beans.

Serve with *chapattis* (Indian flat bread that is traditional in Burundi) or with rice (more recently adopted in Burundi, but common in the United States).

Lucy M. Long
(See "Burundi," Lucy M. Long, *EAFT*, pp. 89–90.)

C

Cajun (North America)

Étouffée, which is sometimes spelled phonetically, A-2-Fay, comes from the French word for smothered. It is most commonly served with shellfish, either shrimp or crawfish. Making étouffée begins with a roux, a technique central to many Cajun dishes. The roux either is cooked to a light brown or blonde for a more buttery flavor, or a darker brown for a deep, nutty flavor.

This version highlights the influence of other ethnic groups on Cajun foodways with the addition of basil and tomatoes, a nod to the many Sicilian immigrants of southern Louisiana.

Étouffée (Smothered seafood)

1 stick butter
1 large onion, diced
2 stalks celery, diced
1 large green bell pepper, diced
2 stalks green onion, sliced
1 large tomato, diced
1 tablespoon tomato paste
3 cloves garlic, minced
¾ cups all-purpose flour
2 pounds shrimp or crawfish tail meat
1 teaspoon dried basil

½ teaspoon white pepper
½ teaspoon black pepper
½ teaspoon cayenne pepper
1 teaspoon Louisiana-style hot sauce (Tabasco, Crystal, or similar)
1 teaspoon Worcestershire sauce
2 cups shrimp stock

To make a roux, melt a stick of butter in a large skillet on medium heat. Slowly add the flour and whisk until blended. Continue to stir the *roux* until it turns a light brown, about the color of peanut butter. Add the onions, celery, bell peppers, and half of the green onions (reserve the other half to garnish the finished dish). Add the dry seasonings, sauces, and garlic and cook until the vegetables are soft (about 15 minutes). Incorporate the stock slowly, adding a small amount at a time and stirring carefully until the étouffée is smooth and thick, about 30 minutes. Add the shrimp or crawfish and simmer until mixture is smooth and the shrimp are cooked.
Serve over white rice and with a few green onions on top.

A note about seafood stock:
Buying your seafood whole can create the opportunity to make a simple seafood stock. Boil the shells from two pounds of large shrimp (or about 5 pounds of crawfish) along with about a cup each of onions and celery, two cloves of garlic, and a bay leaf in 1½ quarts of water. After an hour, strain out the vegetables and shells.

Graham Hoppe with Joe Vuskovich
(See "Cajun," Graham Hoppe with Joe Vuskovich, *EAFT*, pp. 91–94.)

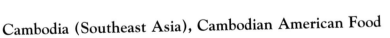

Cambodia (Southeast Asia), Cambodian American Food

For many Cambodian Americans, rice is typically served at every meal in some form or another and is accompanied by three to four dishes, such as curries, soups, vegetable mixtures, fish, or duck, plus condiments (similar to Asian Indian chutneys) served alongside. Celebration meals would include ten or more dishes. Curries are a basic part of the Cambodian food culture and are familiar to many Americans. They can easily be adapted to mainstream American tastes by altering the spiciness. Many of the ingredients can now be found in mainstream groceries, international supermarkets, or Southeast Asian markets.

Khmer Chicken Curry
Serves 4

Curry paste ingredients:
- 1 one-inch piece *galangal*, peeled and sliced (substitute fresh ginger root or powdered ginger in a pinch)
- 2 one-inch pieces turmeric root, peeled and sliced OR 2 teaspoons powdered turmeric
- 2 cloves garlic, chopped
- 1 stalk lemongrass, sliced thin (or substitute dried lemongrass powder)
- 4 shallots, peeled and chopped OR ½ onion, diced
- 2 pieces *kaffir* lime leaf, sliced OR 2 lime leaves sliced (substitute regular lime leaves or add the juice of one lime, about ¼ cup of lime juice. Fresh really does taste better!)

To make paste: Blend in food processor until a paste and add 2 tablespoons hot water.
Other ingredient (see below for combining with paste):

- 1 can coconut milk (not sweetened or coconut cream)

Curry ingredients:
- 1 sweet potato, cubed
- 1 onion, diced
- 1 carrot, sliced
- 4–6 long beans cut into one-inch pieces OR ½ to ⅔ cup green beans (one-inch pieces)
- 1 chicken breast, sliced or cubed (your taste)
- Fish sauce to taste—maybe 1 tablespoon (it will not taste fishy!)
- 1 small tablet palm sugar OR 2 tablespoons brown sugar
- ¼ teaspoon salt
- 4 star anise
- ½ cup water OR good-quality chicken broth (if broth already contains salt, do NOT add more)

In a large saucepan, heat coconut milk to a simmer on medium-high heat, add curry paste, and cook for 10 minutes (simmering) with sugar, sweet potato, carrot, onion, and long beans or green beans. Add cubed (raw) chicken and simmer for about 15–20 minutes. Add salt, star anise, fish sauce, palm sugar, and water. Stir and cook until vegetables are tender and chicken is cooked through. Do not let vegetables get mushy. Serve with steamed jasmine rice or baguette.

Rice: Start rice cooking at the same time coconut milk is heating. A traditional method of judging water to rice ratio: put desired amount of rice (1 cup dry is good for this recipe, which will make 2 cups cooked) in a saucepan, add a pinch of salt, put tip of thumb touching top of rice and add water until water reaches first knuckle. Heat rice, water, and salt to boiling, covered. Turn temperature down so that rice simmers for about 10 minutes. Turn off and leave on burner until curry is ready.

Rachelle H. Saltzman
(See "Cambodia," by Rachelle H. Saltzman, *EAFT*, pp. 94–98.)

～

Cameroon (Middle Africa), Cameroonian American

Cameroon is referred to as Africa in miniature, which means it encompasses a bit of every part of Africa—culture, climate, religion, and more. There is the rain forest, the desert, savannah, grassland, and everything in between. There are over 250 dialects spoken in Cameroon. As these dialects differ, so do the foods that come from them. A national dish is "bitter leaves" stewed with smoked fish and ground peanut paste. Spinach is often substituted for the bitter leaves in the United States, partly because of the bitterness but also because of lack of availability. Also, it is common in Cameroon to stew fish and beef (and other available meats, such as pork or chicken and shrimp) together, a taste that does not always fit the American palate. Peanut-based dishes, such as chicken in peanut sauce, tend to be popular among Americans, but many Cameroonians find chicken in the United States to be soft and "mushy" since they are used to older, laying hens. Many of the ingredients for Cameroonian food are unavailable in the United States, so individuals traveling back home frequently bring ingredients with them, freezing them to save for special occasions. Some ingredients can be obtained from African and other ethnic groceries as well as health food stores, but substitutions are common. Fish and seafood are also optional, since they sometimes give a "fishy" flavor they are not always suitable for American tastes.

Ndole (Beef and fish stew)

2 pounds stew beef (optional)
1 large dry (smoked) fish (optional)
1 pound shrimp (optional)

2 cups raw groundnut paste (can use peanut butter)
1 cup fresh bitter leaves (or dry bitter leaves—soak overnight)
2 packs fresh spinach (washed and chopped)
1 tablespoon fresh ground garlic
2 medium onions, chopped
½ cup crayfish (crushed) (optional)
1½ cups vegetable oil
2 cups water
2 fresh ground habanero peppers (optional)
Salt to taste
4 boullion cubes

Wash, season, and cook beef until tender; wash, cut, and steam fish, or cook until tender; wash, clean, and prepare shrimp.

In a large pot, heat one cup oil. Add one of the chopped onions, salt, and garlic, stir well. Reduce heat, and add groundnut paste. Cook for about 45 minutes, stirring occasionally to keep the groundnut paste from burning. Add water and beef. Stir well, and cook for about 30 minutes. Add bitter leaves, spinach, crayfish, and peppers. Add dry fish, shrimp, and boullion cubes. Reduce heat, and cook for about another 25 minutes. In a frying pan, pour in the remaining oil, and add remaining onions. Lightly sauté, and add to stew.

Serve with *miondor*, *bobolor*, boiled rice, fried plantains, boiled plantains, or food of choice.

Steamed Fish

2 whole fish (In Cameroon, red snapper, sole, or mackerel would be the fish of choice, but salmon is a popular alternative in the United States.)
4 medium tomatoes (diced)
1 medium onion (chopped)
2 tablespoons ground *njangsang* (native spice)
2 tablespoons ginger, fresh ground
2 tablespoons garlic, fresh ground
1 teaspoon ground *jowe*
1 teaspoon ground country onion (native spice)
1 teaspoon ground *beh beh* (native spice)
2 fresh ground habanero peppers
¼ cup olive oil
2 bouillon cubes
Salt to taste

Banana leaves for wrapping

Wash and cut fish to desired sizes. Mix all ingredients together. Marinate fish in mixture. Wrap in leaves and steam for about an hour and a half. Serve with fried plantains, rice, boiled plantains, and other sides.

Ceci Tchakounte Tadfor
(See "Cameroon," Elinor Levy and Ceci Tchakounte Tadfor, *EAFT*, pp. 98–102.)

~

Canada (North America), Canadian American Food

Canadian food culture, like the United States's, is a multicultural one built upon the native First Peoples' culinary traditions. The French and British were the dominant colonizers, and their legacy remains today in language, music and dance forms, and food. Meat-filled pastries were common in both countries and carried over to Canada, although this version reflects French Canadian cuisine. Canadians in America generally have a sweet tooth and oftentimes maintain a fondness for butter tarts, Nanaimo squares, *tarte au sucre*, and other traditional sweet desserts.

Tourtière (Meat pie)
Pastry crust: this recipe makes 3 double-crusted pies

- 5 cups flour
- 1 tablespoon sugar
- 1 teaspoon baking soda
- 1 pound lard (Tenderflake) cut into small cubes
- 1 beaten egg in a measuring cup filled with the following:
- 2 tablespoons lemon juice or vinegar and topped to 1-cup mark with ice water

Mix flour, sugar, and baking soda with a fork in a large bowl. Then add lard, beaten egg, and lemon juice (or vinegar) water mixture and stir wet and dry ingredients together. Use a pastry cutter to mix the dough, and then work the dough with your hands until you are able to form 6 patties. Chill for an hour so before rolling out to fit in your 9-inch pie plates.

Filling:

    1½ pounds ground beef
    1½ pounds ground pork
    1 large onion, finely chopped
    2 garlic cloves, finely chopped
    ¼ cup fine breadcrumbs
    1 teaspoon salt
    1 teaspoon savory
    ¼ teaspoon cloves (or to taste)
    ¼ teaspoon cinnamon (or to taste)
    About 1 cup of water; add slowly to mixture to get thick consistency

Brown the pork and beef slowly in a large pot. Drain and then rinse the fat off. Add the onions, garlic, and salt. Add the remaining spices a little at a time and adjust to your taste. Roll out pastry to fit your pie plate. Sprinkle about ¼ cup of fine breadcrumbs onto the bottom of the crust. Pour in the cooked meat mixture. Cover with a top crust. Be sure to cut small steam vent holes in the top crust. Brush top crust with a beaten egg mixed with a little water. Bake at 350°F for about 40 minutes.

Bailey M. Cameron
(See "Canada," Bailey M. Cameron, *EAFT*, pp. 102–5.)

～

Cape Verde (Western Africa), Cape Verdean American Food

The Cape Verde islands off the western coast of Africa were uninhabited until Portuguese explorers arrived in the mid-fifteenth century. The transatlantic slave trade brought Africans and other Europeans to the volcanic islands that are currently inhabited by about 525,000 people. Cape Verdeans are a multiethnic people, and most are of Creole descent (mulattos) and scattered all over the world. Since the late eighteenth century, and mostly by way of New Bedford, Massachusetts, Cape Verdeans came to the United States as textile or (seasonal) cranberry workers, whalers, or stevedores. Today it is estimated that about five hundred thousand Americans are of Cape Verdean descent, and the majority live in southern New England. Cape Verdean Americans tend to identify with Portuguese heritage, and their foodways are strongly influenced by Portuguese cuisine.

Staple foods include pork, beef, a variety of beans including lima and kidney, cabbage, carrots, corn (which was imported by the Portuguese to the islands), eggs, onions, rice, and fish. Seasonings include paprika, bay leaves, garlic, and onions.

The national dish of Cape Verde, *cachupa*, also called *manchupa*, is a stew of corn (or hominy), beans, greens, and meat or fish, and recipes vary from household to household. It can be found in two forms: *povera* (poor or everyday) and *rica*. Rica has additional ingredients, usually sausage (*linguiça*), or richer cuts of meat. Cachupa is sometimes fried and served with an egg; this is the form typically found in Cape Verdean restaurants. In the United States, *cachupa* became known as *manchup(a)* and means home to Cape Verdeans.

Cachupa à la Maria (Stew)

1 cup dried fava beans (field beans)
1 cup dried stone beans (*feijao pedra*) (black beans can substitute)
½ cup lima beans (butter beans)
2 small mackerels, whole
4 garlic cloves, crushed
White pepper
White vinegar
1 large onion, in pieces
4 cups yellow corn kernels
1 cup white corn kernels
1 pound pork ribs, salted
2 spring onions, in rings
1 white cabbage
1 cassava (root) (can substitute with potato)
10 to 15 potatoes, medium size
1 bunch yellow cress
1 bunch fresh coriander
2 *chouriços* or *linguiça* sausage, sliced
Olive oil
Salt
Stock powder

Soak the fava beans and stone beans in plenty of cold water overnight. Butter beans do not need soaking. Clean the mackerels and do not remove the heads. Cut the fishes in 2-inch pieces, put them in a bowl, sprinkle with the garlic, white pepper, and 2 tablespoons of vinegar. Put the onion and yellow corn in a large stockpot with ample water. Bring to a boil and cook for around 10 minutes. Drain the dried beans. Add the white corn, all the beans, and salted meat. Add boiling water, and simmer for 1½ hours.

Slice the outer leaves of the cabbage finely and leave the rest in large chunks. Cut the cassava in about 1½-inch slices. Peel the potatoes and cut larger ones in half. Chop the yellow cress and coriander leaves. Add everything to the stockpot. Put the sliced *chouriço* and mackerel on top. Cover the pot and simmer for 15 minutes. Sauté the spring onions in a bit of olive oil, in a skillet. Add to the pot and add salt or stock powder to taste. Let the *cachupa* rest for 15 minutes. Take the mackerel out of the pot, remove the bones and heads, and put the pieces on a serving plate. Arrange the large cabbage pieces, cassava, potato, *chouriço*, and meat on a large serving plate and the rest of the *cachupa* in a soup bowl. Put the plates and bowl on the dinner table.

Karin Vaneker with Susan Eleuterio
(See "Cape Verde," Susan Eleuterio, *EAFT*, pp. 105–6.)

~

Caribbean, Dutch (Americas, Caribbean), Antillean American

Referred to as the Dutch West Indies for much of their history, the six Caribbean islands of Aruba, Bonaire, Curaçao, Saba, Saint Eustatius, and Saint Maarten were held by the Kingdom of the Netherlands until 1954. In 2010, Aruba, Curaçao, and Saint Maarten became separate countries within the kingdom, while the others were integrated into the Netherlands and are formally referred to as the Dutch Caribbean. Most of the inhabitants live on Aruba, Bonaire, and Curaçao, and few have immigrated to the United States.

The geography and history of the Dutch Antilles resulted in two distinct cuisines, with European (Dutch, British), African (primarily brought as slaves), Asian (Chinese, Indian, Malay, Indonesian), Jewish, and American (Brazilian, Venezuelan) influences. Antilleans are fond of (very) sweet and colorful cakes. This recipe for pineapple cake will be familiar to many Americans because of its similarity to the pineapple upside-down cake popularized by women's magazines in the 1950s.

Bolo di Anasa (Pineapple cake)

3 ounces butter
3 ounces sugar
1 can pineapple slices (10 slices)
10 candied cherries

4 eggs
11 ounces self-rising flour
1 teaspoon baking powder
¼ teaspoon salt
10 ounces castor sugar
10 ounces butter

Preheat oven to 350°F. Melt the 3 ounces of butter over moderate heat in a saucepan. Pour the melted butter in a 10-inch cake pan, and cover the sides with a bit of butter. Sprinkle the 3 ounces of sugar over the bottom. Arrange the pineapple slices on top of the melted butter and sugar and place a candied cherry in the center of each pineapple slice.

Melt the 10 ounces butter over moderate heat in a saucepan. Meanwhile, put the sugar and eggs in a large bowl, and using an electric mixer on high speed, whisk until light and fluffy. While whisking, slowly pour in the melted butter.

Put the flour, baking powder, and salt into a large bowl and gradually add the sugar and egg mixture. Use a fork or the mixer on low speed to stir it into a uniform batter. Carefully pour the batter over the pineapple slices, and put the cake on a rack in the middle of the preheated oven.

Bake for about 45 to 50 minutes, until a toothpick inserted in the center of the cake comes out clean. Cool the cake on a rack for about 10 minutes, and use a dull knife to loosen the edges. Put a plate on top of the cake and carefully turn the cake around, remove the cake pan, and let the cake cool completely.

Karin Vaneker
(See "Caribbean, Dutch," Karin Vaneker, *EAFT*, pp. 107–9.)

～

Central African Republic (CAR)
(Middle Africa), Central African American Food

Located literally in the center of the African continent, the Central African Republic (CAR)'s cuisine reflects a mix of indigenous foods with vegetables and fruits originally brought from the Americas (such as corn, peanuts, sweet potatoes, tomatoes, chili, and cassava) with influences from Arabic slave traders and European colonization. Indigenous ingredients include fish, wild game, insects, bananas, yams, okra, millet, onion, rice, and palm oil. Dough (*gozo*) made from cassava or sorghum is a basic staple, along with cassava *fufu*, the doughy staple served with stews and dishes with sauces throughout west and central Africa.

CAR has been rocked by civil war for a number of years, and numerous refugees have fled to other African nations prior to immigrating to the United States, making it difficult to ascertain the number living here.

Boeuf aux Gombos (Beef with okra)

1½ lb. stewing beef
3 tablespoons peanut oil
2 onions
2 tablespoons tomato paste
10 to 12 okra
Salt
Chili pepper (powder or 1 piece*)

Slice the onions and cut the meat into dices. Heat the oil in a marmite (Dutch oven) and brown the meat on all sides. Add the onion slices, and sauté on medium-high heat for about 5 minutes. Stir frequently and add the tomato paste, about ¼ teaspoon of salt, and a pinch of chili pepper powder. Sauté for a few minutes and cover the beef with water. Place a cover on the pot and simmer the stew on low heat for about 1½ hours. Meanwhile, rinse the okra and cut these in rings of about ½ inch. Add the okra, salt, and chili pepper to taste and simmer for another 30 minutes. Serve hot with *fufu* balls (cassava porridge) or plain rice.

* Instead of chili pepper powder, add 1 red chili pepper. The chili pepper will release its spiciness during the cooking process, but the longer it is cooked the hotter the dish will become. Therefore, taste the stew after 30 minutes and eventually remove the chili pepper.

Karin Vaneker and Lucy M. Long
(See "Central African Republic," Susan Eleuterio and Lucy Long, *EAFT*, pp. 109–10.)

～

Central Asia (Central Asia), Kazakhstan, Kyrgyzstan, Tajikistan, Turkmenistan, and Uzbekistan American Food

Central Asia stretches from the Caspian Sea in the west to China in the east. In the north it is bordered by Russia and in the south by China, Iran, and Afghanistan. Sometimes Central Asia is also included, but in general the core region of the Asian continent encompasses the former Soviet republics

Kazakhstan, Kyrgyzstan, Tajikistan, Turkmenistan, and Uzbekistan. Central Asian cuisine is firmly rooted in the traditions of its nomadic peoples, who featured dairy products, such as heavy cream, yogurt, cheeses, and butter, and meat products, especially those that could be preserved through drying and smoking. The cuisine also reflects the Silk Road and trade for grains, such as wheat, rice, millet, and sorghum, and for fruits and vegetables, such as muskmelons, watermelons, pomegranates, onions, garlic, quinces, apples, pears, figs, and persimmons.

Relatively few immigrants from Central Asia have settled in the United States, but those who do hold on to some of their culinary traditions, and there are several restaurants in major urban centers featuring those foods. Two dishes that carry strong memories of cultural heritage and also tend to be well received by mainstream Americans are steamed dumplings (*manti*) and rice (*plov*). These are eaten for both everyday or celebratory meals.

Plov, also called *osh*, is ever present in Central Asia. Traditionally eaten with the right hand, the rice pilaf commonly consists of generous quantities of (rendered mutton) fat, vegetable oil, cubed meat, rice, onions, carrots, and cumin. Depending on the region and occasion, raisins, chickpeas, dried fruit, and spices such as turmeric, star anise, coriander, and chili pepper are added. Tea always accompanies *plov* and Central Asian meals.

Steamed or boiled dumplings with minced meat, (mutton) fat, and onions are also popular throughout Central Asia and are called *manti, manty*, or *mantu*. They are often topped with butter, served with a sauce from vinegar and chili sauce, sour cream, tomato sauce, or fresh onions. In Afghanistan it is common to eat manti with a yogurt sauce.

Plov, Osh, Pilaf, Pilau, Pulau (Rice)

1 pound mutton or beef, cubed
¼ cup vegetable oil (sheep tail fat would be preferred for some versions of the dish)
1 garlic bulb
1 large onion, small pieces
3 carrots, shredded
1 teaspoon salt
1 teaspoon black pepper
1 teaspoon cumin powder
1 teaspoon coriander powder
1 teaspoon smoked paprika powder

2 cups rice (long grain such as basmati)
4 cups vegetable stock
½ cup raisins
1 pinch of saffron

Heat half of the oil in a Dutch oven and brown the meat cubes on all sides. Add the garlic and simmer on very low heat for about 1½ to 2 hours. Put the meat and garlic in a bowl and drain the fat of the meat in a separate bowl. Meanwhile, rinse the raisins and soak them in a bowl with boiling hot water; let cool. Soak the saffron in a bit of hot water. Sauté the onions in half of the reserved fat until golden brown, about 5 minutes; stir frequently. Add the shredded carrots. Sauté for a few minutes and add the salt, pepper, and spices. Add the rice and raisins and the remaining fat, cover with stock, and simmer about 30 to 60 minutes, until all the liquid is absorbed. Add salt and pepper to taste. Stir in the meat, heat through, and serve hot.

For a vegetarian *plov*, omit the meat and garlic bulb, sautéed onions, and add about 3 crushed garlic cloves.

Manti, Manty, Mantu (Steamed dumplings)

2 tablespoons vegetable oil
1 pound minced meat (mutton or beef)
1 teaspoon fine sea salt, or more, to taste
1 teaspoon freshly ground black pepper
1 teaspoon turmeric
2½ teaspoons coriander
5 tablespoons tomato paste
2 large yellow onions
1 package (100) wonton wrappers (for steamed dumplings)
½ cup Turkish yogurt
3 garlic cloves, minced
1 teaspoon dried mint
Salt

Heat the oil and sauté the minced meat until brownish. Add the salt, pepper, and spices. Stir and simmer for a few minutes. Add the tomato paste and about ½ cup of boiling water. Simmer for about 10 minutes and let it cool. Meanwhile, chop the onions into very small pieces, add to the meat mixture, and mix. Taste and add salt or pepper.

Place several wonton wrappers on a clean surface and use a small spoon to put a heap full of meat in the middle of each wrapper. Fill a small cup with water and add a teaspoon of oil. Moisten your fingers with the water and moisten the outer edges of the wontons. To close the dumplings: bring together two opposite edges of the wrappers, seal together, repeat with the other edges, and seal the edges of the dumplings completely. Cover the dumplings with a damp tea cloth and steam in batches.

Bring water to boil in a pot with a steamer. Lightly oil the steamer surface and place the dumplings, not touching each other, in the steamer, and steam for about 10 minutes.

Meanwhile, lightly beat the yogurt, stir in the garlic, add a pinch of salt, and spread a thin layer on a serving plate. Arrange the steamed dumplings on the plate, cover with yogurt, and garnish with mint. Serve hot.

Karin Vaneker and Lucy M. Long
(See "Central Asia," Russell Zanca, *EAFT*, pp. 110–15.)

~

Chad (Middle Africa), Chadian American

Few Chadians have sought opportunities in the United States, but those who have tend to maintain strong ties with their cultural heritage and other members of their ethnic community. Sharing food is one way of strengthening those ties.

Millet is the basic Chadian staple. It is cooked into balls, pastes, and pancakes and eaten with stews such as *daraba*, a favorite dish. Rice is sometimes used as a substitute for millet and for another staple grain, sorghum. These grains, along with cornmeal, are used to make a grainy porridge called *boule* that is oftentimes eaten for breakfast. Meals are communal experiences where people sit on the floor around a shared plate set on a mat, although, traditionally, men and women eat separately. Chadean Americans keep some of these customs, but they are adapting their food and eating habits to their new circumstances.

Daraba (Stewed eggplant and sweet potato pie)

20 fresh okra, chopped
3 tomatoes, chopped
1 sweet potato, cubed

1 eggplant, cubed
1 cup of spinach, finely shredded
Beef or chicken stock, cubed (Maggi brand is frequently used in Africa)
¾ cup peanut butter
Salt
Cayenne pepper

Put vegetables in a large pot, cover with water, bring to a boil, and then simmer until tender.

Mix in three-quarters of a cup of peanut butter and a cube of beef or chicken stock and simmer to thicken.

Season with salt and cayenne pepper and serve with millet balls.

Alan Deutschman and Sarah Tekle
(See "Chad," by Alan Deutschman and Sarah Tekle, *EAFT*, pp. 115–17.)

～

Chile (South America), Chilean American Food

Pastel de choclo is a meat and corn pie made with *choclo*, the Quechua word for the tender, fresh corn of the season. Unlike North American corn breads, the *pastel de choclo* is more the consistency of a corn pudding, not unlike the Mexican *pastel de elote*, also made with fresh corn. In some large urban U.S. cities, a cook may find *choclo* in a Latin American grocery market. Often made with beef or chicken, the *pastel de choclo* represents the blending of two cuisines: the corn pastry of indigenous South Americans with the European-inspired spices and seasonings of the filling.

Pastel de Choclo (Corn pie)
Serves 8

3½ pounds chicken (either chicken breasts, for milder flavor, or chicken
    thighs for heartier flavor)
2 cups chicken stock
½ cup seedless raisins
3 tablespoons olive oil
2 medium onions, finely chopped
Salt
1 teaspoon ground cinnamon

24 small pimiento-stuffed green olives, rinsed and halved
3 hard-boiled eggs, sliced
½ cup butter
3 cups corn kernels (thawed, if frozen)
1 can creamed corn
1 tablespoon sugar
2 teaspoons salt, or to taste
4 eggs
Sweet paprika
Sugar

Preheat oven to 350°F. Put chicken and stock in large casserole. Bring to boil, cover, and simmer over low heat until chicken is tender, about 45 minutes. Cool chicken in stock. When cool, remove skin and bones, and chop chicken into 1-inch pieces. Put raisins to soak in cold water for 10 minutes. Heat oil in pan. Sauté onions at medium low until soft, about 5–8 minutes. Season with salt and drain. Add raisins, cinnamon, and chicken. Set aside.

To make topping, melt butter in saucepan. Blend corn kernels and creamed corn to puree. Pour into saucepan and mix in melted butter. Stir in sugar and salt. Cook over very low heat, beating in eggs one by one. Cook, stirring with spoon, until mixture has thickened, about 10 minutes. Let mixture cool slightly. Butter a 2-quart casserole dish and spoon in ⅓ of corn mixture, patting it up the sides of the casserole dish. Spoon in chicken mixture. Layer olives and chopped hard-boiled eggs over chicken mixture. Cover with the rest of the corn mixture. Sprinkle sugar lightly over top of corn mixture, scratching top with fork tines to make grooves. Bake for 1 hour, until topping is set and lightly browned. Serve hot.

Lois Stanford
(See "Chile," Lois Stanford, *EAFT*, pp. 117–20.)

〰

China (East Asia), Chinese American Food

Chinese cuisine is highly varied, with at least eight major regional cuisines: Cantonese (*Yue Cai*), Sichuanese (*Chuan Cai*), Anhui (*Hui Cai*), Shandong (*Lu Cai*), Fujianese (*Min Cai*), Jiangsu or Huaiyang (*Su Cai*), Hunan (*Xiang Cai*), and Zhejiang (*Zhe Cai*). These eight major regional cuisines correspond with the major cardinal points in China.

Immigrants of Chinese heritage have introduced and adapted their food-ways to the United States, leading to the creation of Chinese American ethnic food. These immigrants come from the People's Republic of China, Hong Kong, Macau, Taiwan, Southeast Asia, and other parts of the global Chinese diaspora. There are now an estimated four million individuals who claim Chinese heritage in the United States, representing the largest Asian American ethnic group.

The foodways of Chinese Americans are diverse, based on the region of China from which they claim their heritage. The first presence of a Chinese community dates to the nineteenth century when the 1849 California gold rush brought them to the central valley of California. Coming primarily from an area in southern China (modern-day Guangdong Province), they brought with them variations of Cantonese cuisine, which quickly came to represent Chinese food in general. They successfully established restaurants serving inexpensive and versatile dishes that could easily be adapted to whatever ingredients were available and to local tastes, then took their cooking (and business acumen) throughout the nation, oftentimes following the building of railroads and the development of shipping ports along rivers. They also "invented" new dishes, such as chop suey, specifically for American customers. It wasn't until the 1960s that other regional Chinese cuisines were introduced into mainstream American food culture and American palates opened up to some of the spicier cooking styles. Today, most urban centers boast numerous Chinese restaurants, and restaurants frequently offer dishes from different regions. However, Cantonese-style cooking still tends to define Chinese food for many Americans.

An example of a Chinese dish that is common among Chinese Americans but not usually featured in restaurants in the United States is *congee*, also called *jook* (Cantonese) or *zhou* (Mandarin). A common breakfast food in Chinese households, congee varies in style from region to region and household to household. At its most rustic, it is rice boiled in water to the consistency of mush. Commonly associated with the cooking of the Guangdong Province, Cantonese cuisine, there it is prepared with an aromatic stock base, filled with meats and/or seafood, and topped with aromatic herbs, pickles, and peanuts. Congee also reflects socioeconomic well-being as a plain, watery porridge suggests lean times while a thick, silky version filled with seafood suggests wealth and abundance.

Turkey congee is adapted from the Cantonese style of congee. Until relatively recently, the overwhelming majority of Chinese Americans traced their origins to Guangdong Province. Like many new Americans, they adopted and adapted American holidays and customs. Many embraced Thanksgiving and faced the same day-after dilemma as other Americans: how to deal with leftover turkey. Fusing Cantonese cooking techniques with American ingredients, congee is the quintessential Chinese American dish. It makes a lovely breakfast on a chilly fall morning or a light, soothing supper after a day of feasting.

Congee, Jook, or Zhou (Turkey rice porridge)

Turkey bones (At least half of a turkey carcass, around 7 pounds. More bones result in a stronger stock.)
2 scallions
2-inch slice of ginger
14 cups of water
1 cup raw white rice (preferably an aromatic long-grain variety like jasmine)
2 cups cooked, shredded turkey meat
2 tablespoons salt
Pepper, to taste (preferably white pepper to avoid contrast with the congee)

Optional garnishes: Crushed dry-roasted peanuts, chopped cilantro, sliced scallions, finely julienned ginger, preserved mustard tuber pickles (zha cai), soy sauce, and sesame oil are traditional Cantonese toppings. Feel free to experiment. Shredded iceberg lettuce, strips of roasted seaweed, fried shallots, and crispy wontons are other possibilities.

Place turkey bones, ginger, and scallions in a large stockpot and add water. Put the stockpot on the stove, turn to high, and bring to a boil.

While waiting for the stock to reach a boil, measure out one cup of raw white rice and place in a large bowl. Rinse under cool water until the water runs clear. Drain, and add in fresh water, just enough to cover the rice. Toss in a generous pinch of salt. Let soak for about one hour.

Once the stock reaches boiling, lower heat to medium and skim foam from the stock. Let simmer for one to two hours, after which remove and discard bones, scallions, and ginger.

Add the rice to the stock, raise the heat to high, and return to a boil. Once boiling, lower heat to medium low and cook until desired consistency. Congee can be thin and watery to thick and gruel-like. The Cantonese prefer their congee to be "cottony," when the grains of rice have broken down and the porridge is very smooth.

Add shredded turkey and salt to the pot. Stir well, and let the turkey cook through.

To serve, ladle congee into generous-sized soup bowls. Garnish with toppings, and season to taste with soy sauce, sesame oil, a few cracks of white pepper, and/or salt.

Like other soups, congee tastes even better the next day. Congee can be frozen in plastic containers and reheated.

Willa Zhen
(See "China," Willa Zhen, *EAFT*, pp. 121–29.)

～

Colombia (South America), Colombian American Food

Soups figure prominently in Colombian American culinary culture. This is particularly true for people with coastal roots and those of other Caribbean descents. The traditional *sancocho* or *sopa* can be used as a main or a side dish, depending of the size and quantity of ingredients used. *Sofrito* is a basic starter for a variety of soups. The term *sofrito* refers to the side preparation of several basic ingredients such as peppers, onion, garlic, tomatoes, cilantro, and spiced with salt, pepper, chili peppers, vinegar, or other liquids such as red wine, according to personal taste. The mixture is chopped coarsely and sautéed in olive or canola oil. This is then added to dishes (soups, meats, vegetarian) to enhance the flavor and nutritional benefits. The present recipe lets the reader choose his or her favorite seafood or fish; whatever choice sparks the imagination! The beauty of soups in general is that variety is built into them, and by changing one or more ingredients to suit taste and budget or to accommodate religious, cultural, or local produce availability, the "creation" will likely be a dish enjoyed by guests and family alike.

Sancocho de Pescado (Fish soup)
Serves 8 to 10 people

Sofrito
- 3 tablespoons olive oil
- 1 large onion
- 6 large garlic cloves, peeled and chopped
- 3 large bell peppers; 1 each green, red, yellow; remove seeds and chop coarsely
- 1 large bunch cilantro; clean and remove the harder stems
- 1 12-ounce can of diced tomatoes and green chilies

8 cups water
½ cup coconut milk (optional)
2 to 3 tablespoons condensed skim milk (optional)
2 large ears corn, peeled and cut into 1-inch pieces
1 firm, yellow plantain, peeled and cut into 1-inch pieces (unripe bananas may be a substitute. Have fun experimenting!)
4 medium-sized potatoes, peeled, sliced, or chopped into 1-inch pieces
3 celery stems, cut diagonally into 1-inch pieces
3 medium-sized carrots, peeled, sliced diagonally
1 medium-sized yellow squash, seeds removed, cut into 1-inch pieces
1 large sweet potato, peeled, cut into 1-inch pieces
1 cup frozen green peas
1 to 2 pounds fish (grouper, red snapper, tilapia, or salmon), cut into medium-sized pieces and season with salt, black pepper, turmeric, and cumin as desired (usually one teaspoon of each, then add according to taste)
A dash of hot sauce (optional)
Camarones (shrimp) or any other shellfish (optional)

Add the olive oil to the skillet at medium heat, and add all the *sofrito* ingredients in the given order. Cook gently, stirring, for 5 minutes. Have the water simmering in a separate stockpot. Add the *sofrito* to the water and stir. Start adding all the vegetables, season, and cook gently at low heat for 1 to 2 hours, or until all the ingredients are tender. Add fish (and the milk if desired) and cook for additional 10 to 15 minutes. Stir well, adjust seasoning, and serve accompanied by steamed white rice. Add wedges of ripe avocado as a side.

Carmen Sofia Dence
(See "Colombia" by Carmen Sofia Dence with Susan Eleuterio, *EAFT*, pp. 129–32.)

Comoros (East Africa), Comorian American

An archipelago of islands between Mozambique and Madagascar, Comoros was on Bantu (from continental Africa), Persian, Arab, and Portuguese trade routes, and many of its residents were taken away as slaves as well. The Portuguese "discovered" it in 1505, and it was a French colony from 1841 to 1975. Comorians today are Arab African and predominantly Sunni Muslim. French, Arabic, and Comoran are official languages. Comorians are more likely to immigrate to France and other French-speaking island nations than to the United States.

The country today is very poor, with half of the population below poverty level; however, an Internet website refers to it as a culinary paradise, partly because of the variety of cultural influences that can be found there, particularly in urban centers. Vanilla is a major agricultural export and an ingredient in many dishes, such as lobster boiled in vanilla sauce. Rice is also a basic staple and is frequently prepared with local spices in a style similar to Indian rice puddings.

Ladu (Rice dessert)

¾ cup rice
¾ cup powdered sugar
⅓ cup ghee (clarified butter)
¼ teaspoon cardamom powder
2 teaspoons coarsely grounded black pepper

Grind the rice coarsely with a mortar and pestle or in a blender. Combine the sugar and pepper in a bowl. Put the ghee in a pot, and melt over low heat. Add the rice, and stir constantly until the rice is done. Stir in the cardamom. Poor the rice onto a large plate, and cool and mix with the sugar and pepper mixture. Divide into equal portions, and with moist hands form into 7 balls or brick shapes. Let these dry and cool completely, and serve.

Karin Vaneker
(See "Comoros," Lucy M. Long, EAFT, pp. 132–33.)

∼

Cook Islands (Polynesia, Oceania), Cook Islander American Food

The British occupation of the Cook Islands introduced foreign livestock for commercial purposes, with goats being one of the few successes and now comprising the majority of the Cook Islands' livestock industry. Originally introduced by Captain Cook to create a domesticated supply of protein on the islands, goats heavily outnumber cows due to their diverse foraging diets and their ability to survive with a limited water supply. They became a much-loved addition to the local cuisine, so much so that the livestock industry cannot meet local demand, with roughly eleven thousand tons of goat meat imported each year from New Zealand. One of the most popular recipes using goats is *Puakani'o Ta'akari*, made with coconut and seawater.

Puakani'o Ta'akari (Goat meat in coconut cream)

½ pound goat meat
1 can of coconut cream
Sea salt and water mixture
1 onion
Turmeric powder

Put half a pound of raw goat meat in a large saucepan. Salt the water with sea salt until the salinity is similar to ocean water (around 3.5 percent). Place the saucepan on medium heat until boiling. Once boiling, cover the goat meat and let boil for 2–3 hours. Meanwhile, peel and chop the onion into medium pieces. After 2–3 hours, rinse the goat meat in sea salt water and drain. Add the can of coconut cream, onions, and turmeric powder to taste. Place the saucepan back onto medium heat and simmer until the coconut cream softens the onions.

Eric César Morales and Dillon Tautunu Smith
(See "Polynesia," Eric César Morales and Dillon Tautunu Smith, *EAFT*, pp. 512–19.)

～

Cornwall (Western Europe), Cornish American Food

By far the most famous and distinctive Cornish food consumed today in the United States is the pasty, a hand-held pastry traditionally stuffed with beef, potato, and rutabaga. It has a significant role as the regional food of the Upper Peninsula of Michigan.

While widely acknowledged to be Cornish in origin, the pasty has several iterations in the Upper Peninsula. The "traditional" Cornish dish is made with beef, potato, and rutabaga, while the Finnish version is beef, potato, and carrot. Historically, many other variations on the traditional pasty have been a part of the Upper Peninsula food vernacular, including the Cornish-attributed star-gazing pasty (a fish-filled tribute to Stargazy pie). In the contemporary pasty shop, there are many more variations on the traditional pasty, including breakfast pasties, dessert pasties, pizza pasties, empanadas, and even chicken pot pie pasties.

When ordering a pasty in a Upper Peninsula pasty shop, the question asked is "With or without?" The item in question is rutabaga. The next question is "Catsup or gravy?"

Traditional Cornish Pasty

Crust:
3 cups flour
1½ cups suet (Crisco or lard are preferred substitutes; 1½ sticks butter sometimes), cold and cut into bits
1½ teaspoon salt
6 tablespoons water

Make crust: In a large bowl, combine flour and salt. Use your hands to mix in the cold butter; mix until the consistency of a course meal. Add water one tablespoon at a time to form dough. Toss mixture until it forms a ball. Knead dough lightly against a smooth surface. Form into a ball, dust with flour, wrap in wax paper, and chill for 30 minutes.

For filling, mix together:
1 cup carrots, diced
1 cup rutabaga, diced (note, the rutabaga should be diced slightly larger than the potatoes) (Rutabaga can be optional; use 2 cups carrots instead.)
3 pounds potatoes, diced
2 cups onion, diced
2 pounds ground beef (traditionally, the beef would be chipped or diced, not ground)

Divide the dough into a dozen (4 ounce) balls. Allow to warm to room temperature, and then roll each ball into a 10-inch oval.
Put about 3⁄4 of a cup of filling in the middle of each piece of dough.
Use the edges of your hands to seal the pasty. Add a "dab" of butter on each.
Then crimp the edge. (The style of crimping is an important marker of ethnicity!)
Bake for one hour at 350°F.

Amy Reddinger
(See "Cornwall," Amy Reddinger, *EAFT*, pp. 133–34.)

～

Costa Rica (Central America), Costa Rican American Food

In Costa Rica, no breakfast is complete without this pleasing combination of yesterday's rice and beans, either accompanying or combined with eggs. It can also be dressed up with fried ripe plantains and a hunk of fried cheese to make a light dinner. In its most basic form, *gallopinto* is simply leftover rice and beans fried together in a little oil. The small Central American red bean is hard to find in the United States, so black beans, which are a similar size and texture, have been substituted here. Kidney beans would be too large and starchy, and white beans don't provide the deep red-brown color that characterizes this dish. This dish is found throughout Central America and parts of the Caribbean and can be found in most restaurants in the United States featuring those food cultures.

Gallopinto

4 cups leftover white rice
2 cups cooked black beans (instructions below)
½ cup bean liquid
1 cup finely chopped onions
1 clove garlic
Oil to cover bottom of pan
1 cup cilantro, finely chopped
Salt and pepper to taste
2–4 eggs, beaten (optional)
1 cup finely chopped Roma tomatoes (optional)

Fry the onions and garlic in the oil over medium heat. If you are using tomatoes, add them and stir/mash to make a sauce. Add the rice, beans, and bean liquid and simmer, stirring once in a while. When the liquid is almost gone, add the cilantro. Cook until the liquid is gone. If desired, scramble the egg in a little oil and toss with the *gallopinto*. Season to taste with salt and pepper.

Cooking dried beans:

Soak the beans overnight and drain. Using new water, cook the beans until soft. (The time will vary depending on how old the beans are. Some cooks add a metal spoon to the pot to hasten cooking.) Add a bunch of cilantro and a head of garlic cut in half to the pot for flavor. Add salt when the beans are almost soft. Leftover liquid is great for soups.

Katey Borland
(See "Costa Rica" by Melissa McGovern, *EAFT*, pp. 135–37.)

～

Côte d'Ivoire (Western Africa), Ivorian American Food

Côte d'Ivoire, also known as the Ivory Coast, is one of the countries from which slaves were taken and brought to the Americas. Enslaved Africans also brought certain crops, agricultural skills, and cooking styles, such as rice growing, greens, certain peas and beans, and yams. The last are native to Africa and are an important food there. They are frequently confused in the United States with sweet potatoes, which look and taste similar but are a different botanical species. They have become a staple of southern and African American cooking.

This recipe is similar to sweet potato casseroles popular in the American South and for Thanksgiving meals throughout the United States. While nutmeg is popularly associated with pies in the United States, it is a common spice in much of the cooking in West Africa.

Yam Bake

5 cups yam, boiled and mashed (skins should be removed)
1 egg
1 tablespoon butter, melted or room temperature
1 egg yolk
½ teaspoon nutmeg
½ teaspoon cinnamon

Preheat oven at 350°F. Grease casserole dish or ovenproof pan. Mix mashed yams with 1 beaten egg and butter. Add nutmeg and cinnamon. Pour or spoon yam mixture into dish. Beat egg yolk and pour on top of mixture. Bake for 15 minutes until golden brown. Sprinkle with additional nutmeg.

Lucy M. Long
(See "Côte d'Ivoire," Sarah Wyer, *EAFT*, pp. 137–38.)

∽

Creole (North America), Creole

Creole American food is both the food of an ethnic group and the food of a particular place—New Orleans and the surrounding region. The term was originally used in colonial Louisiana and in the Caribbean to refer to people born in the colonies of parents of foreign origin. Both European and African-descended people were thus Creoles. Today, Creole food is defined by both ingredients and techniques. The former includes extensive use of seafood as well as pork, beef, chicken, and even rabbit, rice, and the "holy trinity," a *mirepoix* made of bell peppers, celery, and onion. Also central to the cuisine are garlic, scallions, peppers (sometimes in the form of pepper sauces such as Tabasco or Crystal, two popular local brands), filé, bay leaf, cayenne, thyme, and various kinds of "creole seasoning" mixes (home cooks often rely on local mixes available in grocery stores, but chefs often mix their own), and considerable amounts of salt.

Garlic and Parsley Shrimp with Rice is a popular dish prepared in a lot of households in New Orleans. It does not start with a roux, and it does not have the Creole holy trinity of green pepper, onions, and celery, but it does rely on local seafood, which is central to a lot of Creole cooking. I learned it from Chef Michel Fouqueteau, who demonstrated it at the Crescent City Farmers Market in 2005. Chef Fouqueteau, who passed away in 2008, cooked in a number of New Orleans Creole bistros, including Flagons and Christians (the latter was housed in a former church in midcity). He suggested cooking the rice in saffron-soaked fish stock. The dish is sometimes served with spaghetti instead of rice.

Garlic and Parsley Shrimp with Rice
6 Servings

> 2 pounds medium shrimp, peeled, deveined
> ½ teaspoon salt
> ½ teaspoon red pepper flakes
> 4 tablespoons olive oil
> 1 cup parsley
> 6 garlic cloves
> 3 tablespoons white wine
> Lemon juice

Prepare rice for 6 in advance, keep warm.

In a food processor, chop together parsley, garlic, and 2 tablespoons olive oil. Set aside.

In a skillet, heat remaining 2 tablespoons olive oil over medium high heat. Sauté the shrimp, red pepper flakes, and salt, for a few minutes, until nearly cooked through. Add the parsley and garlic mixture, let cook for a minute or so, then deglaze the pan with the white wine and cook for another minute. Add lemon juice to taste.

Serve over rice.

David Beriss
(See "Creole," David Beriss, *EAFT*, pp. 142–45.)

∼

Croatia (Southern Europe), Croatian American

In the United States, Croatians from all Old Country regions frequently come together in fraternal lodges and churches, becoming familiar with each other's characteristic foods. Coastal Croatians have adopted many dishes of inland Croatians such as *Sarma* (stuffed cabbage rolls of central European origin), but they were less disposed to prepare coastal seafood dishes or *polenta* (boiled cornmeal) as the typical carbohydrate dish.

Sarma (Stuffed cabbage and sauerkraut)

    2 large heads of cabbage, fresh or brine-pickled
    1 can (48 ounce) of sauerkraut
Filling:
    1½ cups chopped onion
    1 tablespoon butter
    1 pound ground pork
    1 cup ham or smoked pork loin, chopped
    1 pound ground beef
    2 eggs, beaten
    4 cloves garlic, minced
    3 tablespoons chopped parsley
    1 tablespoon salt
    ½ cup long-grained rice, uncooked
Sauce:
    4 tablespoons butter
    ¼ cup flour
    ½ cup chopped onions
    1 tablespoon paprika
    1 can (6 ounce) tomato paste
    3 cups broth (beef, chicken, or vegetable) or water

Preparing the cabbage leaves:
Fill a large pot ⅓ full of water and bring to a boil. While waiting for water to boil, remove the cores of two large heads of cabbage. Place cabbage in water for five minutes to blanch. Remove from water and let cool.

Filling:

Sautée chopped onion in butter until brown. Let cool. In a large bowl combine with meats, eggs, garlic, parsley, salt, and rice. Mix well with hands. Set aside.

Open and drain canned sauerkraut. Spread ⅓ of the sauerkraut evenly on the bottom of a large pot. Carefully remove blanched leaves from cabbage heads (about 20 leaves). Using about ⅓ of meat mixture, form a sausage and place on the core end of the cabbage leaf. Tuck in sides of leaves and roll up cigarlike toward the edge of leaf. Place roll on sauerkraut, seam side down. Cover layer of cabbage rolls with more sauerkraut, then continue layering rolls and sauerkraut until all cabbage rolls are in the pot. Finish with a layer of sauerkraut.

Sauce:

In a pot, melt butter and add flour, stirring constantly over low heat until flour is golden brown. Add chopped onion, paprika, and tomato paste. Stir well. Slowly pour in broth or water, stirring until mixture is smooth. Pour sauce over cabbage rolls. Cover pot and simmer over low heat for 3 hours. Let stand for 15 minutes before serving. Top with sour cream and garnish with freshly chopped parsley.

Recipe by *Stephanie Vuljanić-Lemke*

Čevapčiči (Spiced meat rolls)

Of Turkish origin, this variant includes pork, showing Balkan Christian influence.

1 pound ground pork
1 pound ground beef
1 slice bread, soaked in milk and drained
1 egg
1 cup finely chopped onions
3 large cloves of garlic
2 teapoons salt
1 teaspoon pepper
1 tablespoon chopped red pickled peppers (hot banana peppers are good as well)
2 tablespoons chopped pickled jalapeño peppers (adjust for your taste)
1 tablespoon finely chopped parsley
1 teaspoon baking soda
Vegetable oil for frying

Mix and knead together all ingredients for five minutes. Taking about 1–2 tablespoons of meat mixture, form little finger shapes about 2 inches long and ¾ inches in diameter. Grill, broil, or fry the *čevapčiči*, until they are well browned and thoroughly done.

Recipe by *Stephanie Vuljanić-Lemke*

Brudet (Seafood stew)

Northern Adriatic version of the ubiquitous Mediterranean fish soup. The saffron is a French or Spanish borrowing.

1 pound cod filet (or other flaky fish), cut in ½-inch slices
½ pound cleaned squid, cut as above
½ pound shell-on shrimp
1 28-ounce can whole peeled tomatoes
2 medium onions, coarsely cut
5 cloves garlic, sliced
¼ cup olive oil
4 cups seafood stock
2 cups dry white wine
3 bay leaves
½ cup chopped parsley
Oregano, thyme, or marjoram to taste
(optional) saffron threads to taste
1 cup polenta, cooked as per instructions on package, or 3 cups cooked
    polenta

Shell the shrimp, reserving the shells. Add these to fish stock and boil gently in a covered saucepan for 40 minutes. Discard shells and reserve the stock.

Sauté onions and garlic in a soup pot on medium heat for about 5 minutes. Add tomatoes and their liquid, breaking them as they heat. Add reserved stock, wine, and bay leaves and boil for one hour. Add fish and herb seasonings and boil for 20 minutes. Add squid and shrimp and continue boiling for 10 minutes. Serve in bowls over polenta.

Richard March and Stephanie Vuljanic-Lemke
(See "Croatia," Richard March, *EAFT*, pp. 142–45.)

～

Cuba (Americas—Caribbean), Cuban American Food

Traditional Cuban cuisine is a fusion of culinary cultures of many people, including the Taínos, the Spanish, West Africans, Chinese, and those from the United States. Cuba's proximity to Florida has impacted its history and culture and has resulted in a great deal of cultural interchange, especially since the state of Florida shares some of the history of colonization under Spanish rule. Today, Cuban cooking is commercially available in the United States in restaurants of all categories—from kiosks to upscale dining establishments. So-called Cuban-style sandwiches are popular in many more trendy spots. Cuban Americans have held on to many of their culinary traditions, maintaining them at home and using them to celebrate life cycle, religious, and national holidays. They actively promote their food and are participating in the development of Nuevo Latino cuisine. They also adapt their techniques and recipes to new and available ingredients. For example, for an easy dessert of guava slices and cream cheese on a cracker, they might instead wrap a piece of American cheese single around a slice of guava paste.

***Ropa Viej* ("Old clothes," shredded beef and vegetables)**
Serves 6 to 8

    2.5 pound flank steak, cut in half
    2 bay leaves
    ¼ cup Spanish olive oil
    1 large onion, cut in half and thinly sliced
    1 large green bell pepper, cut in strips
    2 to 3 garlic cloves, finely chopped
    2 cups drained and chopped canned whole tomatoes or prepared tomato
        sauce
    ½ cup cooking sherry
    Salt and freshly ground black pepper to taste
    ½ cup drained canned early sweet peas for garnish, optional
    ½ cup chopped, drained pimentos for garnish

Place the beef and a bay leaf in large saucepan, and cover with salted water. Bring to a boil and then lower the temperature to low heat, covered, until the meat is tender, 1 to 1½ hours. Remove the meat to a plate and let it cool. Cut it into 2-inch chunks. Save the stock if you'd like. Heat the oil in a large skillet over low heat and add the vegetables until the onions are tender, 6 to 8 minutes. Add the tomatoes, sherry, and the other bay leaf. Cook uncovered another 15 minutes. Shred the meat and season with salt and pepper. Add to the tomato mixture and simmer on low for 30 minutes. Remove the bay leaves, and garnish with pimientos and peas. You can make this a day or two in advance. Let it cool before putting it in the refrigerator. When you are ready to serve it, heat it slowly in a skillet, about 30 minutes.

Yucca with Lime Mojo (Cassava in lime sauce)
Serves 6

3 pounds fresh or frozen yucca
3 tablespoons salt (I would use 1 tablespoon)

For the mojo:
½ cup lime juice
4 garlic cloves, chopped (or 6–8)
½ cup olive oil
1 teaspoon salt
½ teaspoon black pepper

Peel the yucca, cut it in half lengthwise, and then again into 3-inch chunks. Put the vegetable in a soup pot. Cover with cold water and add the salt. Boil. Reduce heat to medium and cook, covered, about 30 minutes or until the yuca is pierced easily with a knife. Combine the lime juice, garlic, salt, and pepper in a bowl or mortar. Let it sit for ½ an hour. When the yucca is done, drain and put in a serving bowl. Heat the oil and carefully toss the lime and garlic mixture into it—beware of splatter! Let the garlic cook a little; some of it may turn a bluish green at the edges. Do not brown the garlic! Take it off the burner and pour over the yucca.

Marsiella Veiga
(See Cuba," Marisella Veiga, *EAFT*, pp. 145–52.)

～

Czechoslovakia (Eastern Europe), Czechoslovakian or Bohemian American

Bohemian Americans are a population as diverse as their origins, and their foodways reflect the multitude of historical influence. Both the language and food are richly seasoned with Polish, Austrian, German, and Hungarian flavors as well as Czech. Signature imported Bohemian dishes are inspired by the integration of the European sensibility about using everything, wasting nothing, and the American emphasis on quantity. Schnitzels, sausages, strudels, and goulashes are all borrowed from neighboring countries, yet Bohemian cooks add a distinctive twist. For example, Czech dumplings include farina and sometimes stale bread, whereas those of other nations might be made purely from potatoes. Meals typically begin with soup, focus on a main course, and end with a sweet desert.

Both *kolaches* and dumplings are central to Bohemian culinary identity. The former is for special times and holidays, particularly Christmas. The later is typical Sunday fare, served with a big meal. Leftover cold dumplings are often sliced into bite-sized pieces, seasoned with salt and pepper, and fried the next day, often in scrambled eggs.

Sweets are popular ways to conclude meals and to celebrate holidays: *roski* (almond horns); *palacinka*, crepelike pancakes filled with fruit, jam, chocolate, and topped with whipped cream; *ovocné knedliky*, buttered, powdered-sugar-coated dumplings filled with fruit such as cherries, apricots, or strawberries, are examples. A sweet that is finding its way outside of the ethnic kitchen and into mainstream American bakeries is the kolache. For Bohemian Americans, purchasing store-bought brand-name jams, such as Smuckers, for the centers of kolaches was a true sign of success.

Grandma (Stepanek) Merskin's Dumplings

4 medium-large potatoes (Idaho)
2 cups flour
½ cups farina (Cream of Wheat)
2 eggs
Salt

Boil potatoes with peel on. Drain when done. Flour a board and take skins off potatoes. Put the potatoes through a ricer on top of flour. Salt according to taste. Sprinkle farina over potatoes, and put eggs on top of the mix. Knead together and roll into a long roll. Cut off into pieces and let sit for a half hour or so. Then put pieces into boiling water for 20 minutes.

My Grandmother's *Kolache* (Stuffed sweet pastry)

½ pound butter
2 egg yolks (don't beat, will drop in whole)
1 whole egg
½ pint sweet cream or ½ pint canned milk
¼ teaspoon salt
3 tablespoons sugar
1 ounce fresh yeast or 2 dry packages
1 teaspoon vanilla
3¼ cups flour
Filling for center of cookie (typically jam or preserves)

Cream butter, add sugar, and cream again. Add eggs and cream or milk and mix. Crumble/drop in the yeast and add the vanilla. Sift flour and salt and add to butter and egg mixture and mix until dough is well combined. Let freeze (or refrigerate) in a flour-dusted bowl overnight. The next day, take out half of the dough at a time. Roll out ¼-inch thick on a floured board. Cut in to rounds (using a small glass). Put on ungreased cookie sheet. Make a dent in the center of each circle and put in the filling. Let rise for 10 minutes. Put in a moderate oven, and bake until gold brown. Sift powdered sugar over the top when cool.

Debra Merskin
(See "Czechoslovakia," Debra Merskin, *EAFT*, pp. 152–55.)

D

Democratic Republic of Congo (West Africa), Congolese Americans

Many of the traditional ingredients basic to the Congolese diet are not available in the United States, and immigrants have had to either find substitutions or emphasize those ingredients that are available. Rice, corn, and beans, therefore, are highlighted, and *fufu* might be made out of cornmeal or even cream of wheat. In urban centers and in areas with a high concentration of African immigrants, many Congolese Americans source specialty ingredients at African markets, and they purchase more readily acquired ingredients, such as meat and veggies, from mainstream grocery stores.

Madeso Beans
Adapted from ImmigrantKitchens.com

1 pound dried red beans
Small red onion, sliced thinly (white onion can be used)
½ cup green pepper, sliced thinly
½ cup olive oil
1 tablespoon tomato paste
1 nutmeg nut
3 bay leaves
1 teaspoon salt

In a large bowl, cover dried beans with water and soak for 8 hours or overnight. Place beans in a large stockpot, cover with water, and simmer until soft, about 40 minutes. Strain and cool, then return to the large stockpot.

In a skillet, fry onions in ¼ cup olive oil on medium-high heat. When onions are translucent, add green pepper. After another minute, add tomato paste, and stir until the oil becomes red in color. Add enough water to make a sauce out of the thick paste, and cook for about five minutes.

Grate about ⅓ of the nutmeg nut (about 1 teaspoon) into the sauce. Add 1 teaspoon of salt. At this point, you may need to add additional water so the sauce is neither watery nor too thick. Cook for about 15 minutes more on low heat, then pour sauce over the cooked beans. Add bay leaves, and cook beans with sauce, covered, for approximately 15 minutes on medium-low heat, stirring occasionally.

Serve with rice and hot sauce.

Emily Hilliard
(See "Democratic Republic of Congo," Emily Hilliard, *EAFT*, pp. 157–59.)

Denmark, (Northern Europe), Danish American

Danish food is little known in mainstream American food culture and is misrepresented by the pastry known as a *Danish*. Danes in the United States and in Denmark do prepare and consume a lighter and flakier variant, but in Denmark it is associated with Vienna. Within American communities where Danish ethnicity is highly visible, one of the most common traditional foods is the seemingly humble æbleskiver (*aebleskiver*). The name translates as "apple slices," and this spherical, pancake-like food sometimes includes apple slices in the batter. It is made in a special cast iron pan that contains seven to nine holes. These resemble muffin tins and are sometimes sold by the noninitiated under that rubric.

In America, æbleskiver sometimes is eaten as a breakfast food, but more typically it is served with pancake syrup and other American condiments, and may be accompanied by *medisterpølse*, a Danish pork sausage. Occasionally, when cooked at communal dinners, it is even made from packaged pancake/waffle mixes. An æbleskiver dinner may be held as a fund-raiser for churches and civic organizations.

Aebleskiver (Pancake puffs)

Recipe, used with permission, from Sara Andersen, Danish immigrant to Audubon, Iowa, from Nykøbing, Falster

2 cups buttermilk (evaporated milk can also be used)
2 cups sifted flour
2 teaspoons baking powder
½ teaspoon salt
2 tablespoons sugar
3 eggs

Beat egg yolks.

Sift baking powder with the flour. Add sugar, salt, milk, flour, and baking powder.

Add stiffly beaten egg whites.

Place ¼ teaspoon shortening in each hole in the *ableskiver* pan after it is heated.

Fill each hole approximately ⅔ or ¾ full. Bake over a low heat on the stovetop.

When ½ baked, turn the *ableskiver* with a hatpin or knitting needle. (Look for the browning around the edges and the breaking of bubbles in the mixture.) Cooked until browned on both sides.

Serve with jelly, applesauce, powdered sugar, or syrup.

Gregory Hansen
(See "Denmark," Gregory Hansen, *EAFT*, pp. 159–64.)

~

Djibouti (East Africa), Djibouti American

Located in the "Horn of Africa," on the northeastern part of the continent, Djibouti borders the Red Sea (with Yemen across the sea), Eritrea on the north, Ethiopia south and west, and Somalia to the south. Islam is the dominant religion and shapes the food culture, which also displays influences from French and Indian cuisines and is similar to that of neighboring countries. Djiboutians make a flat bread similar to but smaller and flatter than Ethiopian *injera*, called *lahoh* (Yemini name) or *canjeero*, but also made with *teff* flour. The bread is eaten with stews (*maroq*) and for breakfast might be served with butter (or Indian *ghee*) and honey. The cuisine relies heavily on seafood, but also includes beef, camel, and goat. A signature dish is a spicy beef soup called *Fah-fah*, and vegetables are also stewed and spiced to make *yetakelt wet*. Meals can include rice or pasta with meat or rice and lentils. These are usually served with sauces, *bere-bere* or *niter kibbeh*, and a banana—the latter is a custom often continued in East African restaurants in the United States. Indian influence on the cuisine is seen in the preference for tea over coffee, the popularity of small triangular pastries, *sambusas*, and the use of cumin to flavor a common oat porridge called *garoobey*.

Although many Djiboutis leave as refugees, sources claim less than three hundred individuals are in the United States, and they are usually included with Somalians.

Skoudekharis (Rice with cardamom)

1 pound lamb or mutton shoulder in pieces
2 cups basmati rice
5 tomatoes, peeled, deseeded, and cut in pieces (or 1 can of tomatoes)
4 tablespoons ghee or oil
1 tablespoon tomato paste
2 yellow onions
1 red onion
4 garlic cloves, minced
2 red chili peppers
1 teaspoon cumin (ground)
6 cardamom pods
2 pinches of cinnamon powder
Salt
Pepper
Coriander leaves, torn

Cut the yellow onions in small pieces. Cut the red onion in half and slice finely. Heat the ghee or oil in a large skillet and pan-fry the pieces of meat light brown on all sides. Add the onion pieces and slices and sauté over moderate heat. Add salt, pepper, garlic, tomato pieces, chili peppers, and tomato paste. Stir in the cumin, cardamom, and cinnamon. Cover with water, stir, and cover the skillet with a lid. Simmer gently for 45 minutes, until the meat is done. Add the rice, stir, and bring to a boil. Cook the rice for 5 minutes on moderate heat and let it simmer on low heat for 10 minutes. Check the water during cooking, and if necessary add more water. Taste and add more salt and pepper if necessary. Serve hot, garnished with coriander leaves.

Karin Vaneker and Lucy M. Long
(See "Djibouti," Lucy Long, EAFT, pp. 164–65.)

⌢

Dominican Republic (Americas—Caribbean), Dominican American Food

A popular dish in the Dominican Republic is *sancocho*, which translates to stew. Found in many other Latin American cultures but called by different names, *sancocho* is most commonly made with approximately five different kinds of meat. However, due to cost, many Dominican Americans make it with whatever meat and vegetables they have on hand. *Sancocho* is often paired with rice, as most Dominican dishes are, and a few slices of avocado. Because it takes so much time to make, it is usually reserved for special occasions. For those Dominicans in the United States, *sancocho* is still a popular dish, but it often includes different substitutions due to the difficulty in finding certain ingredients in the United States. A simplified recipe is given below.

Casabe, also known as cassava bread, is another popular Dominican dish. A flat bread made from *yucca* (cassava) flour, it originated with the native Taíno people of the Dominican Republic. It is a long-argued tale that this bread is what drove the people of Spain to conquer the land of the Dominican Republic. In the United States, casabe is most often bought at local Dominican or Latin American grocery stores.

Sancocho (Stew)

3 pounds chicken
2 pounds bone-in pork shoulder, cut in 1½-inch pieces off bone
2 pounds bone-in beef, cut in 1½-inch pieces off bone
1 pound goat meat, cut in 1½-inch pieces
2 pounds Italian sausage
4 large plantains, unripe and cut into medium-sized pieces
1 pound potatoes
2 pounds peeled and washed *yucca,* cut into small pieces

2 pounds Spanish pumpkin or butternut squash, chopped up
3 ears corn, on the cob, cut into 6 pieces each
1 pound yams, cut into medium-sized pieces
6 liters water
5 tablespoons vegetable oil
1 ¼ tablespoons oregano
4 ½ teaspoons salt
3 medium-sour oranges (or 4 lemons)
2 tablespoons celery, chopped
2 green bell peppers, cut into large pieces
3 medium-sized onions
2 tablespoons minced garlic
Oregano, thyme, and parsley to taste
2 chicken bouillon cubes
2 teaspoons vinegar
2 tablespoons Worcestershire sauce

Cut the three pounds of chicken into pieces (the size does not matter). Wash all of the meat, except the sausages. Take the three sour oranges and rub them on all of the meat, including the sausages. (This is a popular marinating technique among Dominicans in the Dominican Republic and in the United States.) Add the oil, herbs, onion, garlic, Worcestershire sauce, salt, and pepper to a large stew pot. Once the seasonings begin to simmer and the garlic begins to roast, add the beef and brown. This should take approximately 20 minutes. Add the pork to the stew pot and allow it to simmer for 15 minutes. Add a very small amount of water, but only enough so it does not stick. Add the goat meat and sausage to the stew pot and allow it to simmer for another 15 minutes. Add the chicken and the chicken stock made from the bouillon cubes to the pot, and allow it to simmer for approximately 10 minutes. While the chicken and stock is simmering, boil the water in a separate pot, and then add the vegetables. Simmer the vegetables for approximately 10 minutes. Add the vegetables and the water to the meat and allow it to simmer, until the veggies are soft. Remove about half of them from the pot with a slotted spoon or strainer, place in a small, heatproof bowl, and mash. Once the vegetables are mashed, return them to the pot and allow the stew to thicken. Add in the two teaspoons of vinegar. Once thickened, the stew is finished. Serve in a bowl with a side of white rice and a side of sliced avocado.

Casabe (Cassava bread)

1 pound peeled, washed, and salted yucca

Finely grate the yucca. Squeeze the yucca with a cheesecloth or wet paper towel until as much liquid as possible has been drained from it. Break up any lumps, spread on a baking sheet, and place in a refrigerator (for no more than an hour) to dehumidify the yucca. Heat a cast iron skillet to medium heat until very hot, but do not add any butter or oil. When ready, place some of the grated yucca in the pan and flatten out using the back of a spatula. When the bottom is golden (about 1 minute), flip and cook the other side until golden as well. Serve warm, or cool it first to create the appearance and texture of a cracker. Casabe is a plain-flavored bread, and thus is often made by mixing in different seasonings, such as cheese or garlic to the yucca before refrigeration.

Alexandria Ayala
(See "Dominican Republic," Alexandria Ayala, *EAFT*, pp. 165–69.)

E

Ecuador (South America), Ecuadorian American Food

In Highland Ecuador, as well as throughout the Andes, potatoes represent an important staple that is prepared many different ways. When indigenous farmers first domesticated potatoes in the Andes, they bred and developed a multitude of varieties, adapted to different ecological conditions and with different cooking characteristics. Now in the United States, Ecuadorian Americans can find different kinds of potatoes, but they pale in comparison to the choices available in South American markets. Cheese is often combined with potatoes, as in the favorite dish below, *llapingachos*, a cheese and mashed potato patty. In Ecuador, *llapingachos* are sometimes made with cassava or mashed yucca, but in North America, rarely would these root crops be available. *Llapingachos* are often served with a peanut sauce (recipe below), baked or fried pork, and a tomato and lettuce salad on the side.

Llapingachos (Cheese and mashed potato patty)
Serves 8 as side dish

2 pounds potatoes (Russets work better than boiling potatoes)
1 onion, finely chopped
½ pound white cheese, crumbled
2 tablespoons butter
1 teaspoon salt

Sauce:
½ pound peanuts, roasted and ground
½ cup evaporated milk
3 tablespoons onion, finely chopped
3 tablespoons butter
Cilantro, chopped, and 2 hard-boiled eggs, chopped

Wash, peel, and boil potatoes until tender. Mash them and mix with 1 tablespoon butter, and salt to taste. Let rest to cool, about ½ hour to 45 minutes. Melt remaining tablespoon of butter. Sauté onions until soft, about 5 minutes. Add crumbled cheese to onions. Shape the mashed potatoes into patties and stuff them with the cheese-onion mixture. Refrigerate and let sit for ½ hour to chill. Cook them on hot, greased griddle. If you don't have a griddle, lightly grease a frying pan and fry on both sides until lightly browned.

Sauce: sauté the onions in 1 tablespoon butter. Add the peanuts and milk. Cook over medium heat until the sauce thickens, about 10 minutes. Serve with the fried potato patties. Garnish with chopped cilantro and chopped hard-boiled egg, if desired.

Lois Stanford
(See "Ecuador," Lois Stanford, *EAFT*, pp. 171–73.)

⁓

Egypt (North Africa), Egyptian American Food

Egyptian immigration to the United States is a relatively recent phenomenon.

Contrary to what one might expect, most Egyptian Americans are not Muslims but Coptic Christians (often called Egyptian Orthodox here). The word *Egypt* derives from the Latin word for "Coptic."

Some Egyptians would consider *koshari* to be the national dish, and it is one that translates well to the American context since all the ingredients are readily available. It can also be adapted in countless variations. Since it is labor intensive, it is usually a special occasion dish.

Koshari (Rice, macaroni, and bean dish)

1 pound smallish pasta (elbow macaroni is suitable, as are *ditales*)
2 cups (dry) short-grained rice
2 cups garbanzo beans (canned, drained; or prepared from dried)
2 cups lentils (green or red) (canned, drained; or prepared from dried)

2 14-ounce cans crushed tomatoes
Chili flakes or other hot peppers
2 onions, thinly sliced
7–10 segments garlic
Vinegar, salt, and pepper to taste

To prepare: First, fry the sliced onions until they are light brown and crunchy (do not burn). Set aside. Then, prepare a tomato sauce from the garlic and crushed tomatoes; additional spices may be desired, such as cilantro or parsley (*kusbara w bagdonis*). Take about a quarter of the sauce and add chili flakes or other hot pepper, along with some vinegar, to create a very hot sauce. Finally, cook and drain all of the starches and set aside in separate bowls.

To serve, each individual ingredient is placed on a buffet or simply on the dining table, and each person helps himself or herself to a portion of each, topping it all off with the fried onions and a quantity of hot sauce commensurate with the individual's courage and heat tolerance!

Many Middle Eastern and Mediterranean cultures pride themselves on serving a variety of "mezzes," or small, bite-sized appetizers as an accompaniment to any meal, or as a meal in itself. Here are two Egyptian dishes that could form part of a mezze platter or could be served as accompaniments to a meal or as a stand-alone snack. The rice stuffing can also be used, with or without the addition of ground meat, to fill rolled grape leaves (similar to Greek dolmas); the cooking method is the same.

Ma'ashi (Rice-stuffed vegetables)

Choose the vegetables you want to stuff: zucchini, small eggplants (such as Japanese eggplant), or green peppers are standard, but you could also use potatoes, firm tomatoes, cabbage leaves, or other vegetables. Cut the tops off zucchini (or similar) and hollow them out. Then prepare the stuffing; all spice can be adjusted to taste.

2 cups short-grained rice
1 bunch cilantro
½ bunch parsley
Small bunch of fresh dill
2 small onions or one medium, minced or diced
1 tomato, diced
Tomato paste (1 tablespoon or to taste)
2–4 cloves garlic, minced
6–8 cardamom pods (crush lightly)
1 teaspoon ground cumin

½ teaspoon ground coriander
½ teaspoons black pepper
¼ teaspoon white pepper
5–6 bouillon cubes OR canned stock (usually chicken or vegetable flavor)
Olive oil as needed
Optional: ½ to 1 pound ground beef or lamb

Wash and drain the rice in several changes of water.

If using, brown the meat in olive oil or lard; add all of the spices to the meat (except cardamom pods).

Chop all herbs, the garlic, and tomato; add to the drained rice with a bit of olive oil. Now add the spiced meat (if using), or add all of the spices *except* the whole cardamom pods. Stuff your vegetables (or roll leaves) with the mixture.

Arrange the stuffed vegetables upright in a large, heavy-bottomed pot; add the cardamom pods. Prepare bouillon (or heat stock) in a separate pot and pour the hot liquid over the vegetables just to cover. Bring to a simmer on the stovetop, then cover with a tight-fitting lid and continue simmering until rice is cooked and vegetables are tender but still firm (about 30 minutes). If desired, finish in a 350°F oven to cook off some of the liquid and brown the top of the dish.

You may have some stuffing mixture left over; have a jar of grape leaves on hand so you can use it up!

Baba Ghannoug (Eggplant dip)

The Egyptian pronunciation varies slightly from the Lebanese spelling we usually see, *baba ghannoush*. Of course you can buy this ready made in most supermarkets, but the homemade version is so much better! The oven-roasted eggplant is key. This is a basic recipe for a snack-sized amount (approximately 2 cups, 6 servings); it can easily be doubled.

1 medium eggplant
¼ cup tahini
1 tablespoon lemon juice
1 tablespoon olive oil
1 teaspoon vinegar (dose carefully to taste)
1–2 cloves garlic, minced and crushed
½ to 1 teaspoons cumin
¼ to ½ teaspoon ground white pepper
Chopped cilantro and parsley to taste (at least ¼ cup each)

Roast the eggplant at 350°F for about an hour, until thoroughly softened but *not* dried out. Allow to cool, then scoop out the flesh, removing as many of the seeds as possible. Chop the eggplant flesh into small chunks.

Stir the eggplant into the tahini, adding a bit of water to "loosen" the mixture, then add the other ingredients; stir vigorously to incorporate. Adjust seasonings to taste. Serve with fresh pita wedges or pita chips.

Kristie Foell
(See "Egypt," Kristie Foell, *EAFT*, pp. 173–75.)

El Salvador (Central America), Salvadoran American Food

The *pupusa*, a stuffed grilled corn cake, is the national dish of El Salvador. Eaten as a side dish or snack, they have recently become popular in the United States, and they are frequently sold by Central American food trucks and restaurants and by specialty shops called *pupuserías*. They are also found in Honduras, leading to some discussion over place of origin. Pupusas are traditionally served with *curtido* (a pickled cabbage and vegetable slaw) and a thin tomato salsa. Making *pupusas* and the accompaniments at home among Salvadoran Americans is often reserved for days off or special occasions.

Pupusa de Frijoles y Queso (*Masa* cakes with bean and cheese stuffing)
Makes 8 *pupusas*.

2 cups instant corn flour *masa* (Maseca brand can be found in Latin markets or Latin sections in larger grocery stores)
¼ teaspoon salt
2 cups water (more or less, as needed)
½ cup refried black beans
1 cup shredded mozzarella cheese (not preshredded bags)
Vegetable oil

Mix the beans and cheese in a bowl and set aside. In a separate bowl, combine *masa* with salt. Add water to the *masa* gradually, mixing with your hands, until you form a moist dough that will not crumble. Divide the dough into 8 equal portions and roll each portion into a ball. With wet hands, take the first dough ball and pat it between your hands until it forms a small disc. Push the center of the disc in to form a bowl shape in your hand. Place about a tablespoon of bean and cheese mixture in the dough bowl. Form the dough around the filling (wetting hands as needed to close cracks in dough), pinching it closed to seal in the filling. Lightly pat the dough ball back and forth between your hands to make a thick, round disk (about ¼-inch thick and 4 inches in diameter), keeping the filling encased in dough. Repeat with remaining dough balls.

Heat a lightly oiled skillet to medium-high heat. Cook each pupusa for 2–3 minutes on each side until golden brown. Cover with tin foil as you cook the rest of the pupusas. Serve with *curtido* and salsa.

Curtido (Cabbage slaw)
Makes about 4 cups.

It is best to make the *curtido* several hours or a day before serving.
½ head cabbage, shredded
1 carrot grated
½ large onion, thinly sliced
1 jalapeño or other chili pepper, minced
½ tablespoon fresh oregano, finely minced
¼ cup white vinegar
2 tablespoons sugar
¼ teaspoon salt

In a bowl, cover cabbage and carrots with boiling water. Let sit for 10 minutes and drain, pressing to release liquid. Add sugar and salt to vinegar and stir until dissolved. Combine all ingredients in one bowl; toss to evenly coat. Add more salt to taste if necessary. Cover and let sit for a few hours or overnight in refrigerator.

Annu Ross
(See "El Salvador," Annu Ross, EAFT, pp. 175–79.)

England (Northern Europe), English American Food

England provided one of the primary foundations for American foodways, and many of its food traditions have been adapted and become "all American." Contemporary English food is as ethnic as any other cultural group's within the mainstream food culture it helped to create. Some foods, such as scones, tea, roast beef, and fish and chips, that could be considered English, are eaten throughout the United States, so assimilated that they are no longer identified as "English." There also are pockets of culture in which a tradition has been maintained and handed down over generations. An example is a cake named for Smith Island, an island off the eastern shore of Maryland that was settled by farmers from the southern coast of Britain (Dorset and Cornwall), who came to the area via Virginia in the first half of the seventeenth century. The settlers developed a ten-layer cake that is eaten on an everyday basis. It can be made "from the stump" (from scratch) or from boxed cake mixes. Yellow cake with chocolate frosting is the traditional recipe, but variations include moist layers of fig, banana, coconut cake, and chocolate peanut butter icing.

Smith Island Cake with Chocolate Icing
"From the stump" (From scratch)

2 cups sugar
2 blocks soft butter
5 eggs
½ cup evaporated milk (an island staple)
½ cup water
2¼ cup sifted flour
1 teaspoon baking powder
1 tablespoon vanilla

Preheat oven to 350°F. Grease and flour baking pans. (Five is an ideal number, depending on how many fit in your oven. Cakes may result in differing number of layers depending on batter distribution). Cream butter and sugar well. Beat eggs separately and add to creamed mixture. Add vanilla. Mix evaporated milk and water together. Alternately mix in flour and evaporated milk. Add baking powder in last cup of flour. Use large spoon or ladle to distribute batter to cake pans. Use only enough to make quarter-inch pancake-thin layers. Place as many layers as your oven accommodates in a preheated oven. Bake for 6–8 minutes, until you can touch the top of each layer without it sticking to your fingertip or edges begin to turn golden. Remove layers from oven and let cool in pans. Use knife to loosen edges. Spread frosting on each layer and on the top and sides. Clean emptied pans with paper towel, then regrease (and flour), add batter, and bake. Repeat, cook, and ice/frost until completed. (Number of layers will vary, but ten is ideal.)

Chocolate Icing

2 cups confectioners' sugar
1 cup (or less) evaporated milk
5 heaping tablespoons unsweetened powdered chocolate
1 stick softened unsalted butter
½ teaspoon vanilla

(Icing can be prepared cold or on stovetop.) Put butter, sugar and evaporated milk in a medium saucepan. Cook and stir over medium low heat until warm. Add chocolate and cook to melt. Cook over medium heat for 10–15 minutes, stirring occasionally. Add vanilla. Icing will be thin but thickens as it cools. Add evaporated milk to thin, as it thickens while spreading on each layer, top and sides.

Elaine Eff
(See "England," Lucy Long and Elaine Eff, *EAFT*, pp. 179–83.)

⌒

Eritrea (East Africa), Eritrean American (also Ethiopian American) Food

Traditional Eritrean foodways are similar to those of Ethiopia. Both use *injera*, the spongy, sour, fermented flat bread usually made from *teff*, eaten with spicy stews, sautéed greens, and sauces. History and geography, however, have created some significant differences: Eritrea's location on the Red Sea ensured a more prominent place for seafood. Eritreans are more likely to cook with tomatoes, a legacy of their country's decades as an Italian colony and also of the somewhat warmer climates created by lower elevations. The Italian influence has also made pasta dishes, such as spaghetti and lasagnas, an enduring part of the Eritrean diet. Additional subtle differences between Eritrean and Ethiopian cooking lies in the Eritreans' more varied vegetarian options and unique use of seeds like *intat'e* (flax seed) and grains like *hilbet* (combination of *fava* beans and lentils to create a fluffy paste).

Kawlo (Cabbage)

⅓ cup olive oil
1 onion, thinly sliced or cubed
Salt to taste

½ teaspoon black pepper
1 teaspoon curry powder
1 teaspoon ground ginger
1 teaspoon crushed garlic
1 head cabbage, sliced
1 bell pepper (sweet pepper, can mix colors)

Heat the oil over medium high heat. Sauté onion for about 5 minutes. Stir in the seasonings (salt, pepper, garlic, ginger, curry powder) and toast for a minute. Add in the cabbage, and cook, stirring occasionally, for about 8 minutes.

Reduce the heat to medium-low, cover, and occasionally stir (gently) until cabbage is cooked through.

Alicha (Mild vegetable stew)
Cabbage is optional but usually found in restaurants.

1 cup olive oil (or oil of your choice)
1½ cups red onion, sliced
1 tablespoon ginger (optional)
2 tablespoons garlic
6 potatoes, peeled, washed, and quartered
5 carrots, peeled, washed, and quartered
1½ pounds green beans, ends off and washed
1 medium chili pepper, halved (jalapeno or milder. Dish is not supposed to be hot.)
Salt and pepper to taste
2 tablespoons curry powder and turmeric (optional)
2 tablespoons cilantro or parsley, chopped

Cook onions and garlic in oil until transparent. Add curry powder, ginger, and turmeric (if using). Add green beans and cook for 5 minutes on medium heat. Add carrots and cabbage and cook for 10 about ten minutes Add potatoes, and reduce heat and cover, stirring occasionally, until potatoes are cooked.

Salt and pepper to taste. Throw in cilantro/parsley and chili pepper right before serving.

(An alternative is to steam vegetables separately by type, then roast.)

Kitcha fitfit (Breakfast made of flat bread)

5 cups wheat flour
Water (lukewarm)

1 teaspoon salt
2 tablespoons oil
Ghee/clarified butter
Bere bere
Yogurt

Mix flour and water in increments to form a paste. Add a pinch of salt and a tablespoon of oil. Heat pan and pour paste in it. Begin on high heat and steadily decrease heat as bread cooks. Flip when bottom side browns. When both sides brown, remove from heat and cut up in small pieces. Alternatively, you can buy ready-made unleavened bread and simply heat on pan (before tearing in to pieces). In a separate pan, heat/melt ghee and *bere bere* and add flat bread pieces. Mix well and make sure each piece is well coated. Serve with yogurt and black tea spiced with cardamom.

Intat'e (Flax seed sauce)

1 onion, diced
1 tomato, crushed
1 tablespoon garlic
Bere bere (optional)
4 tablespoons flax seed (toasted and ground)
Juice of 1 lemon
Salt

Dice and cook onions and tomatoes in very little oil until tender; add a teaspoon of *bere bere* and garlic and cook for about 5 minutes. Pour flax seed in, cook and stir for 1 minute, add water, cover and let simmer for 10–15 minutes. Salt to taste and squeeze lemon juice when ready to serve.

Sarah Tekle
(See "Eritrea," Alan Deutschman, *EAFT*, pp. 184–86.)

～

Estonia (Northern Europe), Estonian American Food

Estonian American food shares many traits with the ethnic traditions of Germany, Russia, Scandinavia, and Baltic Europe. Pork is the favored meat, in addition to *seapraad* (roast beef), *verivorst* (blood sausage or "black pudding"), and fish, notably salmon and herring. Common vegetables include potatoes, cabbage, carrots, and beets. Berries grow prolifically in Estonia and are a staple of traditional cooking. Interestingly, cranberries, which are indigenous to the United States, have been imported and are grown there commercially. They have been adopted into Estonian food culture, making it easier for Estonian Americans to make their traditional dishes for American holiday meals, such as Thanksgiving and Christmas. The pink, fluffy dessert called *roosamanna* is a frequent part of holiday meals.

Roosamanna (Berry juice pudding)

2 cups cranberry juice (or other tart berry juice)
¼ cup sugar
3 tablespoon farina (quick-cooking semolina or cream of wheat)

Bring the juice to a boil. Mix the sugar and farina, pour in the boiling juice, and whisk vigorously. Simmer at low heat for around 3 minutes; whisk often. Moisten the inside of a bowl with cold water, and pour in the hot mixture. Let cool for around 15 minutes or more. Whisk the mixture until creamy and thick. Chill before serving. Serve with whipped cream or, more traditionally, cold milk.

Karin Vaneker
(See "Estonia," Nicholas Hartman, *EAFT*, pp. 186–87.)

～

Ethiopia (Eastern Africa), Ethiopian American

Located in the Horn of Africa, Ethiopia is the continent's second-most-populous country. Political instability, ethnic conflict, drought, food insecurity, and lack of employment have driven many Ethiopians from home, oftentimes immigrating to neighboring nations before immigrating to the United States.

Food plays a major role in maintaining and celebrating cultural identity among Ethiopian Americans. Because Ethiopian cuisine is composed of numerous regional and ethnic variations, it is difficult to identify a single set of common foods. One that all agree upon, however, is *injera*, a flat, slightly sour, fermented pancake usually made of *teff*, a grain native to Ethiopia and Eritrea. The foundation of the traditional meal, *injera*, is eaten with stews (*wats* or *shiro*) and *gomen* (sautéed greens, usually turnip greens, collard greens, or kale). These dishes are frequently cooked in a spiced butter, called *niter kibbeh*, and flavored with *bere bere*, a mixture of multiple spices (chili powder, paprika, cayenne pepper, ground ginger, salt, garlic powder, onion powder, grated nutmeg, black cardamom seeds, coriander seeds, fenugreek seeds, whole allspice, cloves, and cinnamon).

Ethiopian restaurants have met with popular success in major cities in the United States, and the serving style is part of the appeal. A large *injera* is laid on a platter with portions on top of numerous meats and vegetables. Additional *injera* are used to dip by hand into the food, while the bottom layer soaks up juices and flavors.

Miser Wot (Birsin in Eritrean restaurants) (Lentils)

2 cups small red or brown lentils (green and yellow split peas can also be used)
5 cups water
1 teaspoon salt
1 onion, minced
1 whole garlic, minced
1 tomato, diced
chili powder (preferably *bere bere*)
1 lemon

Place 2 cups of lentils and salt in 4 cups water. Bring to boil, then cover and simmer for 20 minutes. In another pan, sauté 1 onion in oil. Add tomato and cook. Add chili powder. Add water to make it soupy. Then add garlic. Add lentils to sauce mixture and simmer for 20 minutes until liquid is reduced but the dish is not dry. Squeeze over top 1 whole lemon.

Doro Wat (Chicken stew)

Niter kibbeh (spiced butter)*
Bere bere (spice mix)
1 whole chicken, skinned, traditionally cut into 12 pieces (cut slits in thighs and thicker parts, so spices penetrate)
12 eggs, boiled
2 lemons, juice (rind of 1)
Kosher salt
2 pounds red onions, finely diced (Sweetness comes from the lengthy cooking and softening, or honey could be added.)

1 tablespoon minced garlic
1 tablespoon minced fresh ginger
1 tablespoon tomato paste
¼ teaspoon freshly ground black pepper
1¼ cups chicken stock or low-sodium chicken broth

Wash chicken thoroughly using salt, lemon juice, and lemon rind. Put the chicken in a bowl (not metal) and toss with lemon juice and 1 teaspoon salt. Let stand at room temperature for 30 minutes.

While the chicken is marinating, prepare a bowl with ice water. Bring a medium saucepan of generously salted water to a boil, enough to cover the eggs by 1 inch. Carefully add the eggs, bring back to a gentle boil, and cook for 6 minutes. Transfer the eggs to the ice water and, when cool to the touch, peel. Set aside; do not refrigerate or they will not warm up in the sauce.

Put onions in a large skillet over medium heat. Cook, stirring constantly, until golden, about 10 minutes, taking care not to burn. You may need to reduce the heat as the onions dry out.

Increase the heat to medium high; add ⅓ cup of the *niter kibbeh*, ¼ cup of the *bere bere*, the garlic, ginger, tomato paste, and black pepper, and cook, stirring, for 1 hour. Add the chicken, turning to coat well with the butter mixture, and then leave the chicken skin-side down in the pan.

Add the chicken stock, bring to a simmer, cover, reduce the heat to low, and cook at a gentle simmer until the chicken is very tender, about 40 minutes. Remove the lid, increase the heat to medium and simmer, stirring occasionally, until the liquid is reduced and the sauce is very thick, about 45 minutes, occasionally spooning the sauce over the chicken.

Remove the pan with the chicken from the heat and add the eggs, turning to coat them in the sauce. Cover the pan and let rest for 5 minutes. To serve, place the chicken thighs and eggs on *injera* or serving plates, and spoon the sauce over. Starting the onions in a dry pan is traditional for this dish and adds a toasty taste. Just be careful not to let the onions burn.

* Niter Kibbeh (Spiced butter)

1 pound unsalted butter
1 tablespoon chopped fresh ginger
1 teaspoon whole allspice berries
1 teaspoon fenugreek seeds
1 teaspoon dried oregano
½ teaspoon turmeric
6 black cardamom pods, crushed lightly with a knife blade

2 cloves garlic, coarsely chopped
1 small yellow onion, chopped

Melt the butter in a small saucepan over medium-low heat, swirling occasionally. Stir in the ginger, allspice, fenugreek, oregano, turmeric, cardamom, garlic, and onions and bring to a simmer. Simmer until the butter is clear and the milk solids remain on the bottom of the pan, about 30 minutes. Reduce the heat to low if the butter is boiling too quickly, if it burns it will taste bitter. To finish the *niter kibbeh*: Line a strainer with a dampened cheesecloth. Skim the foam from the top of the butter and discard. Ladle the butter through the strainer, leaving behind the milk solids on the bottom of the pan.

Sarah Tekle
(See "Ethiopia," Heidi Busse, Mulusew Yayehirad, Almaz Yimam, and Janet C. Gilmore, *EAFT*, pp. 187–94.)

F

Federated States of Micronesia (FSM) (Micronesia, Oceania), Micronesian American Food

A traditional method of cooking food throughout Micronesia is in an underground oven, called an *uhm*. The uhm is made by placing volcanic basalt stones on top of a fire, thoroughly heating them until the wood is completely consumed, and then spreading them out over a patch of earth. Food is placed on top, layers of banana and taro leaves are put above the food, and the meal then slowly bakes, with the scent of the wood and the leaves slowly infusing the food.

A popular dish baked in an *uhm* from the Federated States of Micronesia (FSM) is *pihlohlo*. This dish is always present at special occasions, and women are culturally expected to know how to make it. It continues to be an important food among Micronesians in the United States, and in the absence of a traditional *uhm*, the recipe has been adapted for conventional ovens.

Some staples in Micronesian food culture are generally not available in the United States, except in major cities.

Pihlohlo (Banana sponge pudding)

8 ripe bananas, peeled
1 cup tapioca starch
1 can coconut milk

¼ cup sugar
1 banana leaf
1 tablespoon vegetable oil

Mash the bananas in a large bowl. Mix in tapioca starch. Stir in coconut milk until you reach a thick, viscous consistency, adding in a tablespoon of water at a time if necessary. Add sugar to desired level of sweetness. Rub oil on one side of the banana leaf and place the leaf in a casserole dish with the oil side up. Pour the mixture on top and fold the leaf over the mixture, tucking the sides of the leaf into the dish. In lieu of banana leaves, pour mixture into greased casserole dish and cover with aluminum foil. Bake in a regular oven for 30 to 45 minutes at 375°F.

Eric César Morales
(See "Micronesia," Eric César Morales, *EAFT*, pp. 419–24.)

～

Fiji (Oceania, Melanesia), Fijian, Pacific Islander, Melanesian American Food

Also see entries for Melanesia and other islands: Papua New Guinea, Solomon Islands, and Vanuatu.

The largest group of Melanesians to immigrate to the United States comes from Fiji, and they started arriving in the 1950s. These include both native Fijians and Indo-Fijians, and their foods contrast, although the former have borrowed spices from the Indian culinary heritage—turmeric, ginger, and chili peppers—as well as the flat bread, *roti*, that is often used to scoop up sauces and stews.

Rourou (Taro leaves)

1 bundle of taro leaves (*rourou*)
Grated ginger (1 inch)
½ quart coconut milk (*lolo*)
1 onion, cut into small pieces
Salt

Method 1: Wash and tear up or cut the taro leaves in small pieces. Put 3 cups of water in a pot, bring to a boil, and add the pieces of taro. Boil for

15 to 20 minutes and stir continuously. Drain and squeeze out the excess liquid. Put the taro, coconut milk, onion, and grated ginger in the pot. Stir and bring to a boil, stir, and then simmer on very low heat. Add salt to taste.

Method 2: Wash and tear up or cut the taro leaves in small pieces. Heat oil in a pan, add half of the onion pieces, stir-fry until golden brown (at this stage grated ginger or garlic can be added). Add the taro leaves, 2 cups of water, and salt. Bring to a boil, then lower the heat and simmer for 15 to 20 minutes until the taro is tender. Add the coconut milk and the remaining onions, stir, and bring to a boil. Serve immediately.

Karin Vaneker
(See "Melanesia," Karin Vaneker, *EAFT*, pp. 407–11.)

～

Finland (Northern Europe), Finnish American Food

Finns began to arrive in the United States in large numbers in the late nineteenth and early twentieth centuries, bringing with them varied and discrete food cultures. The process of immigrant Finns becoming ethnic Finnish Americans can be seen in their foodways. Some immigrant foods from Finland now exist only as memories; some dishes were abandoned and others preserved, but other dishes were nearly forgotten have been revived. Changes in the function, significance, and symbolism of foods took place. Some dishes considered everyday in Finland have special meaning in the United States, expressing Finnish American ethnic identity.

Pannukakku or *Kropsu*, an oven pancake, is one of the Finnish American comfort foods. It can be eaten as a snack, light supper, breakfast, or dessert. There are many variants of this recipe.

Pannukakku or *Kropsu* (Oven pancake)

3 eggs
2 cups milk
1 cup all-purpose flour
Pinch salt and sugar
Butter

Slowly whip the flour into the egg and milk mixture until all has been absorbed and the mixture is smooth. Add salt and sugar. Let this mixture sit for about a half-hour. Heat the oven to 400°F. Place four Pyrex pie pans in the oven and melt a generous heaping tablespoon of butter in each. Divide the above mixture between the pans. Bake until the mixture puffs up and is golden. When you remove them from the oven, the *kropsu* will deflate. Remove from pans and serve one *kropsu* per person with jams; lingonberry, thimbleberry, and cloudberry jams are some Finnish American favorites.

Yvonne Lockwood
(See "Finland," Yvonne Lockwood, *EAFT*, pp. 195–200.)

～

France (Western Europe), French American Food

French cooking has historically been portrayed as fancy and gourmet, and although Julia Child introduced French cooking into American homes starting in the 1960s, it is still considered inaccessible to many Americans. Similarly, French habits around food have long been held as the pinnacle of healthfulness and are being emulated by some Americans. The two dishes included here represent home cooking among French Americans that are accessible to most cooks.

Boeuf Bourguignon (Beef burgundy)

This hearty beef stew is a favorite at Sunday meals. It gets its name because two of its main ingredients—beef and red wine—are central in traditional Bourguignon cooking. This dish is traditionally served with garlic toast; fresh *tagliatelle* macaroni noodles or steamed potatoes can be substituted.

This recipe can also be done in a crockpot. Serves four.

1 pound beef (shoulder or other stewing meat), cubed
4 onions, chopped
1 *bouquet garni* (if none is available, make your own by tying together thyme, parsley, and bay leaf with cooking twine)
1 bottle red wine (pinot noir); or ½ bottle of red wine and 1 ½ cup broth (vegetable, chicken, or beef)
2 tablespoons flour
Butter and olive oil
Salt, pepper
1 bunch carrots, chopped
¼ pound crimini or button mushrooms, quartered
Parsley (for garnish)

Thoroughly pat dry the cubed beef and brown it in olive oil in a large, heavy pot. Leave plenty of space between pieces of beef to avoid steaming. Set aside. Use the olive oil, butter, and flour to make a *roux*; once the *roux* is golden (in about 2 minutes), add the onions and allow them to soften. Add the beef, mushrooms, carrots, *bouquet garni*, salt, and pepper; pour in the red wine and broth combinations until covered. Simmer over low heat for at least 3 hours. Serve with flat noodles, steamed potatoes, or garlic toast.

Sole Meunière (Miller's sole)

Hailing from Rouen, in Normandy, this method for cooking fish requires a dredging in flour, which is where it gets its name. This dish is an old French classic, having been around at least since the sixteenth century, when it was quite popular. The simple preparation allows sole, a delicate, light fish, to showcase its flavors, which it could not do under heavier sauces. *Sole meunière* is typically served with steamed and buttered new potatoes (*pommes de terre vapeur*). Serves two.

2 sole filets
3 tablespoons butter
½ cup flour
Salt and pepper
Lemon
Parsley

Clarifying the butter: Place butter in a small saucepan and melt over moderate heat, stirring occasionally to avoid browning. Bring the butter to a light boil. Allow the white parts to cook off (this process is complete once the crackling sound ceases). Remove from heat and strain through a cheesecloth. When refrigerated, clarified butter will keep for several months.

Preparing the sole:
Pat the sole filets dry with a kitchen towel or a paper towel. Place flour, salt, and pepper on a soup plate. Dredge each filet in the flour, making sure to shake off the excess. Place clarified butter in a large frying pan and place over moderate heat.

Once the butter is hot, place sole filets and cook quickly, 3 to 4 minutes per side, until the fish is firm. Remove from heat and add lemon juice and a small pat of butter. Garnish with parsley and serve.

Alexandra Gouirand
(See "France," Alexandra Gouirand, *EAFT*, pp. 200–6.)

～

French Polynesia (Polynesia, Oceania), French Polynesian or Tahitian American Food

The largest of the French Polynesian islands is Tahiti, and citizens of the nation refer to themselves as Tahitians. One of their most traditional and beloved dishes is *Poulet Fafa*. This dish derives its name from the French as well as the indigenous ancestry of the country, with *poulet* being the French word for "chicken" and *fafa* being the Tahitian word for "taro leaves." It is prepared at all special occasions, such as weddings, church events, or family reunions, and it is often sold on Sunday mornings by families at roadside stands. The ingredients for this dish are wrapped in banana leaves and baked for an extended period of time in a traditional underground oven, called an *ahima'a*, which translates as "fire-food." For this purpose, a pit is dug that is roughly three feet deep and four to five feet across. A wood fire is then set in it, and large basalt stones are placed in the fire to heat through. When it has burned down, banana leaves and stems are layered over the stones, the food to be cooked is placed on top, and the pit is covered. In contemporary times, metal sheets and stones are used to cover it so that the same pit can be reused.

Lacking easy access to an underground oven or even banana leaves, Tahitian Americans have adapted the recipe to a conventional oven.

Poulet Fafa (Chicken in taro leaves)

1 ½ pounds of taro leaves or spinach
1 banana leaf (optional)
1 can of coconut milk
5 boneless chicken thighs (cubed)
¼ pound pork butt (cubed)
1 onion (diced)
2–4 cloves of garlic (minced)
2–3 tablespoons of oil
2–3 tablespoons of soy sauce
Salt and pepper to your personal taste

Taro leaves, also known as Tahitian spinach, can irritate the mouth and throat if not prepared first. To prepare:

Wash the leaves and remove the thick part of the stalk as well as any fibrous material. Chop the leaves into 1-inch long strips. Bring a large pot of salted water to a boil, and then add the taro leaves. Reduce heat and simmer for 10 to 15 minutes. Drain them and pat dry using paper towels. If using spinach, you do not need to boil first.

For the *Poulet Fafa*:

Rub oil on one side of the banana leaf and place the leaf in a casserole dish with the oiled side up. Spread half of the cooked taro leaves or uncooked spinach on top of the banana leaf. If you are not using a leaf, place directly on dish. Add in the chicken, pork, garlic, onion, oil, soy sauce, salt, and pepper. Pour the coconut milk over the dish. Place the remaining taro leaves or spinach on top. Fold the leaf over the mixture, tucking the sides of the leaf into the dish, or simply cover the dish with aluminum foil. Bake at 350°F for about an hour.

Eric César Morales

(See "Polynesia," Eric César Morales and Dillon Tautunu Smith, *EAFT*, pp. 512–19.)

G

Gabon (Middle Africa), Gabonese American Food

Gabon is not well known to most Americans, and its cuisine even less so. Its main staple foods are rice, cassava, plantains, and yams, usually boiled and pounded into a mash. These are served with a sauce, soup, or stew with some smoked fish, goat, beef, or chicken, but also bush meat. In Gabon, cooked, dried, or smoked meat from deer, monkeys, river rats, crocodiles, and bats is widely available at markets and street corners, and, in rural areas, they are often life sustaining. Natively grown Gabonese cocoa often gives food a chocolate flavor. Many of these ingredients are not available in the United States, so Gabonese Americans frequent markets run by other Africans, particularly those with a shared history of French colonialism, or find substitutes for them. Indian groceries tend to carry similar spices.

Nyembwe (Chicken with nuts)

3 pounds chicken, cooked and cut into pieces
3 onions, thinly sliced
½ cup palm or macadamia nuts
1 teaspoon cayenne pepper
1 teaspoon black pepper
2 teaspoons salt
2 teaspoons garlic, crushed

Boil the palm or macadamia nuts with ample water in a large saucepan. Cover and boil for a few minutes until the nut skins are soft. Discard the skins, and crush or press the nuts with a mortar and pestle or potato masher. Put the mashed nuts in a pot; add 2 cups of water, the cayenne and black pepper, salt, garlic, and the onions. Stir well. Simmer on a low heat until the sauce thickens, stirring frequently. Add the chicken pieces to the sauce. Heat through.

Karin Vaneker
(See "Gabon," Karin Vaneker, *EAFT*, pp. 209–11.)

Gambia (Western Africa), Gambian American Food

Bordering Senegal and the Atlantic Ocean, Gambia was part of the Senegambia region that was colonized in the mid-1800s and split between France and Britain. Britain took Gambia, and English is the national language, which has made it easier for contemporary Gambians to assimilate into American culture.

As with most other African nations on the west coast, Gambia's people were first brought to the United States as slaves. The American historian Alex Haley made Gambia famous through his story of Kunta Kinte in *Roots*. In the 1970s, Gambians began coming to the United States for educational opportunities, and many have done well in professional fields, settling throughout the country but also establishing small communities and Gambian American associations to maintain ties.

The cuisine of Gambia is similar to that of Senegal, with *jolof* rice and chicken *yassa* (fried in onions), but without the French culinary influence. The basic staple is rice, also millet (steamed), couscous, cassava, peanuts frequently made into a paste (*domodo*), palm oil, greens (spinach or cassava leaves), and okra (called ladies fingers, reflecting British influence). Common proteins are fish, oysters, shrimp, chicken, and beef. Pork is not eaten since the majority of Gambians are Muslim, although the country boasts much ethnic diversity and peaceful interrelations. Dried fish is a staple seasoning, although European-processed seasonings, Jumbo and Maggi cubes, are now popular.

Black Pepper Fish Sauce

2 whole fish (4 filets) tilapia or other firm white fish
1 6-ounce can tomato paste
1 onion

2 cloves garlic
2 Maggi cubes
2 teaspoons pepper
½ cup oil
¼ salt
1 cup water
Rice

Sprinkle fish lightly with ¼ teaspoon salt. Fry in ¼ cup of oil over me-dium-high heat until crisp on both sides. Remove from pan. (The fish can also be reserved and cooked in the sauce.)

Slice onion and garlic very thinly. (Ideally, it would be ground to a paste in a mortar or by food processor.)

Heat ¼ cup of oil in the pan and fry fish on medium high and add onion and garlic.

When translucent, add pepper, then stir in tomato paste and 1 cup of wa-ter. Break up Maggi cube and stir into mixture. Bring to a boil and add fish. Reduce heat and simmer for 20 minutes, or until fish is cooked through, and sauce has thickened.

Serve over rice.

Peanut Butter Soup with Chicken

½ cup oil (palm, peanut, vegetable)
12 cups water
2 cups peanut butter (creamy)
6 chicken thighs
1 teaspoon hot pepper
2 Maggi cubes
1 onion, minced

Sour cream (optional, to add to each bowl of soup when serving)

In large soup pan, fry onion until translucent. Add chicken and lightly brown. Meanwhile, stir 1 cup of water into peanut butter. Then add to soup pot.

Stir with a wooden spoon until smooth, then slowly add the rest of the water. Add Maggi cubes and hot pepper. Simmer for about 45 minutes until soup has thickened. Add a spoonful of sour cream to the soup when served.

Mariama Conteh with Lucy M. Long
(See "Gambia," Lucy M. Long, *EAFT*, p. 211.)

～

Georgia (Western Asia), Georgian American Food

Georgian food is not well known in the United States as a distinctive cuisine, and it is frequently confused with Russian or other Eastern European food cultures. It seems difficult to Americanize Georgian food and, for the most part, purveyors of food from the Caucases region keep it Georgian. In trying to replicate the unique spices, however, American cooks usually look to India for similar tastes. This change in spice is evident in the following recipe.

Khinkali (Curried beef and pork)

4 cups flour
1¼ teaspoons kosher salt, plus more to taste
4 ounces ground beef
12 ounces ground pork
2 tablespoons finely chopped cilantro
1 teaspoon Muchi curry
½ tseapoon crushed red pepper flakes
3 small yellow onions, minced
Freshly ground black pepper, to taste

Stir together flour, salt, and 1¼ cups warm water in a bowl until dough forms; transfer to a work surface and knead until smooth, about 6 minutes. Wrap in plastic wrap and refrigerate dough for 40 minutes. Meanwhile, combine beef, pork, cilantro, Muchi curry, crushed red pepper flakes, and onions in a bowl until evenly mixed; season generously with salt and pepper, and set filling aside. Divide dough into 25 equal pieces, and shape each piece into a ball. Using a rolling pin, roll into a 6-inch ball. Place about 2 tablespoons filling in the center of the round, and fold edges of dough over filling, creating pleats in dough as you go, until filling is covered. Holding dumpling in the palm of one hand, grasp the top of the dumpling where the pleats meet and twist to seal pleats and form a knot at the top of the dumpling. Repeat with remaining dough rounds and filling. Bring a large pot of salted water to a boil. Working in batches, boil dumplings until they float and dough is tender, about 8 minutes. Drain and serve hot. Season with black pepper.

Matthew Reger
(See "Georgia," Matthew Reger, EAFT, pp. 211–14.)

⌒

German-Russian (Eastern Europe), German-Russian American Food

At first glance, these two cruller recipes may appear similar, but they are quite different in appearance as well as taste. Many German-Russian Americans have lived in the United States for five or more generations, yet Volga German and Black Sea German foodways remain surprisingly distinct. The names, ingredients, and preparation methods vary widely. One reason such culinary differences persist is that the two groups seldom settled in the same part of the United States. Volga German descendants still cluster in Colorado, Kansas, Nebraska, and Wyoming, while the Black Sea Germans are most numerous in North Dakota and South Dakota. The two German-Russian cruller recipes that follow are prime examples of how an immigrant group's regional differences and Old Country loyalties can persist for generations in a new homeland and in new surroundings.

Volga German *Grebbel* are traditionally eaten on New Year's Eve and served with *Schnitz' Supp'* (a sweet soup that consists of dried fruit, raisins, flour, cinnamon, sugar, and cream). Today, German-Russian Grebbel can be found any time of the year, and these pastries often are a featured food at "Dutch Hop" dances, weddings, rodeos, and county fairs in Colorado, Kansas, Nebraska, and Wyoming. In a humorous attempt to Americanize the name, younger German-Russians sometimes refer to the ubiquitous Grebbels as "Rebels." Originally made as a pre-Lenten dish on *Fastnacht* (Shrove Tuesday), the Black Sea German crullers now are prepared for special occasions throughout the year—including birthdays, name day celebrations, Fourth of July picnics, and tailgate parties. Some modern *Schlitz-Kiechla* are oval shaped (to resemble footballs!) and served outdoors with warmed-up fruit preserves and hot coffee.

Grebbel (Volga German crullers)

4 egg yolks
4 tablespoons sugar
8 ounces sour cream
½ teaspoon lemon extract
½ teaspoon salt
1 teaspoon baking powder
4 tablespoons butter, softened
4 to 4½ cups flour

Beat the egg yolks and sugar. Add sour cream, lemon extract, salt, baking powder, and butter. Mix well. Add flour and knead the dough until smooth. Let the dough rest 1½ to 2 hours. Then roll out the dough about ⅛-inch thick. Cut into rectangular pieces, approximately 2½ × 3½ inches long. Cut four long slits in the middle of each piece. Gently intertwine and twist the dough strips, then drop into hot oil. Since each cruller will twist and fry up differently, no two will look exactly alike. Be sure to fry in enough hot oil so the Grebbel float. Turn once until golden brown on both sides. Drain on a wire rack or on paper towels. Cool, then sprinkle with powdered sugar. One also can use a powdered-sugar glaze that will give the Grebbel a more festive appearance, especially when a little food coloring is added.

Glaze:
1 cup powdered sugar
1 tablespoon butter, melted
2 tablespoons warm milk
1–2 scant drops food coloring (optional)
Combine above ingredients. Drizzle over Grebbel with a spoon.

Schlitz-Kiechla (Black Sea German crullers)

4 whole eggs, lightly beaten
4 tablespoons sugar
1¼ cups sweet cream
1 teaspoon vanilla extract
½ teaspoon salt
3 teaspoons baking powder
4 cups flour

Combine eggs with sugar, cream, vanilla, and salt. In a separate bowl, mix together the flour and baking powder. Now add the egg mixture to the flour, a little at a time, until a nice dough forms. If dough is too stiff or hard to handle, use some shortening on your hands to work the dough. Let the dough rest for about an hour. Lightly grease a rolling pin and roll out the dough until it is about half an inch in thickness. Then cut dough into oblong pieces, about 3 × 4 inches. Make a single slit (Schlitz) in the center of each piece. Fry in very hot cooking oil or shortening until each piece is golden brown. Be sure to turn so that each side is completely done. Let the crullers cool a bit on wire racks. Serve warm with butter, jam, applesauce, stewed prunes, or stewed rhubarb. In some cases, these crullers are made smaller (roughly half the size of regular ones). After they are deep-fried, they are sprinkled with a generous dusting of powdered sugar. When this is done, the smaller crullers are called *Schnee-Balla* (Snow Balls) to distinguish them from the larger and more traditional Schlitz-Kiechla that are served without any sugar or frosting.

Timothy J. Kloberdanz
(See "German-Russian," Timothy J. Kloberdanz, *EAFT*, pp. 214–17.)

~

Germany (Western Europe), German American

German Americans include a wide variety of cultural heritages, all tied by a shared language. Prior to German unification in 1871, "German" was an ethno-linguistic designation only, not a nationality, and most German-speaking immigrants would have identified as Bavarian, Swabian, Prussian, or even Czech, Hungarian, or possibly Austrian. Some German religious groups—Mennonites, Moravians, Hutterites, Amish, and Pennsylvania "Dutch" (from *deutsch*, the German word for "German")—have remained relatively unassimilated.

German foodways have had widespread influence on American food culture, and some have even lost their ethnic associations. Two dishes that have had tremendous staying power in the United States and are still prepared in German American families that may otherwise have little connection to the "old country" are *spaetzle* and *sauerkraut*. One reason for their popularity is that they use common, inexpensive ingredients. At holidays, these dishes may appear as sidekicks to an American pot roast or a German-inspired *Sauerbraten*; but as everyday fare, they may occupy a much larger share of the plate.

In Germany, *spaetzle* is prepared in two main ways: as a side dish/accompaniment, usually with browned breadcrumbs as garnish, or as a main dish related to macaroni and cheese, called *Kas'spatzen* in southern Germany. In German American cuisine, *spaetzle* are used almost exclusively as a side dish or a substitute for noodles; sometimes they are fried after boiling, but they are usually served without any additional garnish. Feel free to substitute store-bought *Spaetzle*, or plain egg noodles, in this trio of dishes.

Spaetzle (Noodle dumplings)

The basic recipe is extremely simple: flour, water, and salt, with an egg or two added in if times are good. There are two ways to form the noodles: using a

Spaetzlepresse (a potato ricer will do) or "vom Brett" (rolling a slightly firmer dough and chopping it directly from the chopping board into boiling water).

For a smallish batch, start with a cup of flour and ½ teaspoon salt in a mixing bowl; stir in water (and egg, if using) until it forms a gooey batter. The batter should be firm, not runny, but it should be "sticky." If you plan to use the cutting board method, you will want a slightly firmer batter, closer to dough.

Bring a large pot of water to a rolling boil. Taking care not to burn yourself from the steam, put your batter into a potato ricer (*Spaetzlepresse*) and press it into the water. It will come out as multiple "snakes."

Or, if using a cutting board, place your dough on the cutting board and chop it into the water in narrow slices. This will yield a heartier noodle.

Regardless of method, watch the pot carefully and skim the noodles off into a bowl as they rise to the top (this means they are done). Drain and serve as you would any pasta; or briefly fry in butter or lard before serving.

Everyday Sauerkraut (Cooked sweet and sour cabbage)

"Real" traditional German sauerkraut is pickled or fermented in a process that can take days or weeks (this is true of most dishes with "sauer" in their name, like Sauerbraten). This is an everyday variety that can be quickly prepared on the stovetop.

½ to 1 head cabbage, white or red
1–2 tart apples
Shortening (lard, butter, or margarine)
¼ cup dry wine (red or white; only use red with red cabbage)
2 tablespoons vinegar (a red wine or apple cider variety is best)
Sugar (about 1 teaspoon)
2–4 juniper berries
Salt and pepper to taste
Optional: 1 onion; caraway seed

Slice the onion (if using) into thin slivers. Heat oil or shortening over medium heat in a large, heavy-bottomed pan and "sweat" the onion.

Slice the cabbage: this can be done by hand for a more rustic dish or using a meat slicer for thin, even strips. Add sliced cabbage to the pan in batches (as room allows); allow each batch to cook down to make room for the next.

Core and slice the apple (you may wish to peel it first); add to cabbage and simmer briefly.

Add seasonings and adjust to taste. Start out with 2 tablespoons vinegar and 1 tablespoon sugar; adjust proportions to your taste. Then lower heat, cover, and simmer until the kraut reaches desired consistency: about 20 minutes for a still-crisp version, or up to an hour for a version with well-combined flavors.

Same-Day Sauerbraten (Pot roast)

A "real" German Sauerbraten is marinated in vinegar for 2 to 3 days before cooking; this was originally a method of preserving meat. In the hurried American kitchen, though, cooks such as Margaret Foell (my grandmother) developed quicker methods that are just as tasty.

4 pounds rump roast
1½ cups vinegar
3 teaspoon salt
6 tablespoons brown sugar
¼ teaspoon each cloves and allspice
1 teaspoon coarsely ground black pepper
2 teaspoons powdered (ground) ginger
2 bay leaves
1½ chopped onions

Roast meat in uncovered pan at 350°F for 45 (20–30) minutes. Cut into ½-inch slices.

Mix remaining ingredients and layer meat, onions, and juice in pan.

Bake at 350°F about 45 minutes (until tender), turning meat in sauce several times while baking.

Kristie Foell
(See "Germany," Kristie Foell, *EAFT*, pp. 217–21.)

~

Ghana (West Africa), Ghanaian American

Many African Americans trace their roots back to the about five hundred thousand Ghanaians shipped to the United States during the transatlantic slave trade (c. 1517 to. c. 1850). In the 1960s and 1970s and following Ghana's independence in 1957, Ghanaian students started migrating to the United States. Currently there are over one hundred thousand Ghanaians in the United States.

Ghanaian cuisine reflects great diversity, ongoing modernity, and the influence of colonial powers (Portuguese, Dutch, Swedes, Danish, Germans, and British) that competed for a dominant position in the profitable trade from the coast of Ghana, known as the Gold Coast.

Ghanaian food is organized around starchy staples (rice, plantain, yam, cassava, millet, and sorghum). Fresh, dried, smoked, and salted fish are a major source of animal protein, and corn, peanuts, cowpeas, okra, and taro leaves and other spinach-like greens are commonplace. These are used in a wide variety of stews, soups, pastes, purees, and sauces. A hot black pepper sauce, *shito*, is used with traditional dishes but also on spring rolls and white bread. Bakeries specialize in butter bread, sugar bread, tea bread, buns, and more with nutmeg a characteristic flavor. Ghanaian American bakeries and groceries offer these foods in the United States.

Ghanaian Tea Bread (2 loaves)
A classic white (sandwich) bread with sugar and nutmeg.

   6 to 7 cups strong or hard (bread) flour
   2 teaspoons salt
   4 teaspoons instant yeast (2 packages)
   4 tablespoons caster sugar
   2 teaspoons grounded nutmeg
   4 ounces margarine (room temperature)
   2 cups lukewarm water

Put the flour in a large plastic bowl and mix in the salt. Incorporate the yeast, sugar, and nutmeg. Cut the margarine in small pieces and mix these in by hand or with a mixer with a dough hook. Add the water and knead the dough for 8 to 10 minutes by hand or with the mixer. Put a bit of flour on the (kitchen) counter and knead the dough, adding a bit of extra flour at a time until the dough is no longer sticky. Make a ball and put it in a clean, large (plastic) bowl. Cover with plastic film or a bag coated with a little bit of oil. Put a damp kitchen cloth over the bowl and let it rise in a warm spot for about 1 to 1½ hours, until the dough has doubled in bulk. Place the dough on a lightly floured countertop; knead, adding a bit of flour, and divide it in 2 pieces. Roll into oblong shapes. Cover with the greased plastic and a kitchen cloth and let rise for another 30 minutes. Meanwhile, grease bread pans with soft margarine or vegetable oil and heat oven to 425°F. Immediately turn down the heat to 375°F and bake the tea breads for 30–40 minutes. Remove the bread from the pans and let cool on a rack before slicing.

Gari Foto (Cassava cake and scrambled eggs)

Cassava roots are used to prepare *gari*, a coarse meal and the staff of life for many Ghanaians. The roots are soaked, grated, fermented, and sun-dried or roasted; the result of the time-consuming process is a convenience food that is carefully sprinkled and mixed with warm water with salt, used in the same manner as *fufu*, rice, and couscous. Commercially manufactured gari is nowadays widely available in shops and supermarkets in and outside of Africa. Gari is often served with a sauce or stew but is also a key ingredient in *Gari Foto*, which is usually served for breakfast or lunch.

2 cups *gari*
½ cup slightly salted warm water
½ cup (palm or peanut) oil
2 medium onions, finely chopped
3 tomatoes, peeled and chopped
1 garlic clove
6 eggs
Salt
Black pepper

Place the *gari* in a bowl, and sprinkle with water, spoon by spoon while stirring. Evenly moisten the *gari*, cover, and set aside. Heat the oil in a pan, sauté the onions and garlic until tender, add the tomato pieces, and simmer for an extra 2 minutes. Meanwhile, put the eggs in a bowl and beat them with a fork, pour the eggs in the pan, and cook them while stirring. Fold the *gari* into the mixture, add salt and pepper to taste, and serve immediately.

Nkatenkwan (Peanut soup)

1 cup peanuts
1 chicken in pieces
1 quart water
3 tomatoes
1 large onion, in coarse pieces

Use a mortar and pestle or a food processor to pound or pulse the peanuts into a thick paste. Wash the chicken and place with water in a large pot. Bring to boil; add tomatoes and onion. Lower heat and simmer for about 30 minutes. Remove tomatoes and onion with a slotted spoon. Remove skin from tomatoes and pound or mash tomatoes and onions into a paste. Add a few tablespoons of water to the peanut paste; mix and gradually stir into the soup. Simmer soup over low heat for about 30 minutes. Serve with *fufu*.

Karin Vaneker
(See "Ghana, Karin Vaneker, *EAFT*, pp. 221–25.)

⌒

Greece (Southern Europe), Greek American Food

Greek American foodways represent an ongoing interchange between original ethnic recipes, adaption to American conditions, adoption of individually generated recipes, technological innovations, and the international evolution of foodways. They also reflect an unchanging appreciation for flavor, family, friendship, and life in general that underlies the culture. Tarpon Springs, Florida, has the largest percentage of residents with Greek heritage in the United States, and food there is an important carrier of heritage and identity. Greeks first settled in Tarpon Springs to work in the sponge business, and Captain Karistinos makes the recipe below to feed his crew. Katerina Zaronias's recipe for stuffed grape leaves is typical of the way they are made in Kalymnos, the island from which many sponge fishermen and their families came.

Fila with *Avgolemono* Sauce (Kalymnian stuffed grape leaves with egg-lemon sauce)

2 pounds ground beef
1 cup uncooked rice
1 medium onion, chopped
1 8-ounce can tomato sauce
1 tablespoon salt
1 teaspoon pepper
1 cup water
1 jar grape leaves, rinsed
Items for the Cooking Pot:
1 large tomato
1 stick butter
Beef or pork bones

Mix together ground beef, rice, onion, tomato sauce, salt, pepper, and water. In the bottom of the pot, lay one layer of unfilled grape leaves or beef or pork bones. Next, roll about 2 tablespoons filling into the middle of each grape leaf and roll them up (fold sides in, then roll away from you). Layer them tightly in the pot. On top of the rolled grape leaves layer sliced fresh tomato and slices of butter. Add water to the top layer of grape leaves. Cover and cook on medium heat for one hour.

Avgolemono (egg-lemon) Sauce

1 large or 2 small fresh lemons
2 eggs

Squeeze the lemons, then pour the juice into the blender, and add eggs. Blend for 30 seconds, and then gradually add about ½ of the juice from the pot. Pour the mixture over the grape leaves. Shake the pot to make sure the sauce distributes evenly.

This recipe is adapted with permission from Katerina Zaronias and her daughter, Irene Zaronias Ward.

Sponge Boat One-Pot Dinner: Grouper Souper

4–5 pounds whole grouper (preferred), or filets
2 medium potatoes, diced
2 medium onions, diced
½ head of celery, chopped
1 carrot, sliced (optional)
1 teaspoon salt or to taste
1 cup olive oil
5–6 lemons

Put the vegetables into a large pot with just enough water to cover them, and boil until the potatoes and carrots are soft.

If you use a whole grouper, scrape off the scales, take off the gills, and clean out the throat. Add the fish to the pot and simmer about 25 minutes, until the meat is soft. When this is cooked on the boat, the grouper is cut into steaks and cooked with the head and bones, but if you use filets it takes less time to cook. If you have used the whole fish, carefully lift out the pieces so that the bones do not disperse. Remove the bones and skin, then return the rest to the pot.

Squeeze the lemons into the soup, and let it boil 1 minute to incorporate the lemon juice into the soup. Cool the soup slightly, then serve. Serves 4.

This recipe was adapted with permission from Captain Anastasios Karistinos.

Tina Bucuvalas
(See "Greece," Tina Bucuvalas, *EAFT,* pp. 225–34.)

⁓

Grenada (Americas—Caribbean), Grenadian American Food

In Grenada, there is an ever decreasing population due to the high percentages of migration to neighboring islands, as well as to the United States and Canada. The national dish of Grenada, Oil Down, is commonly made by Grenadians no matter where they live. Oil Down is a type of stew with a broth made from coconut milk (straight FROM the coconut shell). In the United States, Grenadians tend to use more meat than seafood in Oil Down due to cost and accessibility. Below is a simplified recipe of Oil Down using ingredients that are more common in the United States.

Oil Down (Coconut milk stew)

Approximately 9 water spinach leaves
1 small stalk celery
1 small stem chive
1 small stem thyme
2 medium carrots, chopped
2 green peppers, chopped
1 pound frozen or homemade dumplings (which are made from kneading together flour, salt, and water)
1½ teaspoons turmeric
1 large, peeled breadfruit (a popular starchy vegetable that can be found in some Asian and Latin American grocery stores)
1 medium onion, thinly chopped
3 cloves garlic, minced
1½ teaspoons sugar
3 cups coconut milk (preferably from the shell, but powdered or canned is suitable)

½ to ¾ pound meat of choice salted overnight (preferably fish, but any meat makes a good substitution)

Take peeled breadfruit and cut into eight separate pieces, and then cut in half. Wash the salted meat, and then rinse with lime juice and water. Remove the skin from the onion, rinse, and cut into small pieces. Remove the seeds from the green peppers and cut into thin wedges. Cut sliced peppers into small pieces. Add cold water to a large saucepan and place rinsed meat in water. Bring to a boil and then drain saucepan. (Repeat this step three times in order to thoroughly remove salt.) Cook meat until tender and drain. Sauté onion and garlic in hot oil until garlic is roasted and onions are translucent. Stir in meat, chive, thyme, celery, carrots, and salt to taste. Add the two cups of coconut milk and turmeric. Stir. Add the breadfruit, sugar, and pepper. Stir. Cook until the breadfruit has absorbed most of the liquid. Add 1 remaining cup of coconut milk and take out the sliced green peppers. Add in the dumplings and the water spinach leaves. Stir and cook on a medium-low heat until there is no liquid remaining. Serve hot.

Alexandria Ayala
(See "Grenada," Alexandria Ayala, *EAFT*, pp. 235–37.)

~

Guam (Micronesia, Oceania), Micronesian or Chamorro American Food

Guam was a stopover for Spanish ships from the mid-1500s to the early 1800s, which encouraged immigration from the Philippines to Mexico to Guam. This history is reflected throughout the local cuisine, with Guam's version of red rice made with the seeds of the *achiote* plant (annatto seeds) brought over from Spain, as well as Guam's own form of tortilla—the flat bread that is a staple throughout Mexico. Unlike Mexico, however, where tortillas are primarily made from corn and are for savory food, in Guam *tatiyas* are usually made with flour and are often sweet as well.

Tatiyas (Sweet flour flatbread)

3 cups all-purpose flour
2 teaspoons baking powder
¾ teaspoon salt

½ cup sugar
¼ cup shortening
¼ cup coconut milk
⅛ cup whole milk
¼ cup water
Butter as a spread

Combine all dry ingredients in a large mixing bowl. Stir in liquid ingredients with a spatula. Once the dough starts taking form, shape it into a ball. Divide into 6 equally sized balls. Place a ball in between two layers of wax paper and compress it into a disc, then flatten it, using a rolling pin, into a disc no more than 8 inches in diameter. Cook at medium-high heat on a flat grill pan, compressing any bubbles with a fork. After the first side is cooked, flip over and butter the top of cooked side. Remove cooked *tatiyas* from heat and cut into quarters.

Chamorro Red Rice

2 cups white rice
1 onion (chopped)
2 tablespoons annatto seeds
½ teaspoon salt
2 tablespoons oil

Soak the annatto seeds in 2 cups of warm water for about 30 minutes. Meanwhile, rinse the rice with cold water. Add salt to the annatto seeds and rub them together until the water becomes red. Strain the annatto seeds above a pot and then bring the red water to a boil. Add the rice, 2 cups of water, salt, oil, and onions. Bring the pot to a boil, then reduce the heat to medium and let the water evaporate. Reduce the heat to low, cover the pot, and fully cook the rice, approximately 15 minutes.

Eric César Morales
(See "Micronesia," Eric César Morales, *EAFT*, pp. 419–24.)

～

Guatemala (Central America), Guatemalan American Food

Guatemalan cuisine is grounded in the prehistoric cuisine of ancient Maya civilizations, a cuisine that was based on maize, chiles, tomatoes, and squashes. This dish, *Jocón*, is a stew enriched by a sauce similar to the *moles* of Mexico, reflecting the Mayan culinary influence. This stew most closely resembles the green moles, or *pipians*, of Central Mexico. This dish may be prepared with chicken, or pork as a substitute. It is traditionally served over rice with fresh warm corn tortillas on the side. Some recipes call for just blending the seeds, but toasting the seeds first brings out the nutty flavor in the sauce.

Jocón Stew (Pumpkin seed and sesame seed stew)
Serves 6

2½ to 3 pounds chicken (breasts for milder flavor, thighs for a heartier flavor)
4 cups chicken broth
2 teaspoons salt
¼ cup pumpkin seeds
¼ cup sesame seeds
2 corn tortillas, torn, soaked in water and drained
1 cup tomatillos, husked and chopped (canned, if fresh not available)
1 bunch cilantro, chopped
1 bunch scallions, chopped
1–5 jalapenos or serrano chili peppers, chopped (depending on spiciness preferred)

Place chicken, broth, and salt in large pot. Bring to boil, then reduce heat and cook over medium low for about 1 hour, until chicken is cooked. Remove chicken, cool, and shred with fingers. Set aside. Strain broth and set aside. Heat dry skillet over medium low. Add pumpkin seeds and sesame seeds to toast. Stir occasionally, toasting until lightly browned, about 5–8 minutes. Grind toasted seeds in a coffee grinder until fine powder. Place seeds, drained tortilla pieces, tomatillos, cilantro, scallions, and chili peppers in blender. Add 1 cup of the strained chicken broth and blend until smooth. Put chicken shreds back into pot. Add pureed seed sauce. Add 1 to 1½ cup of strained chicken broth, stirring slowly, until it makes a thick sauce. Heat over medium heat and then reduce to simmer for 15–25 minutes. If sauce gets too thick, add a little chicken broth. Adjust seasoning and serve, often over rice.

Lois Stanford
(See "Guatemala," Lois Stanford, *EAFT*, pp. 237–41.)

⁓

Guinea (West Africa), Guinean American

Guinea has abundant natural resources, but human rights issues and poverty have recently forced many Guineans to leave, and over fifteen thousand have immigrated to the United States. Guinean American food culture is similar to that of other West Africans in the United States but also reflects French colonial influence in traditions of baking and pastries. It is not well known in the United States, and, if available, it is usually found with other West African cuisines.

Mangoé Rafalari (Spicy mango and smoked fish stew)

12 ripe mangoes, average sized
3 onions, sliced halves
1 cup palm oil
6 smoked *bonga shad* (A type of herring; substitute smoked herring or smoked mackerels.)
¼ cup of *sanfoui* powder (dried shrimp powder)
2 Maggi stock cubes
2 red chili peppers
Salt (to taste)

Peel the mangos and rinse these under cold, streaming water. Put the mangos in a pot and cover with water. Bring to a boil and simmer for 15 to 20 minutes. Use a sieve to drain the mango pieces, set aside.

Flake the smoked fish and remove the bones. Put the flaked fish, onion slices, shrimp powder, and chili peppers in a boil, and mix with a spoon. Heat the oil in a pot and add the fish mixture, stock cubes, and 1 cup of water. Bring to a boil; add the drained mango pieces and salt to taste. Stir, cover the pot, and simmer for about 30 minutes. Taste after 5 minutes and remove the chili peppers if the stew is spicy enough. Serve hot.

Karin Vaneker and Lucy M. Long
(See "Guinea," Lucy Long, *EAFT*, pp. 241–42.)

∼

Guyana (South America), Guyanese American Food

Pepperpot is Guyana's national dish and is of Amerindian origin. It is consumed all year round but particularly during the Christmas season. Pepperpot is made with *cassareep*, a thick, dark brown sauce that is a by-product of the bitter cassava root, various kinds of meats, peppers, and other spices. It is eaten with cassava bread, wheat bread, or rice. Among expatriate Guyanese, pepperpot continues to occupy a crucial place as a culinary marker of Guyanese identity. Guyanese living in large urban areas, such as New York City and Atlanta, Georgia, can effortlessly purchase the ingredients for pepperpot from large open markets or Guyanese vendors. However, since *cassareep* is principal ingredient, and often difficult to obtain outside of urban areas, Guyanese would often travel to Guyana or large metropolitan areas to purchase *cassareep*, or have it mailed to them by friends and relatives. In essence, while some ingredients of pepperpot can be substituted or omitted, *cassareep* is indispensable.

Cookup rice is another principal Guyanese cuisine that Guyanese immigrants prepare as a way of commemorating Guyaneseness and embracing nostalgia. Made with rice, beans, coconut milk, meats, vegetables, and a plethora of spices, cookup rice is a one-pot meal that accommodates the busy schedules of working-class Guyanese Americans while simultaneously providing a balanced diet. Guyanese can choose to substitute canned coconut milk or cream for coconut grated at home, omit some or all meat, and vary the types of peas or beans used, based on personal tastes, allergies, or other factors.

Pepperpot (Cassareep stew)

1 ½ pounds beef
1 pound pork
½ pound trotters (tripe) or cow's heels (use other types of organ meats or red meats as desired; chicken is not commonly used in pepperpot)
½ pound pig tail
1 ½ cup cassava cassareep (or to taste) (*Cassareep* is the principal ingredient in pepperpot, and it has a unique taste. There is no real substitution for cassareep, although some may use brown sauces made from burnt sugar and/or flour. However, in those cases, it's no longer pepperpot but "brown stew.")

1 red hot pepper
1 ½ sticks of cinnamon
2 ounces brown sugar (or to taste)
1 pinch of salt (or to taste)
2 stalks basil (marri'd man poke)
1 bunch fine-leaf thyme
1 large onion (finely chopped)
2 garlics (finely chopped)
6 cloves

Parboil pig tails, then scrape to remove hair and dirt. Pressure cook cow's heel. Boil tripe.

Combine all meats in a large saucepan once they are tender. Add cassareep, pepper, cinnamon, basil, thyme, onion, garlic, and cloves to meats. Cook on low heat for approximately one hour or until meats are fully cooked. Add salt and sugar to attain desired flavor.

Note: Bring pepperpot to a boil every day to prevent spoiling. Refrigeration not needed.

Eat with cassava bread, dense homemade bread, rice, or starchy staple of your choice.

Cookup Rice

2 small dried coconuts (grated)
1½ cans coconut milk
1½ pint long-grain parboiled rice
2 pounds meat (1 pound chicken, 1 pound beef)
1 pint of dried black-eyed peas
1 small onion (finely chopped)
1 small tomato (diced)
2 green onions or scallions (finely chopped)
3 cloves of garlic (finely chopped)
½ teaspoon finely chopped fresh herbs (fine leaf thyme, thick leaf thyme, and celery)
1 lemon or 1 cup lemon juice
2 bouillon cubes
1 tablespoon butter or margarine (optional)
1 tablespoon browning or soy sauce (for color)
All-purpose seasoning; or salt, black pepper, cumin, basil, red pepper (crushed or finely chopped)

Wash peas; boil or pressure with light salt until parboiled. Clean meats (chicken and beef) with lemon or lemon juice. Season meats with fresh seasonings, all-purpose seasoning, black pepper, red pepper, cumin, and basil. Add browning or soy sauce. For best results, season meat overnight and refrigerate.

Sauté onion, tomato, garlic, and a portion of fresh seasonings. Add seasoned meats to sautéed herbs; stew together until meats are half cooked. Combine parboiled rice, half-cooked meats, coconut milk, bouillon cubes, and butter/margarine. Bring to boil for about 20 minutes; add seasonings to taste. Lower heat, cover pot, and let cook for another 30 minutes or until rice is moist. Serve with vegetable salad, fried yellow plantains, fried fish, or *achar*.

Gillian Richards-Greaves
(See "Guyana," Gillian Richards-Greaves, *EAFT*, pp. 243–48.)

⁓

Gypsy (North America), American Gypsy or Roma American

American Gypsy or Roma American food is not a single cuisine. Following their departure from India sometime around AD 1000, Gypsies dispersed throughout Europe, the Middle East, and beyond. In the process they were fragmented into a great number of national and tribal groups lacking sustained contact with one another and consequent cultural exchange. Only a few of these groups came to America in sufficient numbers to establish real communities, and they came at different times from different places and had considerable cultural differences prior to immigration. It is not surprising, therefore, that there are major differences in the cuisine of these American Gypsy communities.

By far the most important and far-reaching factor shaping what Gypsies eat and how they prepare their food is a complex of beliefs concerning pollution and ritual purity that originated in India. Roma believe in a bifurcated world divided into Gypsy and non-Gypsy, men and women, ritually clean (*wuzho*) and unclean (*marime*). The body above the beltline, especially the head, is considered sacred; that below, especially the genital area, is *marime*. These beliefs are more stringently held in some groups than others and specific practice varies from one group to another, but all Gypsy life, particularly food and food preparation, has been shaped to some degree by these beliefs. American Roma are particularly strong adherents.

A traditional dish prepared both for feasts and everyday use is *Pirogo*.

Pirogo (Egg noodle pudding dessert)

16 ounces egg noodles
2 pounds large curd cottage cheese
5 cubes butter
4 cups granulated sugar
2 cans evaporated milk
1 cup heavy whipping cream
8 ounces cream cheese
6 eggs
1½ cups raisins (optional)

Boil egg noodles according to directions on package. Strain and put in bowl with butter and cream cheese. Mix until melted. In a separate bowl, mix cottage cheese, eggs, canned milk, cream, sugar, and raisins (if used). Combine contents of the two bowls and mix well. Place in baking dish and bake in a 350 degree oven until firm and golden brown, approximately 1½ hours.

William G. Lockwood
(See "Gypsy," William G. Lockwood, *EAFT*, pp. 248–53.)

H

Haiti (Americas—Caribbean), Haitian American

The Republic of Haiti was officially founded in 1804 after it achieved independence from France in a violent slave rebellion, making the country the first free black republic in history and the second independent state in the Americas after the United States. Migration to the United States occurred long before the colony of Saint-Domingue became present-day Haiti; however, few immigrant groups to the United States have been as maligned as Haitians have over the past forty years, and the negative media portrayals have affected the group's assimilation into mainstream American society.

Haitian cuisine shares many characteristics with other Caribbean cuisines, particularly in its use of tropical vegetables. Its culinary influences come primarily from West Africa and the Arawak people who originally inhabited the island, as well as from France and the Middle East. The cuisine favors spicy, bold flavors. Many dishes are seasoned with cloves and scotch bonnet peppers, as well as garlic, scallions, green peppers, and thyme. Tomato paste is a staple in preparing most sauces, and monosodium glutamate (MSG) is present as a flavor enhancer. A seasoning unique to Haiti is *djon djon*, commonly referred to as Haitian black mushrooms, which are dried and soaked in water to procure a black liquid that is used to flavor rice and other dishes. *Tri tri*, tiny dried shrimp, are also used to flavor rice dishes, and raw cashews are used as a luxurious embellishment to many foods.

Few adaptations have been made in the United States to the cuisine, except perhaps the use of some processed foods to supplement fresh products, such as lemonade powder instead of fresh lemon juice. Additionally, Haitian cooks in the United States will add their own seasonings to American dishes to make them more palatable. An example, though, of culinary interchange between the two cultures is a breakfast staple that came about during the U.S. occupation of Haiti—spaghetti with chopped hotdogs—that remains beloved among Haitian Americans.

Haitian Spaghetti and Hot Dogs

> 1 teaspoon fresh minced garlic
> ½ cup finely diced onion
> 4 whole cloves, crushed
> ½ teaspoon fresh thyme
> 1 tablespoon tomato paste
> 1 tablespoon ketchup
> 2 teaspoons hot sauce
> 2 tablespoons vegetable oil
> 4 hot dogs, sliced
> ½ pound spaghetti (around half a package)
> 1 cup pasta water
> Optional: bouillon cube

Boil pasta in salted water and cook until al dente; drain and set aside, reserving at least 1 cup of the pasta water.

Add oil to a frying pan and set heat to medium. Add cloves and bay leaf and fry until fragrant. Add sliced hot dogs and cook until they turn crisp and begin to brown. Add onions, garlic, and thyme and fry until the garlic just starts to turn golden, being careful to constantly stir the ingredients so that they do not burn.

Now add tomato paste, ketchup, and hot sauce along with ½ cup of pasta water and stir to create a sauce. Add salt and pepper to taste. You can also crumble in about a ¼ teaspoon of bouillon cube or more to taste, if you prefer.

Add the al dente pasta and stir until all the pasta is coated in sauce. Simmer for a few minutes until the pasta absorbs most of the sauce.

Carlos C. Olaechea
(See "Haiti," Carlos Olaechea, *EAFT*, pp. 255–60.)

～

Hawaii (Northern America), Hawaiian American Food

Hawaiian food today mixes Asian, European, and Anglo traditions with native Polynesian ones, using ingredients such as raw fish, seaweed, *poi* (mashed, cooked stem of the taro plant), tropical fruits, and commercially processed foods to create some of the most distinctive cuisine in the United States. A standard meal is a "plate lunch," with rice, macaroni salad, and a meat entrée (usually an American or Asian food). Spam has become embraced in Hawaiian foodways since World War II, and many residents joke that it is "Hawaiian steak." Spam *musabi* (pressed rice with spam) is a popular snack. One of Hawaii's most iconic food traditions, the lu'au has been transformed from a ceremonial, religious feast to a social one (and oftentimes a tourist event) and often includes contemporary American favorites along with selected traditional native foods.

Pork *Laulau* illustrates this mixing of culinary cultures, with pork and salted codfish coming originally from Europe but prepared in a traditional Hawaiian manner.

Pork *Laulau* (Steamed pork, fish, and taro leaves)

1 pound salted codfish (rinsed), or butterfish, sliced into pieces
1 pound pork butt, sliced into 1 ½ inch cubes
Hawaiian sea salt to taste
Black pepper (optional)
Taro leaves for wrapping, without stem (a big leafy green, such as collards, or the large leaves from savoy cabbage can be substituted)
Banana leaves (or tin foil) for outer layer wrap. (Banana leaves are not eaten.)

Season fish and pork with sea salt. If using salted cod, rinse fish several times to remove extra salt. Place a handful of meat and fish onto the middle of several taro leaves. (These are meant to be eaten, but will cause the mouth to itch if only partially cooked.)

Wrap securely and place each bundle into a banana leaf (or tin foil) and secure with a string. Place in steamer to cook for four hours or more, until meat is tender and taro leaves are thoroughly done.

Margaret Magat
(See "Hawai'i," Margaret Magat, *EAFT*, pp. 260–63.)

∼

Hmong (Southeast Asia), Hmong American Food

Green papaya salad is a staple in Laos, the homeland of many Hmong Americans. The dish blends crunch with juice, sweet with sour, and, of course, heat. It is also a popular dish in Esan, the northern region of Thailand, and is often on the menus of Thai restaurants abroad. Tastes between Thailand and Laos vary—for a more robust Lao flavor, add the ¼ teaspoon of shrimp or crab paste noted in the recipe.

This dish is always tweaked to please the eater's individual palate—in home kitchens, restaurants, and roadside stands. Many Asian groceries in the United States carry unripe papaya, but chopped English cucumbers or equal parts grated carrot and cabbage can also be used as a substitute. The recipe calls for long beans, a distinctive type of bean that can be up to a yard in length. These are frequently purplish in color but can be replaced with regular green beans. Before green papaya was widely available in the United States, cooks of Hmong, Thai, or Lao descent invented clever substitutions to never be without this essential taste of home.

Taub Ntoos Quab (Green papaya salad)
Makes 4 servings; preparation time approximately 15 minutes

    1 medium-sized green papaya, grated (roughly 5 cups)
    Juice and pulp of 1 lime*
    2 tablespoons sugar*
    3 tablespoons fish sauce* (*nam pla* in Thai and *nuoc nam* in Vietnamese)
    3 diced Roma tomatoes, or roughly 1 pint halved cherry tomatoes
    5 long beans, cut into 1-inch pieces on the diagonal (roughly 1 cup)
    1 large (or 2 small) clove of garlic, minced
    2–3 bird's eye chilies*, minced (red chilies are often hotter than green)
    ¼ teaspoon crab or shrimp paste (optional)*
    Generous handful of roasted salted peanuts, crushed

*These ingredients depend on your palate—start with these quantities, then increase as desired once you mix the salad.

Peel the green papaya, cut it in half, and remove the seeds. Working in pieces, grate the papaya using a food processor attachment, if possible. You can purchase a tool made for this purpose in Asian food stores, but the food processor makes this step blissfully easy. Add grated papaya to a large bowl, taking note that the quantities listed are for roughly 5 cups. Add all remaining ingredients. Stir with a spoon, and once ingredients are integrated, "pound" the salad roughly twenty times with two spoons, stirring occasionally. While a large mortar and pestle is ideal, a big bowl and sturdy spoons will work just as well. Taste and adjust seasonings to taste. Serve topped with a generous handful of peanuts and a slice of lime.

Katy Clune and Dara Phrakousonh
(See "Hmong," Katy Clune, *EAFT*, pp. 263–66.)

⌁

Honduras (Central America), Honduran American Food

Honduran American food utilizes fresh ingredients and is generally not spicy. Foods are typically seasoned with garlic and other herbs and spices. This soup from the Olancho region of Honduras becomes thicker and more stewlike the longer the starchy plantains and cassava cook. It is usually served with Honduran-style tortillas, generally handmade and thicker than the Mexican-style ones found in U.S. grocery stores.

Sopa de Tapado Olanchano (Olancho-style covered soup)
Serves six.

1 onion
2 medium tomatoes
1 green bell pepper
2 cloves garlic
4 tablespoons chopped cilantro
1 tablespoon oil
3 cups water
2 cubes chicken broth
2 pounds dried, salted beef (2½ pounds stew meat can be substituted)
1½ pounds pork butt, cut in 1-inch pieces
1 pound cassava root* (a starchy potato like Yukon gold can be substituted)
3 green plantains
2 green bananas
3 ripe plantains

2 cans coconut milk
Plantain leaves to cover pot (parchment paper can be substituted)
Salt to taste

*Cassava root is sometimes mistakenly marketed in U.S. grocery stores as yucca because of its alternative Spanish name *yuca*.

Chop the onion, tomato, bell pepper, and garlic. In a large pot, cook the chopped vegetables in oil until softened. Remove them from the pot, salt the beef and pork pieces, and brown lightly. Return the cooked vegetables to the pot, stir in the cilantro, and cook briefly. Add water and chicken broth cubes and gently simmer, covered with a lid, until meat is almost tender, approximately 1 to 1½ hours.

While meats are simmering, peel the bananas, plantains, and cassava, and cut into bite-sized pieces. Keep these ingredients separate, as they will be layered individually later. When meats have reached desired tenderness, remove the stewed meat mixture and save the remaining broth in a separate bowl. In the pot, layer the cassava first, followed by a layer of green plantain. Next, place a layer of the cooked meats, using about ½ of the meat mixture. A green banana layer comes next, followed by the remaining meats. Spread the final layer of ripe plantains on top. Pour the coconut milk in with the reserved broth and stir together. Pour the liquid mixture carefully over the layered dish. Tuck plantain leaves down into the pot to cover the soup. Cover the pot, and simmer gently until the plantains are tender, approximately 30 minutes. If plantain leaves cannot be found, parchment paper can be tucked over the soup to keep in the moisture, but some flavor will be lost. Serve warm.

M. *Dustin Knepp*
(See "Honduras" M. Dustin Knepp, *EAFT*, pp. 266–70.)

⌣

Hong Kong (Eastern Asia), Hong Kong American Food

The food culture of Hong Kong is multicultural, multiethnic, and diverse. Blending Chinese, Southeast Asian, Indian, British, and other global influences, their foodways reflect the waves of migration, economic exchange, wars, conflict, and colonialism in Hong Kong's history. As a British colony from 1842 to 1997, locals incorporated new foodstuffs such as bread, milk, butter, and tea with milk and sugar into their foodways.

Hong Kong–style French toast, paired with a silky smooth cup of Hong Kong–style milk tea, is how many like to start their morning. Hong Kongers are notorious for dining out, as restaurants are plentiful and cheap and apartments often contain woefully tiny kitchens. Hungry eaters seek these dishes at *cha chaan teng*, Hong Kong–style teahouses. Similar to American diners, *cha chaan teng* are community lifelines serving cheap, hearty fare. Residents young and old gather to have a bite, chat, and commune. Many Hong Kong residents bemoan the loss of *cha chaan teng* due to rising rent prices and gentrification in older neighborhoods where these establishments once flourished. Contemporary Hong Kong–style fast food restaurants also serve their renditions of these dishes.

Hong Kong immigrants to the United States find themselves adjusting more easily to American foodways than other East Asians. Ingredients such as milk, butter, and white bread are familiar to the Hong Kong palate, just as they are to most Americans. French toast and tea with milk and sugar are also consumed here. But the manner in which French toast and tea are prepared are distinct; notably, the preference for canned evaporated and sweetened condensed milk are holdovers from Hong Kong's past. Even as ethnic Hong Kongers have learned to embrace fresh milk and fresh ingredients in the United States, the taste of the old country means canned milk and their own way of doing things.

Hong Kong–Style French Toast

4 slices white sandwich bread (thick slices work best)
2 eggs
3 tablespoons butter
Toast fillings: peanut butter, fruit jam, or coconut jam (*kaya* jam, available at Asian grocers)
Vanilla extract
1 tablespoon evaporated milk (optional)
Additional butter for serving
Golden Syrup (Can be purchased from the international food aisle at large grocery stores. A popular brand is Lyle's, a British brand.)
Sweetened condensed milk

Spread peanut butter, fruit jam, coconut jam, or a mixture of these condiments on the slices of bread and make two sandwiches. Trim the crusts. Whisk two eggs in a bowl and add in a few drops of vanilla extract, up to ⅛ teaspoon. If desired, add in one tablespoon of evaporated milk to thin out the consistency and for a little extra flavor. Dip the sandwiches into the egg mixture. Let soak for a few seconds on each side, until moist but not soggy. Remove and set aside on a plate.

Take a large, nonstick pan and heat on medium high. Add butter and melt. Place sandwiches on the pan and fry on medium or medium-high heat until golden brown on one side. Flip and fry the other side until golden brown. Remove and serve on individual plates. Garnish with condensed milk, Golden Syrup, or a generous pat of butter. As a general rule, allow one piece of toast (two slices of bread) per person. Each piece of toast needs approximately ¾ of an egg. This recipe can be scaled up or down accordingly.

For a variation, try deep-fried Hong Kong Style–French toast. Pan-frying is less messy for home cooks, but deep-frying produces a far superior texture. Most Hong Kong restaurants serve their toast in this way. If you choose to experiment with deep-frying, give the toast a shorter soak time to prevent spattering in hot oil.

Hong Kong–Style Milk Tea

4 black tea bags (Lipton's is the iconic brand in Hong Kong)
24 ounces water
Evaporated milk
Sugar or sugar substitute, to taste

Place teabags in a saucepan with 24 ounces of water. Turn to medium high heat and boil. Let the tea boil for five minutes. Remove tea bags and discard. Pour tea into mugs. Add evaporated milk to taste. One-and-a-half teaspoons of evaporated milk per 12 ounces of tea produces a pleasantly milky tea. Add sugar or sugar substitute, to taste. Enjoy with Hong Kong–Style French Toast or alone. This strong brew is also a good afternoon pickup.

This recipe is scaled to fill two 12-ounce mugs. The rule of thumb is to use two tea bags per 12 ounce serving.

Willa Zhen
(See "Hong Kong," Mary Gee, *EAFT*, pp. 270–74.)

～

Hungary (Eastern Europe), Hungarian American Food

An iconic Hungarian dish popular among Hungarian and Hungarian American home cooks alike is *Paprikás csirke nokedlivel*, commonly referred to in the United States as "chicken paprikash." Historically the dish derives from *goulash*, which is thought to be the original ancestral food of the early *magyar* (Hungarian) herdsmen and is still considered the country's national dish. In the title of the dish, *paprikás* refers to a type of creamy stew made with onion, pepper, tomato, sour cream, and, most importantly, paprika. The protein used is most often chicken (*csirke*), although mutton (*birkapaprikás*), veal (*borjúpaprikás*), or catfish (*harcsapaprikás*) are often substituted.

Nokedlivel refers to the egg-based dumpling, similar to German *spätzle*, traditionally served with the stew. The dumplings are commonly prepared with a device called a *nokedli szaggató*, a coarse grater specifically designed to slice the soft, moist dough directly into boiling water. The utensil is difficult to find in kitchen stores in the United States, so the dumplings are often made using another method, which involves scraping off pieces of dough stretched thin onto a wooden cutting board with a handle. This was actually the original way of preparing *nokedli* in Hungary before the handy *szaggató* was invented. Ironically, the absence of the utensil in the United States drives many home cooks to return to this traditional practice of their grandmothers. Scraping the dough this way can prove quite cumbersome, however, prompting some modern Hungarian American home cooks to leave the dumplings out of the recipe completely and replace it with macaroni or some other small, store-bought pasta. Others, like my mother, whose recipe follows, bring their precious *nokedli szaggató* with them from Hungary.

A similar dish can be found in other Eastern European food cultures, but the paprika is a defining characteristic of Hungarian cuisine.

Paprikás csirke (Chicken paprikash)

2 pounds chicken thighs (Some recipes call for thighs and wings. In my family thighs are preferred.)

1 large white onion

1 tomato

1 green bell pepper (In the original recipe, Hungarian wax peppers are used, but these are often substituted for green bell peppers as wax peppers are difficult to find in the United States.)

2 tablespoons of oil (Traditionally the same amount of pork lard is used, but as the quality of lard in the United States is quite different from what can be found in the markets of Hungary [and for health reasons too], oil is substituted in this recipe.)

2 teaspoons *édesnemes* ("noble sweet") paprika (In Hungary, one can easily find dozens of paprika varieties, which are all essential to the cuisine. These varieties have been divided into eight grades based on color, heat, and flavor characteristics. The type of paprika used in *Paprikás csirke* often depends on the cook; each Hungarian grandmother seems to have her own preference. The paprika grade most commonly imported and thus most easily found in the United States is the *édesnemes* ("noble sweet"), so Hungarian American recipes often include this one rather than spicier, smokier varieties.)

10 ounces sour cream

1 teaspoon flour

Nokedli (Dumplings)

4 cups of all-purpose flour

2 eggs

2 tablespoons oil

3 ounces milk

1 teaspoon salt

8–10 ounces water

Clean chicken thighs. Divide into upper thighs and drumsticks.

Finely chop onion. Wash and clean bell pepper; slice into quarters. Peel tomato and dice.

Into a pan, add oil. When the oil is hot, add the minced onion and cook it for about 1 minute on low heat. It's important for the onion not to brown, toast, or caramelize but to become glossy and transparent instead.

Remove pan from heat and stir in paprika. Stir carefully and quickly so it doesn't burn (it has the tendency to burn easily if neglected.)

Cook seasoned onions for about a minute, or until the onion and paprika is well incorporated. Add pieces of chicken. Add sliced peppers and tomato, along with a pinch of salt.

Cover pan and cook on low heat until the chicken becomes tender. If necessary, add only a small amount of water at a time. The sauce should be kept as thick as possible.

In a small bowl, combine sour cream, 1 teaspoon flour, and 3 tablespoons of the chicken's cooking liquid. Stir until it dissolves into a homogenous roux. Add roux to pan and shake pan lightly. Do not stir, as this might break the delicate pieces of chicken.

Cook for an additional 4 or 5 minutes on low heat.

For *Nokedli*

Set a pot of salted water to boil.

Combine egg, milk, and oil. Then add the flour and stir until a smooth consistency is achieved.

Add just enough water to make the dough soft and moist but not too wet.

(NOTE: The dough should be prepared immediately before cooking for good and light nokedli. If dough is left to rest for too much time before cooking it will become hard, resulting in chewy, dense dumplings.)

Grate the dough on a *nokedli* grater, allowing the bits of dough to drop into boiling water. If you do not own a *nokedli* grater, scrape dough thin over a wooden cutting board and slice off ⅓-inch pieces into the boiling water.

Cook dumplings until they float to the top of the water. Pour dumplings into colander and rinse with cold water to remove excess starch.

Serve *nokedli* in a pile with *Paprikás csirke* poured over the top.

The dish is garnished with a dollop of sour cream and some paprika sprinkled over the top. It is best served with a light cucumber salad or pickled vegetables on the side.

Lili Kocsis
(See "Hungary," by Lili Kocsis, *EAFT*, pp. 274–82.)

I

Iceland (Northern Europe), Icelandic American Food

Fish soups are eaten regularly in Iceland, and no two soups taste the same since each family has its own recipe. Soup bases vary widely and may include anything from curry or lemongrass to wild arctic thyme, which grows in abundance across the barren landscape. Traditionally, Icelanders use whatever they have available at the time of preparation, with the only consistent ingredient being fish. Dehydrated vegetables and dried herbs are often used when fresh ones are scarce. Icelanders in the United States use a variety of vegetables and fish for this soup. This flexibility makes it easy for them to adapt it to new tastes and circumstances.

Fish Soup
Serves 4 as a main dish or 6 as an appetizer.

> 3 quarts homemade white fish stock
> ¾ pound cod or similar, skinned and cut into ½-inch pieces
> ¾ pound arctic char or salmon, skinned and cut into ½-inch pieces
> ¾ pound shrimp, peeled (shells used for stock)
> 2 tablespoons butter
> ½ cup vermouth or white wine
> 1 tablespoon tomato paste
> 2 large leeks, minced
> 1 large onion, minced

6 cloves garlic, minced
3 stalks celery, finely chopped
Any other vegetables available, cut into small pieces
1 teaspoon each dried parsley and thyme
3 bay leaves
Salt and pepper, to taste
Crème fraîche
Fresh herbs such as dill or parsley for garnish

Melt butter in a large pot. Add vegetables, cook until tender, about 10 minutes. Add vermouth and reduce the liquid by half; add the tomato paste, stir to combine. Add the stock, herbs, and bay leaves. Bring to a boil; reduce and simmer, 30 minutes to an hour. Add fish and cook until just done, no more than 5 minutes. Ladle into bowls and into each bowl stir 1 teaspoon crème fraîche and garnish with fresh herbs. Serve with crusty bread and good *smjor* (butter).

Maggie Ornstein
(See "Iceland," Maggie Ornstein, *EAFT*, pp. 283–85.)

⌢

India (Southern Asia), Indian American Food

India has many regional cuisines, but northern Indian tends to be the best known in the United States. Indian Americans, however, oftentimes continue making and eating the specialties of the region of their heritage. The recipes below offer a sampling of the varieties of regional dishes brought to the United States.

Mughlai Paratha (Filled pancake)
Serves 2
One of our favorite breakfast dishes is *Mughlai Paratha*, a popular snack and street food in West Bengal and Bangladesh. It is basically a *paratha* with a spicy egg (or egg and meat) filling. (There is nothing particularly *Mughlai* about it—this is a word often used for a nonvegetarian version of a vegetarian dish.) The traditional version is deep fried or sautéed on a large griddle (*tawa*). Instead of making *parathas* from scratch, frozen parathas that are sold in any Indian grocery store can be used. Purists may object—but it is delicious!

1 large egg
1 tablespoon finely chopped onion
1 green chili, finely chopped (the amount depends on your taste and the hotness of the chili)
½ teaspoon garam masala or cumin powder
½ teaspoon salt
2 frozen whole wheat or white flour parathas

Beat the eggs and other ingredients with 1 tablespoon of water. Add 1 teaspoon of oil to a frying pan over medium-high heat. When it is nearly smoking, put in one of the frozen parathas. (No need to defrost.) With a small ladle, pour half of the egg mixture on top of the paratha, trying not to let it spill over the bread's sides. Cover the pan.

Cook for two minutes. Then gently flip over the paratha and cook for another two minutes.

Remove from the pan and fold two sides over to create a wrap.

Serve with Indian pickles and hot tea.

Five-Minute Fish with Turmeric and Salsa

Serves 4. Adapted with permission from Colleen Taylor Sen and Helen Saberi, *Turmeric: The Wonder Spice* (Agate: Evanston, 2013)

Preparing Indian dishes can be very time consuming. This dish is very easy to make and is perfect for emergencies, such as the arrival of unexpected guests. It also has the advantage of being fat-free and contains turmeric, a spice that researchers are discovering has benefits in preventing and alleviating such diseases as Alzheimers, some forms of cancer, arthritis, depression, uveitis, and cardiovascular diseases.

4 orange roughy filets or some other firm-fleshed fish
½ teaspoon salt
1 tablespoon ground turmeric
¼ cup (50 ml) thick, ready-made tomato salsa
½ teaspoon ginger chutney (available at Indian grocery stores) or crushed ginger

Mix the salt and turmeric, then rub a generous amount over the fillets. Place them in a microwave-safe plastic bag and add the salsa. Seal the bag and cook at full power in the microwave for 2 minutes. Test for doneness and cook for an additional 30 seconds if necessary.

Shake the fish and salsa into a microwave safe serving bowl or plate. Add the ginger chutney or ginger juice and return the bowl to the microwave, uncovered, and heat for 30 seconds to release the aroma of the ginger.

Serve with rice.

Colleen Sen

Turnip and Chicken Curry

Serves 2–4, depending on the number of other dishes

This is a variation on a Kashmiri dish called *shalgun gosht*, a rich, highly aromatic curry made of lamb and turnips and traditionally cooked overnight in a clay pot over charcoal. This version uses off-the-shelf ingredients and is much faster to prepare.

1 pound turnips, peeled and cut into 1-inch cubes
12 ounces chicken breast, cut into 1½-inch cubes
1 large onion, cut in half and sliced
2 tablespoon minced garlic
2 teaspoon ginger paste
2 tablespoon curry powder
Two 15-ounce cans chopped tomatoes
1 can chicken broth
2 tablespoons vegetable oil
2–3 green chilies, finely chopped

Heat the oil in a large pot. Sauté the onion, ginger, and chilies for 3 minutes. Add the garlic and sauté for 1 minute more, stirring to keep from sticking.

Add the curry powder and mix well. Add 1 can of tomatoes with juice; stir well for 1–2 minutes.

Add 1 can chicken stock and ½ can of tomatoes. Bring to a boil and add the turnips. Cook until they start to turn soft (7–8 minutes). Add water or more chicken stock if you prefer a thinner gravy.

Add the chicken and cook until done (5–6 minutes).

Serve with plain boiled rice and a salad.

Colleen Sen
(See "India," Deeksha Nagar, *EAFT*, pp. 285–93.)

⌇

Indonesia (Southeastern Asia), Indonesian American Food

Indonesian food culture is made up of numerous distinct regional cuisines and is also shaped by the religious traditions of those regions—primarily Muslim, but also Hindu (in Bali) and some Christian. It generally shares ingredients, flavors, and cooking techniques with other Southeast Asian cultures, but three-and-a-half centuries of Dutch colonization also left its mark, most notably in the adaptation of a native feast (*nasi Padang*) into *Rijsttafel* ("rice table" in Dutch), a formal presentation of numerous (up to forty) dishes representing the variety of spices, textures, and ingredients in Indonesia.

Indonesian cuisine is not very well known in the United States, and only a small number of restaurants offer it. The most popular Indonesian dishes among Americans tend to include *sate* (satay), *gado gado* (vegetables with peanut sauce), *nasi goreng* (fried rice), and beef *rendang* (spicy beef curry), most likely because of their similarity to more popular Southeast Asian dishes. *Rijsstafel* is offered at some restaurants, and it tends to refer to a buffet or a style of serving. The *gado gado* sauce can be used on other foods or even for a dip.

Gado Gado Sauce (Peanut sauce)
Makes: about 1 cup of sauce
Time: 30 minutes

¼ cup oil (or just enough to coat the peanuts)
1 (12-ounce) package raw peanuts (about 2¼ cups)
2 to 3 kaffir lime leaves
Sliver of shrimp paste (*terasi*), toasted (optional)
1 tablespoon seedless wet tamarind, or lime juice
3 tablespoons Indonesian palm sugar or packed brown sugar
2 teaspoons salt
1 teaspoon chili paste, such as *samba oelek* (vary amount according to taste)

Pour the oil into a wok or large skillet. Heat the oil over medium heat until it shimmers. Add the peanuts and stir-fry them until the skins turn a darker shade of reddish brown and the insides turn golden brown, about 4 to 5 minutes. Toss them continuously so they cook evenly and don't burn.

When the peanuts are done, scoop them up with a slotted spoon and leave to cool on a plate lined with paper towels. Remove any burnt peanuts; they will taste bitter.

When the peanuts are cool enough to handle, grind them until fine like sand in a food processor or pulverize them with a mortar and pestle; in which case, grinding them until the texture of coarse sand will do.

In a small pot, combine 1½ cups water, the lime leaves, shrimp paste, tamarind, sugar, and salt. Bring to a boil over medium-high heat and then reduce the heat and simmer for about 5 minutes, breaking up the shrimp paste and tamarind pulp.

Using a strainer or slotted spoon, remove the leaves and any remaining tamarind pulp. Add 1 cup ground peanuts and bring to a boil. Save the remaining 1 cup for later. Simmer until thick and creamy, stirring often so that the sauce doesn't stick to the bottom of the pot—about 8 to 10 minutes.

Stir in the *sambal oelek*. Taste and adjust the seasonings.

Serve the peanut sauce with vegetables, over soba noodles, or as a dipping sauce with grilled meats such as satay. Garnish with fried shallots, fried shrimp crackers, and *kecap manis*.

Note: The sauce will keep for up to a week in the fridge. To reheat, add a little water if it's too thick, and warm on the stove or in the microwave.

Yellow Coconut Rice
Time: 45 minutes
Makes: 6 to 8 servings as a as part of a multicourse family-style meal

2½ teaspoons ground turmeric
1 teaspoon salt
1 cup warm water
1½ cups coconut milk
1 plump stalk lemongrass, bruised and tied into a knot
1 *salam* leaf
4 kaffir lime leaves, crumpled
2½ cups long-grain rice
2 cups water
Garnishes:
1 small red bell pepper, cut into strips
1 small cucumber, peeled and cut into coins
Fried shallots
Dissolve the turmeric and salt in the warm water.

In a large pot, bring the coconut milk, lemongrass, salam leaf, and kaffir lime leaves to a gentle boil over medium-high heat. Reduce the heat to medium-low. Add the turmeric water. Tip the rice into the pot and add the water. Bring to a gentle boil, stirring occasionally.

Simmer uncovered until all the liquid has just been absorbed, about 10 minutes. Reduce the heat to low. Cover and cook for 15 to 20 minutes, or until the rice is tender but not mushy; the rice grains should still be separated. If the rice is still hard, make a well in the center of the pot, add a little water, and cook a few more minutes. Halfway through the estimated cooking time, gently fluff the rice with a fork or chopsticks.

Let the rice cool. Fish out the lemongrass, salam leaf, and lime leaves and discard.

On a large serving platter, mound the rice into the shape of an upturned cone. Garnish with red pepper strips, cucumber slices, and fried shallots.

Pat Tanumihardja. Recipes reprinted with permission from *The Asian Grandmother's Cookbook: Homecooking from Asian American Kitchens.* See theasiangrandmotherscookbook.wordpress.com.
(See "Indonesia," by Patricia Tanumihardja in *EAFT,* pp. 293–97.)

Iran (Western Asia), Iranian American Food

Iranian (Persian) cuisine is ancient and was historically influential throughout western Asia, North Africa, and the Indian subcontinent. Persian Americans continue many of their food traditions and make an effort to use authentic traditional ingredients and recipes for everyday meals as well as holidays. *Khoresht-e-Fesenjaan* (or *Fesenjoon*) is one of the most traditional—and delicious and intriguing—Persian dishes. Traditionally made with duck or goose, in the United States it is usually made with chicken. The combinations of ingredients result in a sweet and sour thick sauce with a depth of flavor, texture, and complexity. The dish contains walnuts, an excellent source of omega-3 and protein. Pomegranate molasses, also called syrup or paste, is available in most Middle Eastern and health food stores in the United States. Serve with long grain rice (see recipes).

Khoresht-e-Fesenjaan (or Fesenjoon) (Chicken stewed with walnuts and pomegranate molasses)
6½ cup servings

1 large peeled onion, processed in food processor until smooth
1½ cup walnuts, roasted and processed into paste
1½ pounds boneless skinless chicken or duck breast, thighs, or drumsticks, cut into 2–to–3–inch cubes

1 tablespoon canola or olive oil
1 teaspoon salt
¼ teaspoon ground black pepper
1 cup pomegranate molasses (use 1½ cups if the molasses is not as thick as honey)
¼ cup ice cold water
1–2 tablespoons granulated sugar

Place oil in a medium-sized pot; heat on medium heat. Add processed onion and stir continuously until onions are uniformly golden. There should be no onion juice left in the pot at this point. Add processed walnuts to onions; mix and scrape the mixture from the sides and the bottom of the pot for about 5 minutes to achieve uniform roasting of walnuts.

Add ice cold water to the mixture and mix until it boils. Add the chicken (or the duck), salt, and pepper. Cook about 30 minutes on medium heat or until fork tender (duck cooks slower than chicken and requires longer cooking time).

Lower heat to low medium; add pomegranate molasses. Cover mixture and cook about 20 more minutes until walnut oil comes to the top of the food. (Different brands of pomegranate molasses vary in sweetness. Some are more sour than others and may need added sugar.)

Polo (Persian rice)

4 cups dry basmati rice
4 teaspoons regular or rock salt
4–6 tablespoons of butter (melted) or canola oil, divided in two
Saffron, if desired

Persian rice can be prepared with two different methods. The easiest is boiling. For this method, rice is washed two or three times. For every cup of basmati rice, use 1½ cup water, some salt to taste (1 tablespoon per 4 cups of rice), and 2–3 tablespoons of oil. Cook on medium heat until the water is evaporated. The more elaborate way of making *polo* is an art and requires patience and practice.

In large bowl, wash rice two or three times with lukewarm water and drain. Add lukewarm water until it reaches about 1 inch above the rice level. Add salt, mix gently, and let soak for at least 1 hour or overnight. Water level must be over the rice at all times during soaking (after it is soaked for ½ hour, you might have to add more water). Fill a medium large, nonstick pot ⅔ full with water and bring to a boil. Drain the soaked rice and add it to the boiling water. Stir occasionally (whenever the water starts boiling again) for about 10 minutes. Test rice for softness by pressing a few grains between your thumb and index fingers. It should be al dente, not too soft or mushy. Drain the rice in a colander (with small holes) in the sink, and quickly run cold water on it. This stops the rice from further cooking. Put the pot back on low to medium heat, add 2–3 tablespoons of oil and place a flat, thin bread (*lavash*) or ¼-inch sliced potato with some salt sprinkled on them in the bottom of the pot. Add the drained rice, gently making a mountain with the rice over the bread. Melt 2–3 tablespoons of butter and drizzle it evenly on the rice. Pour saffron water* on the rice and cover it, with the lid covered with paper towels to soak up any precipitated water and prevent it from dripping back on the rice. Keep it on low heat for 30–40 minutes, until the steam rises from the rice. When rice is ready, the bread or potatoes in the bottom of the rice turns into a crunchy, delicious *Tahdiq* (this means "bottom of the pot": *Teh* (bottom) and *dig* (pot)).

*To prepare saffron, add a pinch of saffron threads to ¼ cup of boiling water and steep in a small covered jar or container for about 15 minutes. This can be prepared before the cooking process starts and kept at room temperature.

Shahla Ray
(See "Iran," Shahla Ray, EAFT, pp. 297–300.)

∽

Iraq (Western Asia), Iraqi American Food

The *Makhlama* has a long history and features many of the staples of the Iraqi diet, such as potatoes, onions, butter, eggs, meat, and spices. In other Arab countries, it is known as an *újja* and in the West as an omelet. The *makhlama* is versatile and can be made with meat or vegetables only. It can be served as breakfast, lunch, or part of a light supper.

Makhlama (Omelet)

Lamb, or other meat (if using)
3 medium potatoes, cubed (optional)
1 white or yellow onion, finely chopped
4–5 ripe tomatoes (approximately 2 pounds), peeled, seeded, and chopped

2–3 garlic cloves, chopped
5 eggs
3 tablespoons chives, finely chopped
2 tablespoons parsley, finely chopped
Olive oil for sautéing meat, onions, and potatoes
Salt and pepper to taste
Lemon wedges for garnish

Options: Add curry, chili powder, or cayenne pepper

In a large cast iron skillet (preferred), sauté the garlic and onions in olive oil for approximately 5–7 minutes, or until the onions release their juices. Add meat or potatoes (if using) and continue to sauté until lightly browned. Add the chopped tomatoes, salt, pepper, and any other spices depending on preference. A small amount of sugar can also be added for a slightly sweeter sauce. Continue to simmer for 8–10 minutes until the sauce has thickened. Carefully separate the sauce so that there are shallow holes or spaces for the eggs. Crack an egg into each of the spaces. Cover and continue to cook until desired consistency of the eggs. They can be served "sunny side up" or with firm, solid yolks. Remove and serve on individual plates. Sprinkle with chopped chives and parsley, and place the lemon wedge on the side.

Laura K. Hahn
(See "Iraq," Laura K. Hahn, *EAFT*, 300–5.)

～

Ireland (Northern Europe), Irish American Food

Traditional Irish Shepherd's Pie includes ground lamb and is often called cottage pie. However, American sensibilities dictate that this dish, an Irish pub favorite, include ground beef, making it a more dinner-worthy, sit-down-with-a-fork version of the American classic burger and fries. And it's great as leftovers.

Irish American Shepherd's Pie

2 pounds potatoes
6 ounces sour cream or yogurt
Salt and pepper

1 tablespoon olive or vegetable oil
One medium onion, chopped
2 pounds ground beef (more on the fatty than lean side)
¼ teaspoon mustard powder
16 ounces fresh or thawed frozen corn
½ cup milk or yogurt
4 tablespoons melted butter
4 ounces grated Dubliner cheese (optional)
Smoked paprika (optional)

Heat oven to 350°F. Peel, quarter, and boil potatoes until soft, about 20 minutes. Mash or rice, add sour cream or yogurt, and then salt and pepper to taste. Set aside. While potatoes are cooking, add oil to a large nonstick skillet over medium heat. Cook onions 5 minutes, then add beef. After about 5 minutes, drain excess fat, and then add mustard power; cook until meat is no longer pink. Let cool slightly, and then incorporate corn, milk or yogurt, and salt and pepper. Place meat mixture in ungreased 2½- to 3-quart baking dish. Crown with mashed potatoes. Top with butter and bake for 35 minutes. Sprinkle with grated cheese, and bake an additional 10–15 minutes until heated thoroughly. Remove from oven, sprinkle with paprika, and serve.

NOTE: You can refrigerate the pie for a few days after assembling in step 4. In that case, continue at step 5 after removing from fridge, and increase the total cooking time to about 65 minutes.

Arthur Lizie
(See "Ireland," Arthur Lizie, *EAFT*, pp. 305–9.)

⌒

Isle of Man (Western Europe), Manx American

Food in the Isle of Man in the 1800s was relatively simple by necessity and geography, with barley and herring being prominent staples. Potatoes became prevalent at the beginning of the nineteenth century, and they were quickly superceded by barley and oats. They were cooked in their jackets and eaten with salt herring, mashed and made into potato cakes, and added to stews and hotpots. The common name for mashed potatoes was *tittlewhack*, a word derived from the sound made by the wooden pestle used to mash big tubs of potatoes. When the first new potato of the season was eaten, it was believed to be lucky to make a wish, as it was sure to be granted. Mashed potatoes were frequently mixed with flour, butter, and sugar and cooked on a griddle for potato cakes.

When Manx immigrated to America in the nineteenth century, they adapted to what was locally available, although the recipes passed down through families still feature barley, oats, herring, and potatoes, prepared relatively simply. A favorite bread, which survives in many variations in Manx American families, is *bonnag*.

Christmas *Bonnag* (Candied fruit bread)

2½ cups white flour
1 cup sugar
1 teaspoon baking soda
1 teaspoon cream of tartar
½ tablespoon cinnamon
2 tablespoons butter
8 ounces candied fruit (fruit cake mix)
¼ teaspoon vanilla
1 cup buttermilk

Preheat oven to 350°F. Mix the dry ingredients well together in a bowl and cut in the butter with a pastry blender until it is the size of oatmeal. Mix in candied fruit. Add vanilla to buttermilk, then mix quickly for 1 scant minute. Place in a 9-inch cake pan. Bake about 35 minutes, or until a toothpick inserted in the center comes out dry.

Betty J. Belanus
(See "Isle of Man," Betty J. Belanus, *EAFT*, pp. 309–11.)

～

Israel (Western Asia), Israeli American Food

The food culture of Israel reflects the multicultural makeup of its population, which includes European, northern African, and western Asian descent. While there seems to be an emerging Israeli cuisine mixing Middle Eastern, Mediterranean, and European food traditions, it is difficult to identify foods that are uniquely Israeli. This also applies to Israeli foods available in the United States, and Israelis frequently distinguish themselves from the American Jewish community. Israeli American food, then, is not the same as Jewish food in the United States. An example is zucchini caviar. The dish was invented during the austerity period in Israel (1949–1959) when meat was scarce and people were looking for substitutes for the Eastern European chopped liver. Originally people prepared it from eggplants but, in my opinion, it tastes better when made of zucchini. The dish is often used as an appetizer, a sandwich spread, or a salad in a potluck dinner.

Zucchini Caviar

2 pounds zucchini, cut into thin circles
4 large white onions
4 hard-boiled eggs
½ pound of walnuts/pecans
Breadcrumbs or wheat to your liking
Olive oil
Salt and pepper

In a hot pan, stir fry the zucchini in olive oil. When the pieces are slightly brown add 1–2 teaspoons of either breadcrumbs or wheat to get a bit of crunchy taste, and salt and pepper to your liking. Repeat the process until all the zucchini is fried.

Stir fry 4 chopped onions until translucent. Put the fried zucchini, onions, eggs, and nuts in a food processor. Add salt, pepper, and olive oil if necessary. Chill in the refrigerator.

Liora Gvion
(See "Israel," Liora Gvion, *EAFT*, pp. 311–13.)

⌣

Italy (Southern Europe), Italian American Food

Most Italians in the United States came from southern Italy, so Italian American cookery is based on those regional styles. Although it exploits the greater access to pasta and fresh meat and fish afforded by their improved economic station in the United States, Italian American home cookery remained remarkably rooted in Old World aesthetics and traditions.

Spaghetti with anchovies is a quintessential southern Italian dish that represents *cucina povera*—cookery of the poor—but all classes enjoy it. Since it involves no animal products, it fits the old Roman Catholic rules prohibiting animal products on fast days—namely, Fridays throughout the year,

Lent, and Christmas Eve—when it is a required element of the celebration in many families. The version below originated in the region of Campania, but it includes walnuts. Note that the "condiment" is cooked only briefly, while the spaghetti is boiling.

Known throughout Italy, chicken with potatoes and peas was a festive dish for poor southern Italians. It continued this role among Italian Americans, appearing as a second course after a first course of pasta as part of the Sunday afternoon family meal. Though not typically found in restaurants around the country, a version has become a standard in Chicago's Italian restaurants under the name Chicken Vesuvio.

Spaghetti alle alici e noci (Spaghetti with anchovies and walnuts)
Serves four.

> 14 ounces (400 grams) spaghetti (medium to thick)
> Salt (for the cooking water of the pasta)
> Garlic, sliced (one medium to large clove; too much will then mask the other flavors)
> Black pepper, coarsely ground (or whole peppercorns, crushed) (optional)
> One small dried red pepper (*peperoncino*) or a small piece of a large dried red pepper, crumbled (or dried red pepper flakes) (optional)
> Handful of walnuts, crushed, but not too finely
> 4–5 salted or oil-packed anchovies, cleaned and rinsed
> One or two good-sized sprigs of flat-leaf parsley, minced
> Olive oil (extra virgin), some for cooking, some for finishing

Set a large pot with ample water to boil; add salt to the water but adjust to compensate for the saltiness of the anchovies. While water is coming to a boil, prepare other ingredients: a) slice the garlic thin; b) if using whole black peppercorns and dried red pepper, crush them together with mortar and pestle; c) crush walnuts; d) rinse anchovies and remove any hard bits of bone or salt, then pat them dry with a paper towel; e) mince parsley.

When water for the pasta comes to a boil, set a large pan or a Dutch oven (sufficiently large to hold the cooked spaghetti) over a medium-low flame and add enough olive oil just to cover the bottom of the pan. Add spaghetti to cooking pot. Plan on draining the spaghetti at a very "al dente" stage (i.e., a minute or so before the package's recommended cooking time for al dente).

Add garlic to a Dutch oven and fry gently in oil. Just before it darkens, add crushed black and red pepper, crushed walnuts, anchovies, and half of the parsley. With a wooden spoon, mix the ingredients and help anchovies to break down. If the mixture is cooking too quickly, adjust the flame to low. The anchovies should break down almost completely.

When spaghetti is still very al dente, add a splash or two of cooking water to the pan with the condiment and reserve a further cup of the cooking water. Drain the spaghetti and add them to the pan with the condiment.

Mix spaghetti and condiment and remaining parsley together in the pan and allow them to cook together for a minute or so, adding a little of the pasta cooking water as required to keep the dish moist. When the pasta is still al dente, turn off the flame. Add a drizzle of extra virgin olive oil if desired.

Serve spaghetti in a large bowl. Note: grated cheese is never added to this dish.

Pollo al forno con patate e piselli (Chicken with potatoes and peas)
Serves four.

4 bone-in, skin-on chicken thighs (other cuts can be used)
4–6 medium-sized potatoes (preferably Yukon Gold)
1 small clove garlic
1 sprig fresh rosemary
1 sprig of fresh oregano (or 1–2 pinches of dried oregano)
Juice of one large lemon (ca. ⅓ cup)
1 cup fresh or frozen peas, thawed
Salt
Pepper
Olive oil (extra virgin)

Preheat oven to 400°F. Prepare ingredients: a) wash and pat dry chicken pieces; b) mince the garlic clove; c) strip sprigs of rosemary and oregano and mince leaves; d) cut potatoes into small chunks roughly 1 to 1½ inches along the three dimensions.

Spread about 3 tablespoons olive oil around bottom of the baking dish. Place chicken pieces in the baking dish skin-side down and season them with salt, black pepper, and a little of the minced garlic and herbs. Flip chicken pieces over and place potato chunks around them. (If not peeled, place chunks skin-side down in the baking dish.) Squeeze lemon juice over chicken pieces and potato chunks, then drizzle olive oil over both. Season with salt and pepper and the remaining minced garlic and herbs.

Place baking dish in oven. After 40 minutes, remove and add peas in the spaces around chicken pieces and potato chunks (which will have shrunk). Cook 20 minutes. When the potatoes are soft all the way through, the dish is done. The chicken skin should be fairly dark brown and very crispy while the meat remains juicy. The potatoes should be partially browned on tops and edges and soft inside.

Serve with a simple mixed salad and Italian bread.

Anthony F. Buccini
(See "Italy," Anthony F. Buccini, *EAFT*, pp. 314–23.)

J

Jamaica (Americas–Caribbean), Jamaican American Food

If you are in Jamaica and find your way into any home for Sunday supper, it is almost a guarantee that rice and peas will be waiting for you on the dining room table. Because of its subtly sweet flavor and ability to quell spiciness, this maroon-speckled dish is the smooth yin to a spicy yang (such as jerk chicken). The traditional processes of grinding coconut meat with water, squeezing the pulp in cheesecloth to make the coconut milk, and preparing red peas from scratch are both labor and time intensive. Though there is less novelty, using canned coconut milk and peas are quick alternatives practiced in the United States as well as in Jamaica.

Jamaica's "Rice and Peas" has Caribbean relatives, such as Trinidad's Peas and Rice, Haiti's *Dira Ak Pwa*, and Cuba's *Moros y Cristianos*. In the United States, you can find rice and peas in most Jamaican restaurants and some Caribbean ones.

Jamaican Rice and Peas

1 cup cooked kidney beans
1 cup white rice
1 cup coconut milk
1 cup bean liquid (the liquid remaining from cooking dried beans or liquid from canned beans combined with enough water to fill a cup)
1 or 2 stalks green onion (scallion)

1 scotch bonnet pepper (optional)
Extra water on hand
Salt to taste
Preparing the kidney beans (if not using canned beans):

Soak beans overnight and drain. Add a pinch of salt to the water, and then cook on the stovetop in fresh water until kidney beans are almost soft—the beans will finish cooking with the rice. Remove beans and keep leftover bean liquid.

Preparing the rice:

Combine the coconut milk, bean liquid, white rice, and prepared or canned beans in a pot or rice cooker. Place green onion (scallion) on top of all ingredients. If a peppery taste is desired, place unbroken scotch bonnet pepper on top of rice. If cooking on stovetop, cook on medium heat, stirring occasionally. Keep an eye on the rice, adding water ¼ cup at a time until rice is cooked thoroughly. If cooking in a rice cooker, cook according to manufacturer instructions.

Deion Jones
(See "Jamaica," Amy B. Santos, *EAFT*, pp. 325–27.)

～

Japan (East Asia), Japanese American Food

"Japanese cuisine" suggests to many Americans only a small repertory of popular signature dishes, such as sushi, tempura, and sukiyaki. Japanese food culture, however, is highly diverse; and its ingredients, cooking methods, and recipes are ripe for adoption by American culture.

The richness of Japanese (and, by extension, Japanese American) cuisine is illustrated by a typical home-cooked Japanese-style meal, which consists of rice, soup (*miso-* or broth-based), and a set of several small dishes (*okazus*). Each *okazu* is prepared with different flavors, so that one's palate is variously entertained throughout the meal. One example of an everyday *okazu* is a dish called *namasu*, which consists of strips of marinated daikon and carrot. A refreshingly tangy side dish, *namasu* can accompany any Japanese-style meal. Moreover, *namasu* frequently appears on festive and celebratory occasions, as the white of the daikon and the reddish orange of the carrot create a combination of colors—*kohaku* [red-white]—that symbolizes auspiciousness within Japanese culture.

In Japanese cuisine, meat dishes need not be heavy or drenched in teriyaki sauce. For instance, pork can be tenderized by boiling it in tea. Tea—especially black tea—contains tannins, astringent polyphenolic compounds that break down proteins. Tea helps to eliminate the smell particular to pork, while extended simmering drains excess fat. This makes tea-boiled pork a healthy meat dish in Japanese home cooking. In Japan it would typically be sliced and served as an *okazu*, but other uses are also possible: the pork could be cut into chunks for stir-fry; sliced thinly for sandwiches; or treated as a main dish, perhaps paired with steamed vegetables.

Namasu (Vinegar-marinated carrot and daikon strips)

1 carrot
½ small daikon (usually translated as "radish" or "turnip," it is roughly equal in size to the carrot)
2–3 teaspoons salt
4 tablespoons rice vinegar or apple vinegar
1 tablespoon sugar

Cut carrot and daikon into thin strips; place in bowl. Rub salt into vegetable strips; let stand for about 10 minutes. Wring internal moisture from vegetable strips; place in a separate bowl. Combine vinegar and sugar, then pour over vegetable strips to marinate. Note: Kohlrabi can be substituted for daikon. Add lemon juice and/or salt to taste. For a milder flavor, add shredded apple or persimmon. For a more robust flavor, add chili sauce, chili oil, wasabi, or ginger. This is a nice side dish to complement oily food.

Buta no kocha-ni (Tea-boiled pork)

1–1½ pounds pork
3–4 tea bags (black tea)
Water
½ cup rice vinegar
½ cup soy sauce
½ cup *mirin* (If *mirin* is not available, use *sake*—or white cooking wine—and sugar; *mirin* can be approximated by combining *sake* and sugar in a 3:1 ratio.)

In large saucepan or stockpot, boil enough water to cover pork; add tea bags. Add pork to boiling tea; lower heat when pork's surface is cooked; simmer 1 hour. Combine rice vinegar, soy sauce, and *mirin* in a different saucepan to make a marinade; heat to boil. Place pork in bowl and add marinade; pork should be at least half covered. Allow pork and marinade to cool;

then cover bowl and refrigerate. After a few hours, turn pork over so as to marinate the other side. It is ready to serve after half a day, or the next day.

Note: Oolong, *houji*, or *bancha* tea will work if black tea is not available. One can experiment with flavored black teas, which will infuse the pork with the scent of apple, pear, or other fruits. Star anise, cinnamon, or other spices can be added for alternate flavoring.

Ayako Yoshimura
(See "Japan," Ayako Yoshimura, *EAFT*, pp. 327–37.)

~

Jewish, Ashkenazi (North America), Jewish; American Jewish

Challah is the egg-rich bread traditionally eaten at Ashkenazic Sabbath and holiday meals. Any bread made from wheat, rye, oats, barley, or spelt could be used as ceremonial bread, but this type of bread, made from white wheat flour with oil and eggs, has become the symbol of a festive Jewish meal in the Ashkenazic tradition. A Sabbath meal traditionally begins with two challahs, each made of six braided strands. For the New Year it is traditional to make a crown-shaped challah, and some Sabbaths during the year are associated with special challah shapes, such as a key-shaped challah for the Sabbath following Passover, but these shapes have fallen out of common use. In the United States, challah has become a popular ingredient for French toast on Sunday mornings.

Matzo is an unleavened bread, similar to a large cracker. They are usually sold in American groceries, oftentimes in the international section. Matzo balls, or *kneydlekh*, are a beloved Passover food in spite of their having no historical connection to the holiday. Traditionally they would accompany chicken soup, so butter, a dairy product, would not be a possible ingredient.

Some Orthodox communities do not make matzo balls or other recipes that combine matzo with liquids during Passover because of concern that leavening might occur if matzo becomes wet.

Challah (Bread)

¾ cup warm water
3 packets active dry yeast
4½ eggs (leave over part of one egg for the glaze)

4 yolks (So that you have about 10 ounces eggs and yolks, combined. You can make it more or less yolky depending on your plans for the whites.)
¼ cup olive oil
¼ cup honey
6½ cups bread flour (30 to 32 ounces)
4 teaspoons kosher salt

Dissolve the yeast in the water. Add eggs, oil, honey, flour, and salt and work into a still dough. Knead the dough for about fifteen minutes and allow it to rise, covered, in a warmish place until doubled. Punch down the dough. At this point you can begin shaping the loaves, or allow the dough to rise overnight in the refrigerator.

Divide into twelve pieces and roll each piece into a smooth, seamless sphere. Roll each dough lump slightly to elongate. Go back to dough lump number one and roll each one a little more. Continue until you have twelve ropes about 12 to 15 inches long. Braid into two challahs of six strands each. To braid six strands, fasten them at the top, then move the leftmost rope to the center and the rightmost but one to the left. Then move the rightmost to the center and the leftmost but one to the right. Continue to the bottom and pinch the ends together.

Allow the challahs to rest 40 minutes or so. Preheat oven to 400°F. Brush with remaining half egg beaten with a teaspoon of water and sprinkle with seeds. Bake for 30 minutes or until brown.

Kneydlekh (Matzo balls)

4 eggs, extra large or jumbo
1 cup matzo meal (preferably Streit's)
½ cup melted butter, coconut oil, or olive oil, or a combination (traditionally matzo balls would be made with *schmaltz*, rendered chicken or goose fat)
¼ cup water
1 tablespoon salt
Black pepper
Cayenne pepper
Sweet paprika

Break eggs into a bowl. Season lavishly with salt, pepper, cayenne, and paprika. Add water and olive oil or melted butter. Beat the egg mixture and while beating gradually sprinkle in enough Streit's matzo meal to make a loose, muddy mixture. You will think that it is too soft, and you will be tempted to add more matzo. Valiantly resist this temptation! It is just right when it looks like it is still too loose. Refrigerate the mixture overnight.

Bring one or two (or three) large pots of wildly salted water to a boil. Roll dough into balls the size of walnuts. Lower the flame under the water slightly so that it is simmering serenely. Gently lower the matzo balls into the water. Leave enough room for the balls to double in size. After a minute or two you may raise the heat to boiling and cook, covered, with no peeking for one hour. If you use all whole wheat matzo meal, cooking time is longer and you will want to add a bit more butter. If you use all white matzo meal, cooking time is shorter.

Eve Jochnowitz
(See "Jewish, Ashkenazi," by Eve Jochnowitz, *EAFT*, pp. 337–41.)

~

Jewish, Sephardic (Northern American), Jewish American Food

This recipe is a sweet bread common in the Hispanic world in the fifteenth century before the time Jews were expelled from Spain and, slightly later, Portugal. Similar breads are found as far flung as Japan and China where the Portuguese brought them, as well as Mexico and much of South America where the Spanish brought it. This version is a long-lost cousin brought to Smyrna or Izmir in Turkey, where a Sephardic population settled after 1492. It made its way to New York early in the twentieth century. The cinnamon is a reminder of its essentially medieval roots.

Panezico de Asucare or *Boyos Dulces* (Sweet bread)

4 cups flour
1 cake yeast
1 egg
¼ cup oil
½ cup sugar
½ teaspoon cinnamon
Pinch salt

Warm 2 cups water or milk. Dissolve yeast in center of flour with water. Add egg into hole. Add oil, sugar, cinnamon, and salt to make dough (bring it all together, work until smooth, but do not knead!). Cover for 1 hour; then knead. Cover for ½ hour; knead well.

Form small rolls and knead each roll. Feather top, and top with beaten egg. Let sit while oven warms. Bake at 375°F on a floured pan until done (golden brown, approximately 15 minutes).

Ken Albala

(See "Jewish, Sephardic," by Ken Albala, *EAFT*, pp. 341–46.)

~

Jordan (Western Asia), Jordanian American Food

Jordanians began immigrating to the United States in earnest just after World War II, and the majority has historically been Eastern Orthodox Christian. Their food shares ingredients and dishes with surrounding cultures with differences emerging in how a dish is prepared and served. Typical staple foods for Jordanian Americans are very much the same as they are in Jordan, and many Jordanian ingredients are commonly found in mainstream American supermarkets, while specialized ingredients and prepared foods are available in Middle Eastern or Mediterranean markets.

A favorite breakfast dish throughout the Levant region (Israel, Palestine, Lebanon, Syria) is *foul*, mashed fava beans with olive oil, lemon juice, onion, garlic, cumin, and parsley. Cutting across religious, political, class, and philosophical differences, this ancient dish can be made in a very modern way, since cans of fava beans are sold in many supermarkets and are even available with seasonings according to each culture. The simplest recipe is to open a can, heat the beans, mash, and sprinkle with lemon juice. Chickpeas can also be mixed in. Vegetarian in its most basic form, it can also be topped with eggs or anything else the eater wishes. Jordanian Americans might even sprinkle on za'atar, a seasoning mix of thyme, savory, oregano, sumac, and sesame found in most grocery stores and spread on flat breads to make "Middle Eastern pizza."

Foul (Ful Mudammas) (Breakfast beans)

2 cups fava beans, cooked
½ onion, minced
Garlic (2 raw cloves minced, or 4 cloves roasted, or 2 tablespoons minced garlic)

Olive oil
¼ teaspoon cumin
Salt, to taste (probably not needed, if canned beans are used)
Pepper, to taste
Toppings:
Tomato, chopped
Hard-boiled egg, sliced
Green peppers, chopped
Parsley, chopped

Heat fava beans until soft. Mash, leaving lumps. Mix in onion, garlic, olive oil, and seasonings. Squeeze lemon juice over dish. Add toppings of choice.

Eat by scooping up beans with pieces of pita bread.

Lucy M. Long and Issa Baiz
(See "Jordan," Cecilia Peterson, *EAFT*, pp. 346–49.)

K

Kenya (East Africa), Kenyan American Food

Kenyan food culture mirrors the nation's complex history. The incorporation of Middle Eastern cuisine reflects an enduring influence of ancient Arab and Persian trade routes along the country's coast. With over forty ethnic groups residing within the country, regional cuisines based on cultural food preferences can also be found. The colonial history of the country is also reflected in the food culture, with British food culture and Indian cuisine also included in the country's cuisine. Kenyan immigrants to the United States carry these influences with them, and most households seek to recreate Kenyan dishes on a regular basis. Typical staples in Kenyan American homes include *ugali* (a maize meal paste), chicken or beef stew, *sukuma wiki* (fried kale with onion and tomatoes), *gatheri* (beans and rice with potatoes and peas), rice, bean stew, fruits, and vegetables. Other dishes and snacks such as *pilau, biriani, samosa,* and *nyama choma* (meat, preferably goat, grilled over glowing charcoal) are prepared during special occasions and festivities, including Kenyan public holidays, such as Independence Day, Christmas, and Ramadan. Kenyans also gather in each other's homes on weekends, at church, and as part of professional or business groups. At such occasions, Kenyan food is cooked and eaten along with a celebration of Kenyan culture, which includes speaking Swahili and listening to Kenyan music. Beef stew and rice (*Mchuzi na Wali*) is a staple that most Kenyan Americans make on a regular basis. The meat can also be stored in the freezer and used later.

Mchuzi na Wali (Meat stew and rice)

Mchuzi (Meat stew):
  2 pounds beef, cut into small pieces (Grass-fed beef produces a flavor and
    texture that is closest to Kenyan beef. Also, cuts that have a little mar-
    bling produce a better flavor than lean meat. If using beef with a little
    marbling, reduce the amount of oil used.)
  1 cup beef stock
  1 large yellow onion, peeled and diced
  2 tablespoons cooking oil (vegetable oil or olive oil)
  3 carrots, peeled and sliced
  3 medium-sized red potatoes, peeled and cubed (Red potatoes are pre-
    ferred because they are firm and hold their shape in the stew better, but
    other varieties can be used.)
  Salt to taste
  1 teaspoon tomato paste
  2 garlic cloves (Skip if you don't like the taste or smell of garlic.)

Optional: 1 teaspoon curry powder and red chili pepper added to desired
hotness
  Cook onions in oil over medium-low heat until soft and just beginning to
brown. Add meat, stir, and cover when juices begin to froth. Cook, covered,
until meat juices have dried. Add diced carrots and cook, stirring often. Add
potatoes and cook for one minute, stirring often. If using curry powder and
chili, please add at this stage. Add tomato paste and stir for approximately one
minute. Add beef stock to the pot and mix ingredients well until tomato paste is
completely dissolved. Taste broth, and add more salt to the stew if desired. Simmer over low heat until vegetables are tender and meat is cooked to desired softness. Once meat is ready, add crushed garlic and cook for an additional minute.

Wali (Steamed rice):
  1 cup basmati rice (preferably authentic basmati bought from an Indian
    food store)
  2 tablespoons olive oil
  2 cups water
  Salt to taste, approximately 1/2 a teaspoon

Optional: You can add chicken boullion to the water if a more savory taste
is desired.

Boil water over high heat. While water is heating, put rice in a strainer and rinse thoroughly under cold water. Once water boils, add olive oil and salt. Add rice and reduce heat to low. Cook, covered, over low heat until all the water is absorbed. Remove from heat and keep covered until ready to serve.

You can also add coconut milk to make coconut rice. If adding coconut milk, reduce cooking water by ½ cup. Follow the rest of the steps outlined above. When half of the water is absorbed, add ½ cup of coconut milk and fluff rice gently with fork. Reduce to very low heat. It is important to add the coconut milk later and cook over very low heat so as to prevent the rice from sticking to the bottom of the pan.

Serve meat stew and rice with steamed vegetables of your choice.

Sheila Navalia Onzere
(See "Kenya," Sheila Navalia Onzere, *EAFT*, pp. 351–54.)

Korea (East Asia), Korean American

Traditional Korean cuisine is centered around rice, which is often prepared with beans, barley, or other grains. Accompanying it is a form of soup or stew, grilled fish, or meat. These are often highly seasoned, including combinations of garlic, ginger, red or black pepper, scallions, soy sauce, sesame oil, and sesame seeds. Each meal also includes a variety of side dishes called *banchan*. These small dishes are often composed of blanched, boiled, pan-fried, or steamed vegetables, along with an assortment of pickled items called *kimchi*.

Kimchi is vital to both traditional and modern Korean and Korean American meals. The prevalent form consists of Napa cabbage fermented in salt and red pepper and seasoned with brine, scallions, ginger, garlic, fish sauce, and salted shrimp. Other common varieties of kimchi are made from daikon radishes, cucumbers, mustard greens, and scallions, but every region has its specialties, and every family has its own recipes.

The pungent odor and spiciness of kimchi originally made it unappealing to many American palates, but it has recently been "discovered" and is now a trendy item, partly because of the recognition of the health values of fermented foods. Another Korean dish that tends to be well liked by Americans is *bulgogi*, marinated grilled beef strips. Now popular in "Korean tacos," it traditionally is served with rice and side dishes. For picnics, it is frequently wrapped in lettuce and rice.

Bulgogi (Fire meat)

Marinate overnight in the refrigerator:

1½ pounds beef in paper-thin slices and small pieces, easier to do if the meat is slightly frozen. (Some mainstream American grocery stores actually sell "bulgogi meat" in the deli section. Otherwise, it is usually the meat from the back, between the ribs. A little bit of marbling is good. Other meats can be used, most commonly, chicken or pork.)

4 green onions, chopped

3–4 cloves garlic, minced

1 teaspoon crushed sesame seeds

1–2 tablespoons sesame oil

4–5 tablespoons Korean soy sauce or Kikkoman brand

1–2 tablespoons sugar (brown sugar is an option)

¼ teaspoon black pepper

1 teaspoon ginger, minced (optional)

¼ Asian pear or apple, grated (adds sweetness; if not available, add more sugar)

Mix all ingredients together to form a sauce. Pour it over the beef and mix thoroughly. Let the meat marinate for 15 minutes to an hour, or overnight. (It can also be frozen for future use.)

The traditional method of cooking is to grill on a special slotted pan over charcoal or an open flame (gas ranges work for this). Otherwise, you can either:

- Spread on a baking dish and broil or cook quickly in a frying pan with small amount of beef stock for extra "juice."
- Serve with rice. It can also be wrapped in rice and lettuce leaves for a picnic food.

(For a vegetarian version, use tofu or tempeh. The sauce is delicious on any kind of meat. Also, sliced mushrooms, onions, or other vegetables can be marinated and cooked along with the meat.)

Jonna Adams Goreham and Lucy M. Long
(See "Korea, South," Amanda Mayo, *EAFT*, pp. 354–58.)

⁓

Kyrgyzstan. See Central Asia.

Kuwait (Western Asia), Kuwaiti American Food

Kuwaiti food culture is similar to that of other Gulf nations, being a mixture of Mediterranean, Persian, Indian, and Arabian cuisines. It is an important medium for hospitality, socializing, and family bonds and is shared at gatherings among Kuwaiti citizens who come to the United States primarily as students and are spread across the country at different universities.

Kuwait's "signature" dish is *machboos*, which consists of chicken, mutton, or fish over rice cooked with special spices. Vegetables or eggs may also be added. The *zubaidi* fish, also called pomfret, is considered the national fish and is oftentimes featured at meals. *Khubz*, a large flatbread, is the traditional bread, and is substituted in the United States by other flatbreads from "Middle Eastern" bakeries. A fish sauce, *mahyawa*, accompanies meals, but it is not easily available in the United States. Kuwaiti Americans are also used to purchasing *falafel* (ground chickpea) and *shawarma* (skewer-roasted chicken or beef) sandwiches in their home country, and these are now frequently available in the United States, even from restaurants not associated with Middle Eastern cuisine.

Zubaidi (Pomfret fish) and Rice

1 kilogram (2¼ pounds) *zubaidi* (pomfret fish); in the United States, they use tilapia, lamb, or chicken

1 tablespoon ground spices (ginger, dried lemon, cardamom, cumin, clove, cinnamon, black pepper)

1 cup olive oil

1 tablespoon lemon juice

4 cups water

3 onions, medium size

1 celery stalk, cut into chunks

1 carrot, cut into chunks

1 lemon, cut into slices

2 bay leaves

2 green peppers, cut into julienne

¼ cup raisins

½ teaspoon saffron

3 cup stock

1 tablespoon corn oil

4 cups basmati rice, parboiled
2 cups yogurt
Salt and pepper

Clean the fish and leave it in salted water with some flour for 30 minutes. Rinse and drain in a colander. Make slits on both sides of the fish using a sharp knife.

In a mixing bowl, mix half of the spices, half of the olive oil, and lemon juice, and season with salt and pepper.

Marinate the fish, making sure that the marinade is covering all over the fish and into the slits. Set aside.

Boil water in a large pan. Cut one onion into big chunks, and add it to the water. Add celery, carrot, lemon, and bay leaves. Add the marinated fish and let boil for 5 minutes. Take out the fish and set aside.

Julienne the remaining onions. Heat the remaining oil in another pan over medium heat and sauté the onions. Add green pepper, stirring the mixture for 5 minutes. Add the remaining spices, raisins, saffron, and stock. Season with salt and pepper.

Let the mixture come to a boil, then lower the heat and let simmer for 7 minutes.

Grease a large, nonstick pan with corn oil.

In a large mixing bowl, mix 1 cup rice with yogurt. Spread to cover the bottom of the pan. Assemble layers of the fish, onion mixture, and the remaining rice alternatively, seasoning each layer with salt and pepper, and pressing down slightly.

Cook over medium heat for 5 minutes, lower the heat, cover, and let cook for 15 minutes or until fully cooked. Let cool. Invert the pan over a large serving plate.

Nailam Elkhechen
(See Kuwait," Nailam Elkhechen and Lucy M. Long, *EAFT*, pp. 358–59.)

L

Laos (Southeast Asia), Lao or Laotian American

Lao food culture is similar to that of Thailand, but is not as well known in the United States as Thai. Basic foods include glutinous "sticky" rice, chili peppers, tropical fruits such as papayas and lime, beef, fish, coconut, *pandan* leaves, and spices such as *galanga* and lemongrass. Beef is often chopped and marinated with cilantro, onion, fish sauce, chili, and lime juice and served as *larb*. *Larb*, called the national dish of Laos, is made with chicken or duck at some restaurants in the United States. Papaya salad is a mainstay and is made with shredded green (unripe) papayas, fish sauce, lime, tomatoes, sugar, crab paste, peanuts, chili pepper, string beans, and Asian eggplants.

Kua Mii (Lao fried noodles)
From Nana Sanavongsay ("Cooking with Nana," with permission)

1 pack *banh pho* noodles*
5 heads of shallots chopped
1 clove garlic
1 cup sugar (can use less if desired, ½ cup)
1 tablespoon MSG (monosodium glutamate) (optional)
½ cup vegetable oil
Green onions, sliced
Cilantro, chopped
Fresh bean sprouts, washed and drained

Sliced egg "omelet" (eggs beaten with fish sauce and MSG), fried and sliced
* Wash noodles with cold water and soak, then rinse before adding to sauce.

Sauce:
⅓ cup oyster sauce
⅓ cup thin soy sauce (*sid u how*)
¼ cup fish sauce
1 tablespoon black soy sauce
1 tablespoon black pepper
¼ cup water

Mix all of these to make sauce. Add the black pepper. Add 1 tablespoon
MSG (optional). Taste and adjust as desired. Put a pan on high heat, and
add oil to pan. Add sugar to frying pan; stir. Keep an eye on the pot; *don't
burn the sugar.* As it turns brown, turn the heat down (oil keeps the noodles
from sticking together). Add shallots and garlic; stir fry. Let it cook until the
shallots and garlic are brown. Add prepared sauce plus ¼ cup water.

Add soaked and rinsed noodles. Turn heat to high and keep stirring
sauce into noodles. Stir-fry for about 3–5 minutes; don't overcook the
noodles. (Broth will keep the noodles soft; it's OK if there is some sauce
left, it will soak in later on.) Transfer noodles to a bowl and mix for about 1
minute so it doesn't stick together, then allow it to cool for 10–15 minutes.
Add bean sprouts, cilantro, and green onions. Keep stirring so it doesn't
stick, and then add fried eggs. (You can eliminate the eggs if you want.)
You can refrigerate any leftover sauce. Vegetables and egg slices can be
added as a garnish.

Ma Der Ma Der: "Please enjoy our food."

Sue Eleuterio
(See "Laos," Sue Eleuterio, *EAFT*, pp. 361–63.)

～

Latvia (Northern Europe), Latvian American Food

Rye, not wheat, flourished in the cold, wet Baltic region. For many centuries
rupjmaize, a highly nutritious, dark, dense, sourdough rye bread made with
whole grain rye flour (no wheat), sourdough starter, caraway, sugar, water,
and salt was Latvia's venerated staple food, its staff of life. Other staples
of the Latvian diet include dairy products (eggs, butter, milk, cream, sour

cream, and cottage cheese), pickled fish, especially herring, root vegetables such as potatoes, onions, carrots, turnips, beets, cabbage (for sauerkraut), peas, and beans (dried and later cooked), apples, pears, stone fruit, and a wide assortment of berries, most often made into jam.

Some culinary preferences from the old country remain. Though altered, *rupjmaize* kept its iconic place in the Latvian culinary pantheon. When the oldest generation of émigrés passed away, a small number of bakers, male and female, continued to bake *rupjmaize*. Prior to holidays and special occasions, groups of older women active in local Latvian Lutheran churches (where services were conducted in Latvian) sometimes baked rye bread together in church kitchens for consumption at holidays.

Recently, Latvian American caterers, including some newly immigrated from Latvia, have begun selling *pīrāgi* online. Others offer classes in *pīrāgi* making. Reflecting current American concerns, *pīrāgi* are sometimes filled not with meat but with sautéed vegetables such as onion, potato, mushroom, and cabbage.

Jāṇu siers (Solstice cheese)

> 4 pounds large-curd cottage cheese
> 6 cups milk
> 2 cups cold water
> 5 eggs
> 1 tablespoons caraway seeds
> 4 tablespoons of butter

Smear butter or cooking oil on the inside bottom of a 12-quart pot to prevent the milk from sticking. Add the milk and water. In a food processor, blend the cottage cheese and eggs until the cottage cheese curds disappear. Then add the caraway seeds and mix by hand.

Add the blended mixture to the milk and place the pot on a burner. Cook at medium high until the curds rise to the top and the whey looks greenish. Cook for another ten minutes. Strain the mixture through cheesecloth placed over a sieve. When all the liquid is gone, place the strained semisolid mixture on a large piece of cheesecloth. Bring the edges together to form a round. Place a weight on top of the round and let the mixture stand on the counter (do not refrigerate) until its consistency is semisolid and cheese like. This will take anywhere from 4 to 12 hours depending on the humidity and temperature of the kitchen. Once cheese is properly aged, refrigerate. It will keep for up to a week and can be frozen.

Beware: The mixture will drain as it sits so you will need a large plate or bowl under it to catch the liquid.

Susan Eleuterio
(See "Latvia," Michaele Weissman and John Melgnailis, *EAFT*, pp. 363–66)

~

Liberia (Western Africa), Liberian American

Liberia is located in West Africa and, although thousands of miles away, it has a long history with the United States. The first large migration of Liberians to the Americas occurred during the transatlantic slave trade when enslaved Africans were captured and sent to the Americas. Liberia shares this forced migration with other African nations; however, it is unique in that it was later one of two countries established for free Blacks who wanted to return to Africa. (The other was Sierra Leone, originally a British colony.)

Rice and cassava (pounded into *fufu*) are staple foods of Liberia. Both are eaten with sauces, stews, and soups. Yams, sweet potatoes, semolina, plantain, and green bananas are also used for fufu, and Liberian Americans use whichever ingredients are more easily available in the United States. Staple vegetables are okra, collard greens, cabbage, and eggplant, and meats include beef, goat, chicken, and fish. Aside from goat, most of these ingredients are available in the United States, and some, like beef, are less expensive than in Liberia and therefore tend to be used more by immigrants. Variations on peppersoup are found throughout West Africa, but the soup seems to be especially popular in Liberia and other English-speaking nations (and former British colonies) of Ghana, Nigeria, and Sierra Leone. Peppersoup spice mixes are sold in Liberia and some import groceries in the United States. Goat meat and dried shrimp are popular ingredients in Liberia, but Liberian Americans frequently substitute chicken and fresh or frozen shrimp, partly because they are more easily available, but also because they are more to mainstream American tastes.

Pepper Soup or Peppersoup (Spicy meat soup)

1 pound chicken, cut into bite-sized pieces (goat, lamb, or beef can be used instead)
1 pound shrimp (fresh or frozen)
2 cups chicken broth
1–2 cups water

2 medium onions, quartered
1 garlic clove, minced
2 chili peppers (whole and uncut if eaters do not like it too spicy; otherwise, clean and chop finely)
2 bay leaves
2 tablespoons packaged peppersoup spice mix (if not available, use a combination of allspice, anise pepper, anise seeds, cloves, coriander seeds, cumin seeds, dried ginger, fennel seeds, and tamarind pulp)
¼ to ½ teaspoon salt
¼ teaspoon black pepper
1 tablespoon vegetable oil
1–2 tablespoons lime juice (optional)

Cut onions, peppers, and garlic, and add them to a pot with chicken, water, broth, and oil.

Let it reach a boil, and then let simmer until meat is soft, usually 25 minutes. Add shrimp and other seasonings.

Cook for another ten minutes or until shrimp is cooked. Add lime juice to "brighten" the taste as desired.

Serve with fufu or rice.

Esther Spencer and Lucy M. Long
(See "Liberia," Esther Spencer, *EAFT*, pp. 373–75.)

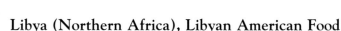

Libya (Northern Africa), Libyan American Food

Libya, located in the Maghreb region of northern Africa, shares in the Bedouin food traditions found in other desert nations in that region: Algeria, Egypt, Morocco, Tunisia, and Algeria. Grains, dates, olives, olive oil, and milk are essential ingredients, but Libya's cuisine also displays influence from its days as an Italian colony. Wheat is made into pasta, especially in the western side of the country, as well as bread (Italian style and used for sandwiches) and *couscous*. Spaghetti and macaroni have become parts of the diet throughout the country. Rice is popular in the East and is usually eaten with lamb or chicken.

Libyan American food is generally the same as other Middle Eastern cuisines in the United States and is usually sold in Lebanese, Jordanian, and Syrian restaurants and groceries. It is sometimes distinguished by the use of pasta in place of rice.

Sharba Libya (Lamb soup)

½ pound lamb meat, cut into small cubes
1 onion, chopped
¼ cup olive oil
1 cinnamon stick
5 cardamom pods, crushed
A few *shaiba* leaves*
3 bay leaves
1 teaspoon black pepper
1 teaspoon (red) paprika powder
1 teaspoon turmeric
1 teaspoon *bzar*** (Libyan spice mixture)
1 tablespoon salt
2 tomatoes, chopped
2 tablespoons tomato paste
½ cup chickpeas,*** cooked
1 tablespoon dried mint
4 tablespoons parsley, finely chopped
½ cup orzo (soup pasta)
6 cups boiling water
1 lemon

Heat the oil in a soup pot. Add the pieces of lamb and chopped onion. Add the cinnamon, cardamom, *shaiba*, and bay leaves. Sauté over medium heat for a few minutes and add the pepper, paprika, turmeric, and salt. Stir and add the tomatoes, tomato paste, and chickpeas. Simmer for a few minutes over medium heat and stir occasionally. Add 2 tablespoons of parsley, mint, and 2 cups of boiling water. Stir, bring to a boil, and simmer over low heat for 45 minutes. Remove the cinnamon, cardamom, *shaiba*, and bay leaves with a slotted spoon. Add 4 cups of boiling water and the rest of the parsley. Stir and add salt, pepper, and spices to taste. Add the soup pasta, stir, and simmer for another 15 minutes or until the pasta is done. Serve with lemon wedges and bread.

* *Shaiba* leaves are referred to in English as black stone flower or *kalapasi* (L. *Parmotrema perlatum*). They are used in Saudi Arabic and Indian cuisine; in the latter they are known as *kalapasi*, *dagad phool*, or *patah phool*.

** *Bzar* consists of equal parts black pepper, cinnamon, cloves, nutmeg, turmeric, ground ginger, and a smaller part of cumin. For this recipe, mix together ⅛ teaspoon each of black pepper, cinnamon, cloves, cumin, and a pinch of nutmeg.

*** Put canned chickpeas in a sieve and rinse them with cold water.

Karin Vaneker
(See "Libya," Nailam Elkhechem and Lucy M. Long, *EAFT*, pp. 375–77.)

Liechtenstein (Western Europe), Liechtensteiner American Food

Only 61.39 square miles in area, Liechtenstein's small population is highly educated and enjoys a high standard of living. Liechtensteiners have little motivation to emigrate, and only 1,200 Americans list the nation in their ancestry, with those individuals living in Iowa and Indiana. Liechtensteiner food is similar to that of Switzerland and Austria, but it does have some of its own specialties. *Ribel* (or *Rebl*), tiny cornmeal dumplings, was traditionally a farmers' dish but is now being celebrated by some restaurants and chefs as a national food. A special type of cornmeal (*ribelmaiz*) is sold in European stores, but cornmeal can be used in the United States.

Ribel/Rebl (Cornmeal dumplings)

1 cups cornmeal
1½ cup milk
½ cup water
1 teaspoon salt
1–2 tablespoons of butter

It's best to use a pot that can be used both on top of the stove and in the oven. If not available, have ready an ovenproof pan to pour the mush into once it is cooked.

Bring milk, water, and salt to a boil.

Slowly stir in the cornmeal.

2 methods: Turn to low heat and simmer 5 minutes, stirring constantly, or simply cover the pot, remove it from heat, and let sit for about 15 minutes.

Then, spread butter on top, and roast the mixture for about 20–30 minutes until it is crumbly. (Some recipes call for gently frying the mixture.)

A fork can be used to stir it to make it crumbly.

Eat *ribel* with a spoon with sour cream, applesauce, elderberry sauce, or cooked cherries.

Recipe by *Thomas Wippenbeck*
(See "Liechtenstein," Hannah M. Santino, *EAFT*, p. 377.)

Lithuania (Northern Europe), Lithuanian American Food

Lithuania was one of the last countries in Europe to accept the potato. Right from the very beginning it was a peasant food, eventually becoming so popular that it was called the "second bread" in Lithuania. By the twentieth century, ethnographers have recorded over four hundred recipes in Lithuania using potatoes, of which the *kugelis* method of cooking is one of the oldest dishes stemming from the Roman times. The *potato kugelis* is the one dish that is iconic for all Lithuanian immigrants to the United States, who started coming in 1850 and continue to the present day. Few Lithuanian Americans know that the kugelis was brought to Lithuania by Ashkenazi Jews (Litvaks) that settled in Lithuania, where they introduced the potato kugel and *latkes* (*bulvių blynai*—potato pancakes) as cheap foods at wayside inns and pubs. From there, the potato kugelis quickly spread to peasant kitchens in the nineteenth century. In America, the Jewish kugel became a metaphor for Jewish cooking. For Christian Lithuanians in America, the kugelis is practically the same.

Potato *Kugelis*

> 5 pounds Yukon gold (they will not oxidize as much as russets and have a buttery flavor)
> 2 cups scalded milk or condensed milk
> 5 brown eggs
> 1 medium onion, finely grated
> 1 pound bacon, finely chopped, fried, with all the resulting fat added to the mixture
> 1 stick butter, melted
> Salt and pepper

The liquid from the grated potatoes can be drained or retained. If drained, the resulting cooked texture will be firmer; otherwise it will be softer. Add the bacon and all the hot grease, hot milk, and melted butter to the grated potatoes. These hot items will greatly prevent the graying of the potatoes. Another method is to add a crushed vitamin C tablet to retard oxidation. Salt and pepper to taste. Pour potato mixture into a Pyrex casserole (10 × 16 inch) dish or into a taller cast-iron pot. The casserole dish will bake quicker at 350°F or in a cast-iron pot at a lower temperature (275°F) and a longer time (2 to 2.5 hours). A more concentrated taste and creamier texture is suggestive of a firm pudding.

Another traditional dish in the repertoire of Lithuanian Americans is *Šaltibarščiai* (Cold Beet Soup). The origins of this soup lie in Lithuania's aristocratic traditions of soups made with beet leaves (*batvinlapiai*) from around the seventeenth century, itself part of a wider culinary cache of cold soups (*šaltsriubės*), especially from fruit and sour leaf plants similar to sorrel. Cold, soured-milk-based versions began to appear in the culinary literature in Lithuania no earlier than the nineteenth century. In the United States, the prevalence of šaltibarščiai recipes in immigrant cookbooks began with the arrival World War II refugees and continues with the most recent immigrants.

Šaltibarščiai is made with beets, cucumbers, eggs, and the green leaves of onions and dill in a base of soured milk. This refreshing cold soup is made exclusively during the summer months and is always served with hot boiled potatoes, though some prefer fried potatoes.

Šaltibarščiai (Cold beet soup)

    2–3 scallions or chives
    1 can of sliced red beets
    1 can of marinated red beets, sliced if available
    1–1.5 cups of cucumbers diced or sliced and quartered
    2 hard-boiled eggs
    1 quart of buttermilk or kefir
    Sour cream or yogurt
    Fresh dill
    Salt
    Water or milk
    Boiled potatoes
    Lemon juice

In the bowl, chop the scallions and mash with ¼ teaspoon salt to release the onion flavor. Add about one cup of buttermilk or kefir and a couple of dollops of sour cream to the bowl and whip until frothy. Then add the rest of the buttermilk. Season for salt; add a drop of lemon juice.

Cut beets into straw pieces. Some folks like a thicker soup by grating the beets. A quick way to cut the slices into straw pieces is to use a wire egg slicer and add to the bowl. No need to add beet liquid from canned beets. Color will turn pink from the beets themselves. If cucumbers are store bought, peel them and chop into small cubes or cut them into slices about ¼-inch thick and add to the soup. Add a couple of green onions and chopped dill and mix well. Peel the hard-boiled eggs and slice with egg slicer. Use the slices of eggs to decorate the top of the soup along with some chopped dill for garnish. The soup should be served chilled for an hour for flavors to mingle. Boil peeled potatoes and dry for a few minutes in the pot with a tablespoon or two of dill. Serve hot as a side to the cold sour milk soup.

Ričardas Vidutis
(See "Lithuania," Ričardas Vidutis, *EAFT*, pp. 377–85.)

～

Luxembourg (Western Europe), Luxembourger American Food

Luxembourg, one of the smallest countries in Western Europe, has a long history of immigration to the United States, starting in the 1630s. There is now a strong and active community of Luxembourger Americans. Although many settled with German Americans and use German as their ethnic language, a number of Luxembourgian settlement areas, and organizations, events, and news publications, have helped them maintain a strong sense of community. The monthly *Luxembourg News of America*, for example, offers traditional recipes.

Luxembourger food reflects the cuisines of its neighboring countries: France, Belgium, and Germany as well as the Netherlands. Traditional dishes are of peasant origin and were easily preserved in the farming communities of Luxembourger Americans. Two stand out as iconic: *traïpen* (*moustraïpen*), a type of sausage made of hog's head, pork blood, and cabbage; and *stärzelen* (*sterchelen*), dumplings made from buckwheat. The traïpen is associated with winter and is ritually served after midnight mass on Christmas Eve.

Stärzelen/Sterchelen (Buckwheat dumplings)

2 cups buckwheat flour
1 teaspoon salt
1 pound bacon, diced (can mix fatty and lean bacon)

4 cups water

Fry bacon in a large frying pan. Let sit while dumpling dough is made. Boil water. Add salt. Slowly add buckwheat flour, stirring constantly with a wooden spoon. Stir until a very thick dough is formed. With a knife, cut dough into small chunks or balls. Drop dough into hot bacon fat and let cook. Make sure the stärzelen are coated with grease.

Stärzelen are served hot, frequently with mustard, but variations include a rich cream sauce or meat gravy.

Hannah M. Santino
(See "Luxembourg," Hannah M. Santino, *EAFT*, pp. 386–87.)

M

Macao (East Asia), Macaense American

Bafassá is a Macaense word that comes from the combination of two Portuguese culinary terms, *abafar* (literally "to smother or suffocate," but in cooking it means to cook tightly covered as in stewing or even steaming) and *assar* ("to roast"). The Macaense term was coined from *abafar* + *assar*, abbreviated to *bafá* + *assá* = *bafassá*. The origin of this dish is probably from the Portuguese pork in *vinha d'alhos*—a garlic and wine-vinegar marinade with the addition of turmeric. This, with a strong Malay influence, was adapted into one of the principal dishes in Macaense cuisine.

The recipes below demonstrate how family recipes of traditional dishes might be modified. In the second recipe, António Jorge DaSilva adds wine instead of water to his mother's recipe, something he prefers in many of his Macaense dishes but which somewhat challenges its authenticity.

Porco Bafassá (Stewed-roasted pork in garlic-turmeric sauce)
Recipe by Olga A. Pacheco Jorge DaSilva. Modified by António and Penelope Jorge DaSilva. Serves 6–8.

2 pounds pork (roast)
1 tablespoon turmeric
½ cup port wine
½ cup rice vinegar
4 cloves garlic, coarsely chopped

Salt to taste
Modified recipe:
3 pounds pork shoulder roast or pork loin
6 cloves garlic, smashed
1 tablespoon turmeric (additional ½ tablespoon for potatoes)
½ teaspoon cumin
¾ cup sweet sherry
½ cup Chinese rice vinegar
2 bay leaves
9 potatoes, peeled and halved or quartered
½ teaspoon white pepper
2 teaspoon kosher salt, add to sauce before cooking

Mix the vinegar, sherry, turmeric, cumin, garlic, and pepper in a glass receptacle to marinade the pork. Puncture meat evenly on both sides with a fork. Place pork in a Pyrex or other baking dish and leave to marinade overnight, or at least 4 hours, turning the meat over once. Baste the pork with the marinade occasionally.

Parboil the potatoes for 15 minutes in water with ½ tablespoon turmeric until they are nearly cooked. Remove the potatoes and set aside. Quarter the potatoes, if they are large.

After the marinade process, remove meat, drain the marinade into a bowl, and set aside. Pat the meat dry. Sear all sides of the meat in a hot cast-iron pan with a little oil—3 minutes each side. Place the meat in a Dutch oven.

Add the marinade then the potatoes on both sides of the meat. Crush a little black pepper over the meat, then sprinkle with about 2 teaspoons of kosher salt, then cover the pot.

Preheat the oven to 275°F, then put the meat in and leave to bake for 2½ hours. After about 1 hour, baste the potatoes with the meat juices and continue to roast the meat.

Slice the meat, arrange on platter, then spoon the gravy over the meat. Place potatoes around the meat and serve. Steamed white rice can also be served with this dish. (Slicing the pork is more traditional than leaving whole.)

Note: The potatoes were originally parboiled in salted water only (no turmeric added) then fried with the pork drippings and its oil. The modified process, instead of frying, is the same as one would use to roast potatoes when cooking a "Sunday Roast" in England.

António Jorge DaSilva
(See "Macao," Mary Gee, *EAFT*, pp. 389–92.)

～

Macedonia (Southern Europe), Macedonian American

Macedonian American food culture is frequently identified as Greek or Bulgarian and is associated also with Turkish, Serbian, Albanian, and generally Baltic cuisines. A distinctive dish developed by Macedonian Americans but now attached to a specific American region is Cincinnati Chili. Slavic Macedonian immigrant brothers, Tom and John Kiradjieff, are credited with creating the Cincinnati Chili craze in Ohio that has flourished into a $100 million industry. It began in 1922 at the Empress Chili Parlor when the brothers spiced a version of chili con carne with cinnamon, allspice, and clove, echoing the spices in *moussaka* (ground lamb, potato, and eggplant topped with béchamel sauce). In 1949 a former Empress Chili chef of Greek descent, Nicholas Lambrinides, opened Skyline Chili; he added hints of cinnamon and chocolate to his recipe, and the chili parlor business in Cincinnati region exponentially expanded. The chili is ordered in a particular way: two-way (chili over spaghetti), three-way (with Cheddar cheese), four-way (with raw onions), or five-way (topped with kidney beans).

Cincinnati Chili
Serves 4

2 tablespoons olive oil
6 cloves garlic, finely chopped
2 medium yellow onions, finely chopped
2 pounds minced beef
1 tablespoon sweet paprika
1½ teaspoons chili powder
1½ teaspoons ground cinnamon
½ teaspoon ground allspice
½ teaspoon ground cloves
½ teaspoon ground cumin
¼ teaspoon coriander
1 teaspoon dried oregano
½ teaspoon freshly ground nutmeg
1 dried bay leaf
Kosher salt and freshly ground black pepper, to taste
2 cups tomato sauce

1 ounce unsweetened chocolate
Red wine vinegar or Tabasco, to taste
¾ pound dried spaghetti
1 15-ounce can red beans, rinsed and drained
4 cups cheddar cheese, finely grated
Oyster crackers

Heat oil in a large skillet over medium high heat. Add garlic and half of the onions and cook, stirring occasionally, until lightly caramelized, about 5 minutes. Add chili powder, cinnamon, allspice, cloves, cumin, oregano, nutmeg, bay leaf, and cook until aromatic. Add beef, salt, and pepper and cook, stirring occasionally, until well browned, 6–8 minutes. Spoon out and discard any accumulated fat. Add tomato sauce and 1 cup water; bring to a simmer, and finish the sauce with chopped chocolate. Taste and adjust seasoning with a dash of red wine vinegar or Tabasco. Reduce heat to low and cook partially covered about 25 minutes. The sauce should be thin.

Bring a large pot of salted water to a boil over medium high heat. Add spaghetti and cook, stirring occasionally, until tender, 8–10 minutes; drain. Put beans into a small pot and cook over medium heat, covered, stirring occasionally, until hot throughout. Divide spaghetti between 4 large bowls. Top with chili, cheese, remaining onions, and beans. Serve hot, with oyster crackers on the side.

Adrienne Hall
(See "Macedonia," Adrienne Hall, *EAFT*, pp. 392–95.)

⌒

Madagascar (East Africa), Malagasy American Food

Although Malagasy people were brought to the United States as slaves during the 1600s and 1700s, their culture was lost, and few Malagasy immigrate to the United States today, preferring to go where French is spoken.

Rice is the basic staple of every traditional meal, although cassava is also relied upon. These are eaten with stews and a pepper sauce. The national dish is *Romazava*, which is prepared with the shredded green leaves of *bredy mafana* (*Acmella oleracea*), a common Malagasy "bitter herb" or green vegetable. It can be substituted with spinach, mustard greens, or watercress. Vanilla is also a common flavoring.

Sakay (Pepper sauce)

5 medium to hot chilies
3 garlic cloves
1 tablespoon ginger, grated
2 tablespoons oil (Palm or peanut oil is preferred, but olive or other types can be used.)
Salt

De-seed and cut the chilies in pieces; crush the garlic. Use a mortar and pestle or food processor to pound the chilies, garlic, and ginger to a paste. Add the oil and salt, stir.

Romazava (Stew of beef and leafy green vegetables)

Oil
2 pounds beef, cubed
1 onion, cut into pieces
4 tomatoes, diced
3 garlic cloves, grated
5 cups hot water
1 tablespoon ginger, grated
1 chili pepper, chopped
2 or 3 bunches green leafy vegetables (such as spinach or mustard greens)
Salt

Heat the oil in a casserole dish; add the onion and sauté for about 5 minutes over medium heat until translucent. Add the beef cubes, stirring occasionally, and sauté for about 15 minutes. Add the garlic, ginger, and chili pepper; stir; add the tomato pieces, bring to a boil, and simmer for 15 minutes. Add 5 cups of hot water and approximately 1 tablespoon of salt; bring to a boil. Meanwhile, clean and cut the green vegetables; add to the stew, stir, cover, and simmer on low heat for about one hour, until the meat is tender.

Karin Vaneker
(See "Madagascar," by Karin Vaneker, *EAFT*, pp. 395–97.)

∼

Malawi (East Africa), Malawi American

Corn (maize) is the most abundant crop and the staple starch in Malawi. It is ground into a fine flour and made into a porridge called *nsima*. This is then eaten with *ndiwo*—vegetable sauces or relishes—and beans, meat, or fish, with the last usually fried. Cassava flour is also used to made *nsima*, but it tends to be associated more with village fare. In the United States, white cornmeal is sometimes used, but cornflour, purchased at international markets, is preferred. Similarly, the sauces are made of leaves that are generally not consumed in the United States—pumpkin, cassava, rape, sweet potato, beans—so Malawi Americans substitute other greens—mustard, collards, kale, cabbage, and Chinese (Napa) cabbage. Peanuts (groundnuts) are also a staple, and groundnut flour is added to the cooked greens to thicken them. Peanut butter is used in the United States.

Nsima (Porridge)

2 cups cornmeal (cornflour or ground maize can be purchased at international markets)
5 cups water
No salt!!

Heat water in large pot until lukewarm. Slowly add half the cornmeal, a spoonful at a time, and stir continuously. Be sure to use a wooden spoon. When it begins to boil, reduce heat to low.

Add rest of cornmeal gradually, stirring it into the mixture. (Stir constantly and flip the *nsima* from the bottom of the pan to the top to keep it from burning.)

Stir and cook until porridge is thick and smooth and doesn't fall off the spoon.

Turn off heat and let stand for several minutes until it can be formed into patties by hand.

Serve patties with *ndiwo* and fish.

Eaters break off pieces, roll it with their hand into a smaller flattened ball, then make an impression in the ball with their thumb, so that the *nsima* can be used like an edible spoon to dip into sauces. (The *nsima* will be very sticky, so plan on washing your hands afterward!)

Ndiwo (Sauce)

3 cups of greens, chopped (Pumpkin leaves are traditional but need to have the outer parts removed. Other greens can be used.)
1 small onion, chopped
1 tablespoon oil
2 small tomatoes, chopped
1 cup water
Salt to taste

Sauté the onions in oil until tender. Add the remaining ingredients, cover, and simmer over medium heat for 5 minutes or until greens are tender. Serve with *nsima* or rice.

Christine Haar and Ariel Lyn Dodgson
(See "Malawi," Lucy Long, *EAFT*, pp. 397–98.)

～

Malaysia (Southeast Asia), Malaysian or Malay American

A distinctive part of Malaysian food culture is *sambal*, a condiment almost always served at the table to be mixed into the food. It might also be added to rice. It adds spice and additional flavor to all dishes. Sambals are chili based with a myriad of possible flavor combinations, and every family—and even individual—has their favorite recipe. These have been brought to the United States and are one of the markers of Malaysian identity, carrying memories of family and heritage.

The following is the most common variation in the southern part of the Malay Peninsula around Malaca and is a Peranakan-inspired version.

Sambal (Chili sauce)

2 teaspoons *belacan* (fermented shrimp paste)
6 long red chilies, coarsely chopped (Fresno or cayenne will work; milder *sambal* can be made with a red Holland bell pepper.)
10 green Thai bird chilies, coarsely chopped (Fresh/unripened, but red ones will work; however, use only 6.)
2 shallots, coarsely chopped

3 cloves garlic, coarsely chopped
Limes as garnish and for added juice to finished *sambal* (Preferably use Calamansi lime. Key limes will work, but if all else fails, use Persian or standard green limes.)

Toast *belacan* by placing in a small baking pan and placing pan in a very hot oven (400°F) for 2 to 3 minutes. *Belacan* can also be toasted by wrapping tightly in foil and placing directly over open flame for 1 to 2 minutes, using tongs to turn the foil package over several times while toasting. It should smell aromatic and shrimpy. Place toasted *belacan* and all remaining ingredients in a food processor, and pulse the mixture until all ingredients are small and about the same size. The finished sambal should be coarse, small, and uniform in size. No salt should added, as the *belacan* is very salty.

Serve with slices of the lime, with a small amount of lime juice squeezed over the finished sambal. It can now be added to rice as a flavoring, to prepared dishes for enhancement of flavor, or be used a marinade for grilled items.

Howie Velie
(See "Malaysia," Howie Velie, *EAFT*, pp. 398–401.)

Mali (Western Africa), Malian American

Home to the city of Timbuktu (now a UN-designated heritage site), Mali's food culture is similar to that of other West African countries, particularly former French colonies. Malian Americans have commonalities particularly with immigrants from Senegal, Benin, Guinea, and Côte d'Ivoire. The chicken *yassa* recipe below illustrates the ways culinary cultures cross over national boundaries. (Compare with the recipe for the same dish in "Senegal.") The second recipe is for a typical dish eaten everyday.

"No matter how long the log lies in the river, it will never be a crocodile" (Malian proverb).

Nono Kumo ani Bashi (Sour milk with bashi)

While I was living in the rural part of Mali, each morning after breakfast several young Peuhl girls would come around with a calabash of soured milk to sell. One of the ways this would be eaten was with the addition of *bashi*. (Bashi is steamed ground millet, that is, a couscous made from millet. It is available in any store selling African foods.)

In America where the high-fat sour milk is not available, the following is done: Start with a serving of plain Greek yogurt, add some sugar or honey to taste, a good tablespoon of peanut butter, and a tablespoon or two of bashi. Stir well; add water to desired consistency. Enjoy.

Chicken **Yassa**

3 Maggi cubes
2 teaspoons fresh ground pepper
3 heaping tablespoons Dijon mustard
Salt, 2 or more teaspoons to taste
1 green pepper
3 large carrots
1 spicy pepper (habanero or poblano chili or at least 1 tablespoon of red pepper flakes)
1 whole chicken
1 small head of cabbage
1 cup of peanut oil
2 pounds potatoes, white or sweet
3 or 4 lemons, juiced
3–4 pounds onions
Water

Cut chicken into pieces. Heat several tablespoons of oil in a Dutch oven with 1 Maggi cube, powdered. Add chicken and sauté. Remove when half done.

Dice peppers; cut potatoes into large chunks; cut cabbage into small slivers; peel and quarter onions.

Add rest of oil to Dutch oven with 2 dissolved Maggi cubes, pepper, salt, and Dijon mustard. Mix well. Add vegetables and chicken. Add water to barely cover. Bring to boil, turn down to simmer, and cook until done, 20–30 minutes. Serve over white rice.

Waraba
(See "Mali," Lucy M. Long, *EAFT*, pp. 402–3.)

⌢

Malta and Gozo (Southern Europe), Maltese American Food

The Maltese American population is small, successfully assimilated, and mainstreamed, resulting in Maltese food and culture remaining obscure outside of Maltese enclaves. Traditional Maltese dishes reflect an eclectic Mediterranean blend of Sicilian, Southern Italian, North African, and British influences. Maltese specialties are not exclusive to Malta, but the addition of spice blends or commercial curry powder differentiates preparations from neighboring cuisines. Pasta is popular among Maltese Americans, and an old-fashioned favorite is baked macaroni.

Imqarrun il-forn (Maltese baked macaroni)
Serves 8

    1 pound penne pasta
    ½ pound ground beef
    ½ pound ground pork
    1 large onion, chopped
    4 cloves garlic, minced
    2 bay leaves
    ½ cup fruity olive oil + more for coating pasta and the dish
    1 teaspoon cumin seeds, crushed
    1 teaspoon cassia cinnamon
    2 teaspoons curry powder
    Cloves, pinch
    ½ cup tomato paste
    Kosher salt to taste
    Freshly ground black pepper
    ½ cup grated pepato Romano cheese

Preheat oven to 400°F. Coat the baking dish with olive oil. Set aside. Cook pasta in boiling salted water until al dente. Coat with olive oil and spread to cool on a large pan. In a heavy bottomed pan, season and sauté meats in a tablespoon of olive oil until cooked; drain fat if desired. Remove meat from pan, put back on medium heat, and add in olive oil. When oil is moderately hot, sweat onions and garlic until aromatic, add in bay leaves and spices and cook about 2 minutes. Add in tomato paste, cook for two minutes, and add meat back in and ½ cup of water and cook. Add in pasta and grated pepato cheese. Taste and season with salt and freshly ground black pepper.

Put into greased dish and bake for 25 minutes until hot and crusty on top with some crisp, dark edges.

Adrienne Hall
(See "Malta and Gozo," Adrienne Hall, *EAFT*, pp. 403–5.)

〜

Mayotte (East Africa), Mahoran American

A territory of France in the Indian Ocean between Madagascar and Mozambique, the islands making up Mayotte are also claimed by Comoros. French is the official language, but residents also speak a dialect of Swahili and other languages from the area. The population is primarily Muslim, but a small portion is Roman Catholic. Mayotte's climate is tropical with a rainy season, and its economy is now heavily dependent on tourism.

Papaya with Coconut and Vegetables

3 green papayas
3 fresh coconuts
1 onion, pieces
3 tomatoes, pieces
1 teaspoon saffron (or turmeric)
Salt
Pepper
Water (2 cups of hot water for 1 cup of coconut flesh)

Cut the papayas in half lengthwise. Use a spoon to scoop out the seeds. Slice the halves into 1-inch pieces and peel these. Cut the papaya flesh into cubes.

Bring water to a boil in a large pot and boil the pieces for 1 minute. Remove with a skimmer.

Crack the coconuts open with a hammer, and collect the water. Use a knife or flat-headed screwdriver to separate the flesh from the shells by putting it between the flesh and the shell. Grate the flesh in a food processor or with a metal grater. Soak the flesh in hot water; allow to cool. Strain and squeeze out the milk. Put the milk in a large pot, add the papaya, onion, tomato, and saffron and bring to a boil. Simmer for 30 minutes; add salt and pepper to taste. Serve with rice.

Karin Vaneker
(See "Mayotte," *EAFT*, pp. 406–7.)

⁓

Melanesia (Oceania, Melanesia), Pacific Islander, Melanesian American Food

Also see entries of individual islands: Fiji, Papua New Guinea, Solomon Islands, and Vanuatu.

(See "Melanesia," Karin Vaneker, *EAFT*, pp. 407–11.)

⁓

Mennonite (North America), Mennonite

Mennonites are a Protestant group originating in Dutch- and German-speaking areas of Europe in the sixteenth century. Because of their radical beliefs of pacifism and adult baptism, they often faced persecution and fled to avoid violence and aggression. Many eventually made their way to the United States where they live in communities spanning a wide range of cultural and religious expressions. Generally known for their work in social justice, peace, mediation, service, and a lifestyle focused on cultivating simplicity, family, community, and mutual aid, some members have long advocated attending to food as a means to achieve these ends.

North American Mennonite foodways are typically hearty and rich in dairy products, potatoes, and farm-raised meats, such as chicken, pork, and beef. Because of the variety of backgrounds of Mennonites and their various diasporic trajectories, it is difficult to describe a unified Mennonite cuisine, though much of it has a distinctive Germanic character. Basic staples include yeast breads, noodles, dumplings, eggs, butter, milk, cheese, pickles, and relishes. Baked goods hold a special place in the culinary culture, often associated with holidays. An example is peppernuts (also called *pfeffernuesse*), made at Christmas time by several Northern European cultural groups. Mennonite peppernuts are sometimes big and chewy and, at other times, as tiny as peas and very hard. Their flavorings range from oil of peppermint to a mixture of ground cinnamon, nutmeg, cloves, star anise, ginger, and black pepper, according to preference.

Peppernuts (Cookies)

From my maternal grandmother in Hillsboro, Kansas.

"The Russian Mennonites in my family prefer their peppernuts (*paypanate* in Low German) very small, spicy, and crunchy, with a taste of anise. We begin to make them around Thanksgiving, putting them in large, airtight containers when done, snacking on them a handful at a time or serving them with coffee. Because of their small size, peppernuts cannot be dipped into coffee—but a few can be put on a spoon and lowered into it for similar effect. With extra help, the process of cutting the dough into hundreds of small, bite-sized pieces for baking can produce gallons of peppernuts that can be enjoyed throughout the holiday season. In order to make these popular morsels last, my grandmother would only bake a portion of the recipe, leaving the rest of the dough in the freezer to take out and bake in smaller batches to ensure that there would still be some at New Year's."

Preheat oven to 350 or 375°F
2 cups brown sugar
1 cup butter
2 eggs
½ cup cream (half and half)
1 teaspoon baking soda
3½ cups flour
½ teaspoon cinnamon
¼ teaspoon nutmeg
⅛ teaspoon cloves
½ teaspoon ground star anise

Cream butter and sugar until fluffy. Add eggs, one at a time, beating well. Add cream and mix thoroughly. Sift half the flour with the spices, baking powder, and soda, and then add it to the wet mixture and mix well. Add remaining flour until it gets difficult to stir. Knead on a board until the dough becomes stiff, adding flour if necessary. Store the dough in the refrigerator overnight or for a number of days to allow the spices to blend. When ready to make the peppernuts, roll out the dough into finger-thin ropes and slice with a sharp knife, dipped in flour. The pieces should be between ¼ and ½ inch long. Place them on a greased baking sheet so they are not touching. Bake at a temperature between 350 and 375°F, depending on how hot your oven runs, and for 6 to 10 minutes. Peppernuts burn easily—and their taste and texture vary according to how brown you want them. We always preferred them more brown and thus crunchy, meaning that we had to be extra careful to make sure they did not burn.

Catherine Hiebert Kerst
(See "Mennonite," Catherine Hiebert Kerst, *EAFT*, pp. 411–14.)

Mexico (Central America), Mexican American

Mexican foodways reflect a mixture of Spanish and indigenous native influences and are differentiated by the geography and traditions of each specific area. Mexican American food showcases migration not only of people but also of ingredients—particularly the chili pepper—and a fascinating history of dishes and preparations, some of which are created in some cases in the United States but are considered Mexican. From fast food to haute cuisine, Mexican ingredients, dishes, and methods of preparation are familiar across the United States, with enormous variations in their connection to authentic traditions and foodways.

Tortillas are a staple in Mexican American foodways and have been widely adopted by mainstream American culinary culture. Tortillas are now the second most popular packaged bread in America. In Mexico, tortillas are typically made from corn that has gone through nixtamalization (soaking in an alkaline solution), but the Spanish introduced wheat flour in the 1600s. Beginning in the 1900s, white flour tortillas became popular in Mexican American cuisine particularly for *burritos*—a tortilla stuffed with meat, beans, and other ingredients and rolled up, but also for tacos and other dishes. They are now characteristic of "norterño" (northern) cooking found along the borderlands of Mexico and the United States. The Mexican bread pudding recipe is a traditional dish for a Mexican American family from Texas who migrated to the Midwest. It combines some of the European influences on Mexican culture prior to annexation of Texas by the United States with Mexican flavorings and tastes.

Tortillas (Flat bread)

    4 cups all-purpose flour
    1 teaspoon salt
    2 teaspoons baking powder
    2 tablespoons of cold lard
    1⅓ cups of warm water

Mix all the dry ingredients—flour, salt, and baking powder—together in a large mixing bowl. Next add the lard until the flour resembles cornmeal. Add water slowly and mix until the dough comes together; place on a lightly floured surface and knead a few minutes until smooth and elastic. Divide the dough into 24 equal pieces and roll each piece into a ball. Preheat your *comal* or use a large iron skillet over medium high heat. Use a well-floured rolling pin to roll a dough ball into a thin, round tortilla. Place tortilla onto the hot, dry comal (or flat skillet) and cook until bubbly and golden; flip and continue cooking until golden on the other side. Place the cooked tortilla in a tortilla warmer; continue rolling and cooking the remaining dough.

Capirotada (pronounced Kah-pee-roh-tah-dah) (Mexican bread pudding)

1 pound of 2–3 day-old stale white bread (other options include: bolillo rolls or French bread)
4 tablespoons of melted butter
1½ cups brown sugar (other option include *panela* or *piloncillo*, if you can find it)
4 cups water
½ cup chopped pecans
¼ cup slivered, blanched almonds
⅔ cup of raisins, soaked in warm water to soften
1 cup of cheese (grated or crumbled), choice of Monterrey Jack Cheese or *Queso Anejo*
3 cinnamon sticks
4 cloves
4 peppercorns
3 star anise (or ½ teaspoon of anise seeds or oil)
2 or 3 Granny Smith apples—peeled, cored, and chopped

Preheat oven to 350°F and lightly butter all sides of a medium-sized casserole dish. Place bread slices in your toaster and butter prior to breaking into bite size pieces *or* you could bake the bread chunks on a cookie sheet and brush melted butter on top and gently toss bread until golden brown. Add brown sugar (or *panela* or *piloncillo*), cinnamon sticks, cloves, peppercorns, and anise to boiling water for about 15 minutes. Boil gently until sugar is dissolved and a dark syrup has formed. Remove spices. In the prepared (lightly buttered) baking dish, place a layer of bread chunks, followed with a layer of apples; next sprinkle some raisins, some of the nuts, and then the grated cheese. Repeat the layers until all the ingredients (except the syrup) are used. With a large ladle spoon, gently pour the syrup over the entire dish, making sure all ingredients have been coated. Bake on a center rack at 350°F for 30 minutes.

Capriotada can be served hot or cold. A scoop of vanilla ice cream on top is especially good.

Gloria Enriquez Pizano
(See "Mexico," Kristina Roque and Susan Eleuterio, *EAFT*, pp. 414–19.)

⁓

Micronesia (Oceania), Micronesian American Food

Micronesia is a series of archipelagos that include Guam, Kiribati, Marshall Islands, Federated States of Micronesia (FSM), Nauru, Northern Mariana Islands, and Palau, but the largest population of Micronesians in the United States hail from Guam and the Marshall Islands. The various populations of Micronesia all use ingredients common across much of the Pacific, such as taro, yams, breadfruit, bananas, coconuts, fish, shellfish, pigs, and chickens, most often prepared in a traditional underground oven, called an *uhm*. Some staples in Micronesian food culture are generally not available in the United States, except in ethnic or specialty markets. Breadfruit is a basic starch but is particularly difficult to find since it is highly perishable. Canned breadfruit is sometimes used; another tropical fruit, jackfruit, frequently found in Asian markets, or plantains or potatoes can be substituted.

Taro is another staple. *Colocasia* taro is one of the four types and many varieties of aroids in Micronesia. Traditionally they are roasted on hot stones, baked in an earth oven, or boiled. They are prepared in their skin or peeled, but are also grated and ground. They are mainly grown for their roots, but in some areas the stalks and leaves are also eaten. The most common substitute for taro leaves is spinach, while potatoes, sweet potatoes, cassava, or parsnips are used in place of the root.

Gollai Apan Lemmai (Breadfruit in coconut milk)

1 large breadfruit
5 cups coconut milk
½ teaspoon salt

Cut the breadfruit into quarters. Peel the skin, remove the core, and cut it lengthwise into pieces. Sprinkle with salt. Pour the coconut milk in a pot, and add the breadfruit pieces. Cover the pot, bring to a boil, and simmer on low heat for about 30 minutes.

Taro with Shellfish

2 cups *Colocasia* taro root, peeled and cut into cubes
1 cup shellfish
1½ cups coconut cream
1 onion, chopped

1 tablespoon oil
1 cup taro leaves
Salt, pepper

Put the taro cubes in a pot with boiling water, and cook until soft, around 15 minutes. Meanwhile, wash the taro leaves, and cut in small strips. Drain the taro. Wash the shellfish, and if necessary remove the shells. Heat the oil in a saucepan. Sauté the onion for 4 to 5 minutes, add ½ cup water and the coconut cream, and bring to a boil. Add the shellfish; simmer for about 5 minutes on low heat. Add the boiled taro root and leaves; simmer for 5 to 10 minutes. Add salt and pepper to taste.

Eric César Morales and Karin Vaneker
(See "Micronesia," Eric César Morales, *EAFT*, pp. 419–24.)

∼

Moldova (Eastern Europe), Moldovan American Food

Traditional Moldovan food culture reflects the influences of a variety of other cultures including Russia, Ukraine, Greece, and Germany. Fruits and vegetables are prominent in the diet and feature products found throughout rural Eastern Europe: beans, lentils, onions, celery, eggplant, and radishes. Dairy products include a national cheese from sheep milk, *brynza*, which is a popular appetizer and is used to stuff a variety of dishes. A wide assortment of meats including beef, chicken, pork, sheep, and goose are important components of the cuisine and tend to be fried, grilled, or baked.

Typical foods associated with Moldovan Americans include *sarmale*, composed of rice, meat, and vegetables rolled in cabbage leaves. Another dish is *mămăligă*, a porridge composed of corn mush and other ingredients. Soups are also popular and are often main courses served midday. Moldavans prefer thick soups, many of which contain a sour liquid from wheat grains, *bors*. It is unlikely that this is available in the United States, but Moldovan American recipes make do with other ingredients, including mealy style potatoes commonly found in American supermarkets.

Moldovan Potato Soup

1 pound russet or Idaho potato, peeled and cut into small dice
1 onion, medium, small dice
1 cup sour cream

1 tablespoon parsley, chopped
2 tablespoons butter
Salt and pepper to taste

Boil the potatoes and onions in approximately 2 quarts of salted water. When vegetables are soft, strain and reserve cooking liquid. Mash potatoes and onion, and add reserved liquid to a desired consistency. Add salt and pepper to taste and bring to a slow boil. Incorporate the sour cream slowly and simmer for approximately 2 minutes. Add parsley and butter. Adjust flavor with salt and pepper.

Charles Baker-Clark
(See "Moldova" by Charles Baker-Clark, *EAFT*, pp. 425–26.)

⁓

Monaco (Western Europe), Monegasque American

Monaco is one of the smallest (.78 square mile) but most densely populated nations in the world, and its citizens enjoy a high standard of living. It is probably best known to most Americans through the 1956 "fairy tale" marriage of American actress Grace Kelly to the Monegasque Prince Rainier III.

Monaco's food is similar to that of surrounding France and other southern Mediterranean cultures, particularly Italian. It does not seem to have a presence in the United States, but the country is known for its seafood and pastries, particularly its signature dish, *barbajuans*, a fried, filled pastry that can be either sweet or savory. Other dishes make use of ingredients common to the Mediterranean region, such as the onions prepared Monegasque style.

Summer *Barbajuans* (Pastry)

For the pastry:
    13 ounces white wheat flour
    ⅓ cup olive oil
    1 egg
    About ½ cup water
For the filling:
    3 ounces onions, chopped
    5 ounces leek, chopped
    8 ounces spinach

8 ounces Swiss chard
8 ounces ricotta
2 ounces Parmesan (cheese) grated
4 tablespoons olive oil
2 eggs
Salt
Pepper
2 cups oil, for frying

Prepare dough by mixing all ingredients in a large bowl until it forms a ball. Cover the bowl and let dough rest in the refrigerator for about 1 hour. Meanwhile, prepare the filling: Put 2 tablespoons of olive oil in a large saucepan and sauté onions and leeks until translucent. Sprinkle with salt and pepper. In a large pan bring water to a boil; add 1 tablespoon salt and blanch (boil) the spinach and chard for about 1 minute. Drain, chop coarsely, and put in a large bowl. Add sautéed onions and leek, ricotta, Parmesan, 2 tablespoons of olive oil, and eggs. Mix well. Add salt and pepper to taste. After dough has rested, roll it into a very thin sheet (about ⅟₁₆ to ⅛ inch thick). Cut into squares and use a teaspoon to drop small amounts of stuffing on each square. Moisten the dough with water around the filling and then fold the dough over to form small raviolis. Heat the oil to 375°F. Drop about 6 to 8 raviolis at a time in the oil and fry until golden brown, about 5 minutes. Remove from oil with a slotted spoon, drain on paper towels, and serve hot.

Oignons à la Monégasque (Monacan-style onions)

1 pound small white onions
½ cup seedless raisins
4 tablespoons olive oil
2 tablespoons tomato paste
1 cup water
½ cup vinegar
1 bay leaf
2 tablespoons chopped parsley
2 sprigs thyme
1 sprig celery
1 tablespoon sugar
½ tablespoon peppercorns
1 teaspoon salt

Rinse raisins with cold water and soak in boiling water for around 10 minutes.

Clean onions by removing the top and tail with a knife. Place in a bowl, cover with boiling water, and set aside for 10 minutes. Drain and peel off skins.

Heat 2 tablespoons of olive oil in a large saucepan; add onions and sauté on moderate heat for about 5 minutes. Stir frequently.

Add tomato paste. Stir in remaining ingredients and bring to a simmer.

Cover pan and simmer the onions on low heat for 30 minutes. Stir occasionally.

Remove the cover and simmer for about 15 minutes. Stir frequently while the cooking liquid thickens and the onions tenderize. Taste and add more salt, sugar, or vinegar.

Cool; remove herbs and spices, and serve with meat or on bread.

Karin Vaneker
(See "Monaco," Hannah Santino, *EAFT*, pp. 425–26.)

⌢

Mongolia (East Asia), Mongolian American Food

Many Americans are familiar with the name Genghis Khan but do not know any details about Mongolia. Similarly, Americans may mistakenly think they are familiar with Mongolian cuisine because of the popularity of "Mongolian barbecues." The concept was actually developed in Taiwan in the 1970s, then brought to the United States. It offers a unique style of service in which consumers fill a bowl with vegetables or other additions before handing it to a cook standing behind a grill who usually starts with selected meats. Some Chinese and pan-Asian restaurants now offer a "Mongolian grill" where the consumer points to their selection of ingredients that are then quickly sautéed on a large grill.

In reality, Mongol people eat primarily meat and milk with some grains. In the past, the meat, called "red foods," was from sheep, horses, deer, reindeer, goats, and camels; in the United States, it is from cows, sheep, and goats. They also eat many "white foods," milk and milk products from all of the animals mentioned above. Milk is consumed fresh, but also allowed to ferment for different amounts of time for different dishes. Milk from horses, they believe, is the most nutritious, but it is difficult to obtain in the United States.

The following recipes have been adapted for American ingredients. In Mongolia, a type of clarified butter, called *orom*, is used. When it is slowly cooked, it separates into two parts: yellow butter (*shartos*) and a protein called "white butter" that is not oily but has texture. *Orom* tastes simultaneously sweet and sour. Since *orom* cannot be found in the United States, sour cream and plain yogurt is added to butter. Mongolian filled dumplings, *buuz*, are typical of dumplings or turnovers found throughout the world. According to a Mongol American cook, meat in the United States tends to be greasy rather than juicy, as is Mongolian meat, so she adds cabbage to make the meat less "oily." Although steaming is more traditional, she also likes to fry the buuz, feeling it gives them more taste and a nice "crunch" to the dough. It is also quicker than steaming.

Hailmag (Cookie dough dessert)

Dessert, but also eaten with milk tea for breakfast.

2 sticks butter (200 grams)
¾ cup flour (200 grams)
6 tablespoons sour cream
6 tablespoons plain yogurt
½ cup sugar (100 grams) (adjust to taste)
¼ to ½ cup milk
Pinch of salt
1 cup raisins

Use a nonstick pan and wooden spoon.
Cook butter very slowly, stirring with wooden spoon (do not burn). When butter melts, gradually add flour, sprinkling it over the butter and stirring constantly to prevent it from sticking to the pan. When flour is browned, add sugar and salt. Then add sour cream and yogurt. Mix well, still cooking slowly over low heat. Add raisins and mix into dough. If dough is dry and heavy, add enough milk to make the dough soft and smooth. Roll dough into small balls. *Hailmag* can be served warm, immediately after making, or shaped into squares and frozen, to be eaten like ice cream.

Munkhbayar Dashzeveg

Buuz (Filled dumplings)

1 pound beef (500 mg), finely chopped (could be lamb, or half ground beef and half finely chopped steak; ground beef makes it less chewy)

1⅔ cups flour (350 mg)
1 onion, finely chopped
5 cloves garlic
½ cup cabbage (100 mg), chopped fine (Personally I like to add a little cabbage in the filling, to make it less greasy, and not bulky.)
Pinch black pepper
1½ teaspoons salt
¾ to 1 cup water

Mix flour and ¾ cup water. Cover dough, and start making filling. Mix finely chopped meat, cabbage, onion, and garlic. Add salt and pepper. Add about ¼ cup water in the mixture if needed to make a dough similar in heaviness to pizza dough.

Cut the dough into small pieces, and flatten the dough with a roller into circles about 1½ inches thin, and make the edge thinner. Put the mixture on the dough circles and start folding/punching it.

To steam *buuz*: Place about 2 quarts water into a steamer and boil. Coat the steamer with vegetable or olive oil. Also dip the bottom of each *buuz* into oil. Place the *buuz* into the steamer. Cover tightly, and cook about 20 minutes. Do not open lid.

When finished cooking, open the lid and fan the buuz with a plastic plate. Serve with ketchup, soy sauce, or spicy sauce of your choice.

Barbara Annan and Munkhbayar Dashzeveg
(See "Mongolia," Jacqueline M. Newman, *EAFT*, pp. 426–29.)

~

Morocco (North Africa), Moroccan American

Moroccan food is heavily spiced (though not spicy) and combines sweet and savory flavors. The most popular dish in Morocco is *tajine*, a stew named after the cookware used: a large earthenware pot with a triangular lid. The dish can be any combination of meat (generally chicken, beef, fish, or lamb), vegetables, even dried fruit, and is easily adapted to American ingredients and tastes. Tajines are traditionally eaten from one pot in the middle of the table, using whole wheat bread to soak up the sauce.

Mint tea is extremely popular in Morocco and throughout North Africa and is usually drunk during breakfast and/or teatime. Used to welcome guests and celebrate religious holidays, it remains important for Moroccan Americans even though the ingredients are frequently found only in Arab grocery stores. The tea can also be made without mint.

Atay B'nanaa (Mint tea)
Takes 5–10 minutes to make. Serves 4.

> 1 tablespoons loose-leaf gunpowder green tea
> 4 tablespoons sugar or to taste
> 2 to 3 stems mint, rinsed thoroughly in water
> 1 liter boiling water

Put 2 tablespoons of gunpowder green tea in teapot. Pour a few tablespoons of boiling water over tea and swirl around. After a few seconds of swirling, pour water out. Repeat twice.

Once tea leaves have been washed and soaked, fill teapot three-quarters full with boiling water and put over medium heat.

When you see bubbles forming on the surface of the tea, submerge the mint leaves in the teapot. Then add 4 tablespoons of sugar. Let tea come to full boil with the green tea leaves on the bubbly surface.

After the tea has boiled for a few minutes, take it off the stove and pour one full glass of tea. Pour the tea back into the teapot and repeat three more times to ensure the sugar is fully incorporated in the tea.

After the fourth time, taste the tea instead of pouring it back into the pot. Add more sugar if desired.

Once sugar dissolves, tea is ready to be served. It should be poured high above the glass in order to create bubbles in the small, clear glass. Add mint for garnish in the glass. Serve with Moroccan cookies, cake, and pastries. Enjoy!

Kefta bil mataisha wa bayd Tajine (Stew of ground beef with tomatoes and eggs)
Takes 45 minutes to 1 hour to make. Serves 4.

Meatballs:
> 1 pound ground beef
> 2 teaspoons ground cumin
> 1½ teaspoons paprika
> 1 teaspoon salt
> ¼ teaspoon black pepper

Stew:
> 2 tablespoons olive oil
> 2 red onions, thinly sliced

6 cloves garlic, minced
4 tablespoons finely chopped fresh cilantro
5 medium ripe tomatoes, grated (discard peel)
1½ teaspoons ground ginger
1 teaspoon ground turmeric
½ teaspoon black pepper
¼ teaspoon ground hot pepper
1 tablespoon tomato paste
4 eggs
Chopped parsley for garnish

Mix ground beef with cumin, paprika, salt, and pepper. Form into small meatballs about ¾ inch in diameter.

Pour olive oil into *a tajine* (or deep skillet with lid). Layer onions, then meatballs, then garlic and cilantro on top. Cook over medium-high heat until meatballs are slightly brown on the outside, about 10 minutes.

Add remaining spices (ginger, turmeric, black pepper) and tomato paste to the grated tomatoes. Spoon mixture onto the meatballs. Cover and cook for another 20 minutes until meatballs are cooked through, stirring occasionally.

Crack eggs into the tajine and allow to cook uncovered for about an additional 5 minutes or until eggs are cooked to your preference.

Garnish with parsley and serve with warm bread.

M. Ruth Dike
(See "Morocco," M. Ruth Dike, *EAFT*, pp. 429–32.)

⌒

Mozambique (East Africa), Mozambique American

Mozambique, on the southeast coast of Africa facing the Indian Ocean, served as a port of trade for Swahili, Arabs, Persians, and Portuguese. The slave trade thrived there—run by Arabs as well as Europeans—and some African Americans have Mozambique heritage.

Portuguese culture has heavily influenced the country's culture, who brought cassava (from Brazil), cashew nuts, sugarcane, corn, millet, rice, sorghum, potatoes, paprika, peppers (sweet and chili), and onions to Mozambique. The cuisine also uses spices from the Portuguese—bay leaves, paprika, chili, garlic, and fresh coriander. Portuguese-based dishes include *pãozinho* (a type of bun), *prego* (steak roll), *rissóis* (battered shrimp), *espetada* (kebab), *pudim* (pudding), and *inteiro com piripiri* (chicken in piri-piri sauce). Piri-piri is the Swahili word for "pepper," and the piri piri pepper developed from chili peppers brought by the Portuguese from South America to parts of Africa. Along the coast, the cuisine is more varied and Portuguese influenced than it is in inland areas. The diet there includes more fruit and rice as well as seafood dishes.

Mozambique dishes and seasonings, especially those based on chili seasoning, are found in many Portuguese American restaurants.

Matata (Clam stew)

2 pounds (fresh) clams
1½ pounds pumpkin, diced
1 onion, diced
1 dried red chili pepper
½ cup unshelled peanuts
2 tomatoes, diced
½ cup manioc or spinach leaves
1 teaspoon salt
½ teaspoon black pepper

Clean the clams in a sieve under cold running water. Wash the manioc or spinach leaves; drain and chop coarsely. Grind the chili pepper, and shell the peanuts and chop into small pieces.

Heat the oil in a large skillet, and sauté the onion on moderate heat, until translucent. Add the peanut and tomato pieces, stir, and add the clams. Crumble the chili over the clams and add 2 cups of water. Season with salt and pepper and bring to a boil. Cover the pot and simmer (on low heat) for 30 minutes. Add the pumpkin pieces and greens. Cover the skillet and simmer for another 15 minutes or until the pumpkin pieces are tender. Serve hot with boiled white rice.

Karin Vaneker and Susan Eleuterio
(See "Mozambique," Susan Eleuterio, *EAFT*, pp. 432–33.)

～

Myanmar (Southeast Asia), Burmese American

Formerly known as Burma, Myanmar shares many aspects of food culture with China, India, Thailand, and its other Southeast Asia neighbors. Burmese food is a distinctive cuisine, however, and three ingredients are particularly important: pork, mango, and *lahpet* (a form of fermented or pickled tea leaves). A Burmese saying tells the importance of these ingredients: *A thee ma, thayet; a thar ma, wet; a ywet ma, lahpet.* This saying translated is, "Of all the fruit, the mango's the best; of all the meat, the pork's the best; and of all the leaves, lahpet's the best."

Burmese Veggies with Hot Peppers exemplifies the belief of many Burmese that a vegetable diet promotes better health and leads to longer lives. It is an ordinary dish that has similarities in Asia, where vegetables and oils are common components in cooking and is typical of traditional dishes that have been carried over in the United States.

Beet greens and *yu choy* (*choy sum*) can be substituted for *bok choy*, and spring onions are an acceptable substitute for leeks. In addition to sunflower oil, sesame and peanut oil are prominent in Burmese cooking. (Burma produces six million tons of peanut, sesame, and sunflower oils annually, but consumes 8.5 million tons of edible oil annually, so it imports about 2.5 million tons.)

Burmese Veggies with Hot Peppers

3 tablespoons sunflower oil
½ cup green bell pepper, thinly sliced
1½ cups red bell peppers, thinly sliced
1½ cups bok choy, sliced
1½ cups snow peas
4 tablespoons baby leeks, sliced (spring onions can substitute)
1 cup carrot, thinly sliced
3 garlic cloves, sliced
⅛ teaspoon fresh red chili, chopped
4 teaspoons tamari soy sauce
Salt
Pepper

Heat oil over high heat in large saucepan or wok until hot (but not smoking). Toss in vegetables and seasonings. Stir-fry for 3 to 6 minutes, stirring 5 to 7 times. Season to taste with salt and pepper. Remove from the heat and serve.

Note: Vegetables should be slightly crunchy. If more tender vegetables are preferred, cook a few minutes longer. Serve with brown rice or noodles. Provides up to 4 servings. It might be served also with the distinctive Burmese green tea salad (*la phet thot*).

Ray P. Linville
(See "Myanmar," Ray P. Linville, *EAFT*, pp. 433–36.)

N

Namibia (Southern Africa), Namibian American

The traditional cuisine of Namibia is similar to South Africa and other Southern African nations. It reflects a similar cultural history but also displays the legacy of German colonization in traditions of beer making and a preference for meat (as steaks), cakes, and pastries. Squash soup represents that thread in their foodways. The small number of Namibians living in the United States may find dishes and products they are familiar with at South African restaurants and shops in the United States.

Butternut Squash Soup

1 butternut squash
About the same weight in carrots
4 tablespoons butter
1 onion
Fresh ginger (about 1 inch)
4 cups vegetable broth
1 can (14 ounce) coconut milk
Salt
Pepper
4 tablespoon lemon juice

Clean the butternut squash, carrots, and onions. Dice the squash, carrots, and onions into small pieces. Heat the butter in a soup pot, sauté the vegetables, add the broth, and simmer for about 15 minutes. Puree the soup with a blender; add the coconut milk, salt, and pepper to taste. Serve hot with a splash of lemon juice.

Karin Vaneker and Lucy M. Long
(See "Namibia," Betty J. Belanus, *EAFT*, p. 437.)

Native American, Pacific Northwest (Northern America), American Indian; Native American Food

Native Americans in the Pacific Northwest gathered plants and berries that grew wild in the region and used the plentiful fish from the ocean, particularly salmon. Cedar planks were frequently used for roasting and smoking meats over an open fire and gave a distinctive flavor. They are still used today, although in an oven as well as on grills.

Cedar Plank Salmon with Juniper-Blueberry Sauce and Roasted Potatoes
Serves 4

2 pounds salmon fillet cut into 4 to 6 portions—keep skin on
1 or 2 cedar planks
3 tablespoons sunflower oil
1 pound small blue or white potatoes
1 tablespoon minced, fresh dill
1 tablespoon minced, fresh chives
1 cup blueberries
4 juniper berries ground in spice grinder
½ cup water
Salt and pepper

Soak the cedar planks in water for 2 to 4 hours. Preheat the oven to 350°F.

Place potatoes in a bowl with ½ the oil. Toss to coat evenly and pour into a shallow baking dish, leaving room between potatoes. Season with salt and pepper. Bake until tender, 30 to 40 minutes.

Place the salmon on the plank, skin side down. Lightly rub the top and sides of each portion of fish with oil. Season with salt and pepper. Bake for 20 to 30 minutes.

Sauce:

In small saucepan, gently toast the ground juniper berries. When they become fragrant, add blueberries and water to the pan. Bring to a boil, stirring constantly, then simmer for about 15 minutes or until berries begin to fall apart. Remove from heat and set aside.

To serve, toss roasted potatoes with minced dill and chives.

Spoon juniper-blueberry sauce over fish.

Stephanie St. Pierre

(See "Native American: Pacific Northwest," Stephanie St. Pierre, *EAFT*, pp. 440–44.)

⌐⌐

Native American, Plains (North America), American Indian; Native American Food

Like other Native American cuisines, the food of the Plains cultures in contemporary times is an amalgamation of practices from the era before contact with Europeans and after. Today, many tribes are reviving traditional food-ways as part of a larger movement to reclaim sovereignty. As a result, many foods and methods of procuring and preparing food that had been neglected or forgotten are being rediscovered and integrated into an exciting food scene all over America.

Prior to being confined to reservations in the mid-1800s, Native Americans of Plains cultures were highly mobile and covered vast swaths of terrain from which to forage for fresh local foods that supplemented their primary food—buffalo. They also traded with tribes from all directions, exchanging supplies of dried flint corn, squash, beans, chilies, and *menomenee* (wild rice) for items such as smoked salmon and acorn flour.

Native diets were healthy, high in essential nutrients. While warriors hunted buffalo, boys snared prairie chickens, ducks, rabbits, rodents, fish, snakes, turtles, lizards, and frogs. Insects were sometimes eaten, as were eggs from ducks and other birds. Fresh vegetables were limited because of the environment but included wild greens, cattails and their pollen, onions, and herbs, berries, seeds, and camas bulbs, along with root vegetables such as bread root, carrot, potato, turnip, and sunchoke. Bark from white pine, willow, and other trees was steeped alone or with herbs as teas for refreshment or medicinal purposes. Small gardens of squash, corn, and beans were planted in summer camps, and honey and maple syrup were collected from the wild to be used as sweeteners.

Meaty Mushroom, Corn, and Turnip Stew
Makes 8 generous servings

2 pounds meaty shank bones cut into chunks (buffalo, venison, elk, lamb, or beef)
8 cups water or stock
1 cup wild turnip cut into large chunks (substitute ½ cup turnip + ½ cup parsnip)
2 cups hominy (presoaked or canned)
1 cup dried wild mushrooms
1 tablespoon dried rubbed sage
1½ tablespoons fresh sage chiffonade (reserve some for garnish)
2 cups sliced green onion (reserve ½ cup for garnish)
¼ cup sunflower oil
Salt and pepper to taste
4 whole acorn squash
To garnish:
Chives
Chilies
Hazelnuts

Place dried mushrooms in water to cover and let sit.

Season the meat with salt and pepper. In a large Dutch oven, heat the oil and brown the meat. Add green onions and sauté until they soften. Add turnips and sauté until they begin to brown. Add some water to deglaze pan. Add the rest of the water and dried sage. Bring to boil.

Add mushrooms and soaking liquid to pot. (Be sure to leave any grit behind when pouring or strain through cheesecloth.)

Lower heat to simmer and cover. Cook about 1 hour. Add hominy, mushrooms, and fresh sage. Continue to cook, covered, at a simmer until meat falls from the bone, about 1½ to 2 hours longer.

Add salt and pepper to taste. (Can also be cooked in a slow cooker.)

To serve, fill bowls with stew, making sure each bowl has several meaty bones. Sprinkle with fresh sage and green onions.

Alternative serving suggestion: Cut acorn squash in half lengthwise and remove seeds. Roast in a 350°F oven until tender but not falling apart. Set aside while stew is cooking. When meat is falling off bones, take bones out of stew and cool. Remove all meat and marrow from bones, chop into small pieces, and stir back into stew. Discard bones. Salt and pepper to taste. Fill each squash with a heaping serving of stew. Reheat if necessary. Garnish with minced chives, hot red chili pepper, and toasted, chopped hazelnuts.

Stephanie St. Pierre
(See "Native American: Plains," Stephanie St. Pierre, *EAFT*, pp. 444–48.)

～

Native American, Southwest (North America), American Indian; Native American Food

Tortillas are frequently thought of now as Mexican, but the process for making them comes from indigenous cultures in Central America. Historically, corn was made into hominy (*posole*) by soaking it in a lye solution (wood ashes), which loosened the hull and improved its nutritional content by releasing niacin. The soaked corn kernels are also ground into meal for bread. Traditionally, grinding corn was accomplished on a *metate* slab (stone with flat surface and raised sides for grinding), and a pestle. Thirty-five to forty hours were required to process the corn to a fine grind to make the *masa*. Grinding and preparing the masa was woman's work; like many other traditional tasks, it was accomplished in a group, where socialization with singing, storytelling, and gossiping help to pass the hours. The young were watched over by the women who modeled this disciplined behavior. Today, flour for corn tortillas can be purchased in many supermarkets, along with ready-made tortillas.

Wheat flour was incorporated into Southwest Native American diets after the reservation system was established in the mid-1800s and food was supplied by the U.S. government. The flour was used to make a flat, pancake-like bread that came to be called "Indian frybread" and is now used as a wrap for "Indian tacos" or covered with butter, jam, or sugar and eaten as a sweet snack or dessert. These replaced corn tortillas in some households.

Corn Tortillas
Makes 16 4-inch tortillas

2 cups *masa harina* (flour and cornmeal mixture)
½ teaspoon salt
1⅓ cups (approximately) warm water

Place the dry ingredients in a medium bowl and slowly add the water, stirring with a fork until the dough comes together into a ball. Knead the dough several times and roll into a log shape about 2 inches in diameter and 8 inches long. Wrap the log in plastic wrap and let it stand 30 minutes. Preheat a cast iron *comal*, skillet, or griddle over medium-high heat. Cut the log into ½-inch rounds, keeping it covered so the dough doesn't dry out. Place one of the rounds between 2 sheets of plastic in a tortilla press and flatten to about ¹⁄₁₆-inch thick. Peel off the plastic and place the tortilla in the preheated pan. Cook for about 1 minute, until light brown speckles appear. Flip the tortilla and cook 30 seconds, pressing down on the tortilla with a small spatula.

Repeat with the remaining rounds. As the tortillas are cooked, stack in a kitchen towel to keep warm. Serve immediately.

Note: This recipe may also be made in a food processor. Place the dry ingredients in the work bowl fitted with the steel blade. While the machine is running, slowly pour the warm water through the feed tube and process until the dough forms a ball. Proceed as directed above.

Indian Fry Bread

> 4 cups all-purpose flour (or 2 cups whole wheat and 2 cups white, all-purpose flour)
> 1 tablespoon baking powder
> 1½ teaspoons salt
> 1½ teaspoons canola oil (replaces the more traditional lard)
> Water
> Oil for frying at 350°F

Mix the flour, baking powder, and salt in a large bowl. Add oil and enough water to make a soft dough. Knead lightly for a few minutes until dough becomes elastic. Shape into balls approximately 3½ inches in diameter and let rest for 15 minutes. Take each ball and pat and stretch by hand until approximately 12 inches in diameter. Fry in oil at 350°F until light and fluffy; turn only once. Drain on paper towels before serving. Makes 10–12 pieces.

Mary Crowley
(See "Native American–Southwest" by Mary Crowley, *EAFT*, pp. 448–52.)

Native American, Woodland (North America), American Indian; Native American Food

The "Three Sisters" of corn, beans, and squash were central to Native American agriculture and food. Grown together, the three crops nourished each other, and eaten together, they complement each other nutritionally. They also were adopted by European colonizers and integrated into what is now thought of as "American" food culture, both individually and together in dishes such as succotash. With the combination available as commercially processed canned or frozen "mixed vegetables" (with carrots substituting for squash), homemade versions of the dish are still made for special occasions. In some families, it is one of the iconic dishes for Thanksgiving. Below is an updated version from a Native American family.

Succotash ("Three Sisters"—corn, beans, squash)

1 cup dry large lima beans (Soak overnight; drain; and remove outside skin; yields 2 cups shelled lima beans.)

Approximately 1 cup of sweet corn—generally two medium ears (You can shell directly from ear or can use previously shelled corn; shelled corn indicates cutting the corn kernels from the cob. If using dried corn, soak for at least several hours [can also cook with beans during first cooking instead of adding later].)

Two cups of pumpkin, cubed into approximately ½-inch cubes (about half of a small pie pumpkin). It is OK to have cubes be of varying sizes as it will impart a nonuniformity to the overall texture of the succotash—for a more uniform consistency/texture, cut into smaller pieces.

Overall prep time is 30–45 minutes (includes removing skins from beans, shelling corn, and preparing the pumpkin—skinning, gutting, and cutting).

Add prepared lima beans to pot, cover generously with water, and bring to a boil; reduce to simmer and allow to cook until beans are soft, about 2 hours. Recommend cooking uncovered on stovetop; reduce water as beans are cooking, but do not allow water to completely cook away or you will burn your beans and possibly damage your pot.

Add spices according to taste: recommend bay leaves (about 4 small to medium bay leaves) and 2 pinches of sea salt; another tasty option is adding several dashes of ground, dried sassafras leaves (filé).

Render fat—about 4 tablespoons of lard (although bacon fat or other fat can be substituted here).

1 small onion (about half a cup), diced; can also substitute equivalent volume of wild onion (be careful to peel and wash the bulb thoroughly to remove all dirt)

2 teaspoons of garlic (roasted garlic gives a nice flavor profile)

Sautée onion and garlic in rendered fat (you can also move the bay leaves from the beans to the onions and garlic at this point).

Add sautéed onions and garlic back into beans and stir.

Add corn and stir.
Add pumpkin and stir.
Put into oven and bake (covered) at 360°F until pumpkin is thoroughly cooked (about 45 minutes).
Remember to remove the bay leaves from the succotash before eating (or just eat around them).

Christopher B. Bolfing
(See "Native American: Woodland Cultures," Christopher B. Bolfing and Justin M. Nolan, *EAFT*, pp. 437–40.)

～

Nepal (Southern Asia), Nepal or Nepalese American

Traditional Nepali food consists of *dal* (lentil soup), *bhat* (boiled rice), and *tarkari* (typically vegetable curry). These items are traditionally eaten twice a day and are an integral part of Nepali identity, as illustrated in the saying: *dal bhat tarkari, mero jeevan sarkari* (lentils, rice, curry; my life is the best). Commonly this dish is accompanied by one or two *achars* (often translated as *pickle*, it is a chunky, fermented sauce). *Achar* is typically made with salt, vegetable oil, and a variety of spices in combination with fruit or vegetables to produce a variety of flavors that may be salty, bitter, spicy, and/or umami. This main dish is also typically accompanied by *dahi* (yogurt), *roti* (flat bread), and occasionally *kheer* (rice pudding). In restaurants, this common combination is referred to as *thali* (literally: plate). Nepal is also known for the internationally famous *momos*, which are stuffed dumplings (usually steamed, occasionally fried) made typically from vegetables or often water buffalo meat.

Nepali food culture is similar to that of northern India, although it typically uses less spice and oil and features more fermented vegetables in the *tarkari*. Nepali Americans frequently shop at Indian groceries, and Nepalese American restaurants are oftentimes mistakenly described as Indian. Be that as it may, Nepal itself tends to be associated with Tibet and Bhutan, and all three are romanticized in the American imagination, partly because of a fascination with the Himalayan Mountains, but also because of Bhutan's concept of Gross National Happiness as a way to evaluate quality of life.

A typical Nepali American meal would include the following dishes:

Bhat (Rice)

2 cups uncooked jasmine rice
4 cups water
1 tablespoon ghee (clarified butter. Can be made at home or purchased in
   ethnic groceries. Regular butter can substitute.)
1 teaspoon salt

Rinse rice then combine all ingredients in a pot. Bring water to a boil, stir
once, and reduce heat to a simmer, covered. Once water level is below the
top of the rice, turn off the heat and set aside, covered.

Dal (Lentils)

1 heaping cup of lentils (typically yellow, but any color is fine)
4 cups water
½ cup chopped onion
2 cloves garlic
1–2 dried red chilis (optional)
1 tablespoon ghee
1 teaspoon turmeric powder
Salt to taste
Cilantro

Soak lentils for 10 minutes, remove any floating items, rinse, and drain.
Combine lentils, water, and spices to a pot. Bring to a boil and simmer
until lentils are mushy, about 30 minutes, stirring occasionally. In a separate
saucepan, melt ghee and fry the onions, garlic, and chilis.
Add to lentils and cook for an additional 3 minutes. Top with cilantro
and serve.

Tarkari (Vegetable curry)

2 tablespoons ghee
1 small onion, chopped
2 small potatoes, chopped
1 large tomato, chopped
2–3 cups of seasonal vegetables (usually cauliflower, eggplant, zucchini,
   green beans, carrots)
½-inch chopped ginger

2–3 cloves garlic
2 tablespoons curry powder OR 1 teaspoon garam masala (purchased in Indian groceries)
1 teaspoon turmeric powder
1 teaspoon red chili powder
½ teaspoon cumin powder
1 teaspoon coriander powder
Salt to taste

Parboil the potatoes.
In a large saucepan, melt the ghee and fry the onions until lightly golden brown. Add the spices, garlic, and ginger and simmer for 1 minute. Add all the vegetables and 1½ cups water. Cook over medium-high heat for 10 minutes until vegetables are tender but not soft, stirring occasionally.
Serve all three items together with *roti*, *naan*, an *achar*, or yogurt.

Matthew Branch
(See "Nepal," Matthew Branch, *EAFT*, pp. 452–54.)

⁓

Netherlands (Western Europe), Dutch American Food

Dutch foodways were one of the foundational colonial cuisines, but they have been largely integrated into mainstream American food culture and lost their ethnic association. Waffles, cookies, and split pea soup have Dutch origins but are now "all-American." The first are treated differently according to ethnicity: Americans usually pour syrup or other sweet toppings on theirs, while the Dutch cut theirs in half and fill them with a thick, caramel-like syrup to make *stroopwafels*. Similarly, cookies are common throughout the year in the United States, but traditional Dutch recipes for the Christmas season are a way for Dutch Americans to celebrate their heritage. Pea soup can be made with or without ingredients traditional in the Netherlands (leeks, celery root, Maggi cubes, Dutch sausage).

Waffle

4 cups all-purpose flour
4 cups white sugar
2 cups melted butter
1 cup water

2 eggs
1 teaspoon cinnamon

In a large bowl, mix the flour, sugar, and cinnamon. Add the melted butter, stir well; add the eggs, stir well. Gradually add the water, stirring, until combined to a thick pancake batter. Cover the bowl and refrigerate, or let rest overnight in a cool place.

The waffles are baked in a piping hot (electric) waffle iron. Put a spoonful of the batter in the middle of the iron, close the iron, and bake until golden brown.

To make a filling: boil ½ cup dark molasses–colored syrup, ⅔ cup of brown sugar, and ½ cup of butter into a soft, thick, caramel paste. After boiling, gradually add a teaspoon of ground cinnamon. Cool the syrup and carefully smear the syrup on one hot waffle, top with a waffle, and eat as hot as possible.

Erwtensoep or *Snert* (Pea soup)

2 cups dried green split peas (rinsed)
15 ounces pork belly (ham hock)
1 pork chop
4 medium potatoes, peeled and diced
2 (winter) carrots, peeled and coarsely sliced
½ celery root, peeled and cut in dices
1 leek, sliced
1 small onion, peeled
1 onion, cut in small pieces
½ bunch celery leaves, finely cut
4 cloves, stuck into the whole onion
1 bay leaf
1 teaspoon salt
½ teaspoon pepper
1 stock cube (meat, vegetable, or chicken)
1 *rookworst* (smoked sausage ring)

Place split peas, pork, and stock cube in a large soup pot; add 4 pints of cold water and bring to a boil. Skim froth off top. Cover and simmer for 45 minutes, stirring occasionally with a wooden spoon. Remove pork with a slotted spoon and set aside. Add potatoes, carrot, celery, leek, and onion pieces to soup pot. Stick cloves in the small onion and add to pot with bay leaf and celery leaves. Add salt and pepper. Simmer for 20 to 30 minutes, until the vegetables are soft and tender. Stir occasionally with a wooden spoon. Cut the boiled pork into small pieces and slice the *rookworst*. Remove the cloves and bay leaf. Use a potato masher to mash the soup to a coarse but smooth consistency. Add pork pieces and sausage slices; add more salt and pepper to taste.

Let soup cool overnight to thicken. Reheat, stirring occasionally, before serving.

Serve with dark rye bread and *katenspek* (boiled, smoked bacon) and a splash or two of Maggi seasoning sauce.

Speculaas (Saint Nicholas cookies)

The Dutch use a *speculaasplank*, a wooden, carved-out board; it is dusted with flour and the dough is pressed into the figures. The excess dough is cut off, and the figures are shaken out and baked with the flat side down. Couples and windmills are popular *speculaas* figures. The boards are often passed down from mother to daughter.

2 cups self-rising flour (or flour with 1 tablespoon baking powder)
Speculaaskruiden (spices):
1 tablespoon cinnamon
¼ teaspoon (each) ginger, nutmeg, cloves
Pinch of cardamom
Salt
½ cup soft butter
¾ cup brown sugar
1 large egg
Optional: 1 tablespoon finely grated lemon peel (zest)

Before baking, they are often sprinkled with thinly sliced almonds.

Mix the flour and spices in a bowl. In a separate bowl, beat the butter and sugar until light and fluffy (around 5 minutes). Add the egg and lemon zest; mix well. Add the flour mixture and stir until combined. Wrap the dough in plastic, and let it rest in a cool place or the refrigerator for an hour or overnight.

Preheat the oven to 350°F. Line 2 baking (cookie) sheets with parchment. Form small, 1-inch balls from the dough; put these on the baking trays about 2 inches apart. Use a glass or flat object to flatten each dough ball. Bake for around 10 to 15 minutes. In the oven, put the rack slightly above the center, and bake the cookies until the edges are browned. Remove from the oven and let the cookies cool on a wire rack.

Karin Vaneker
(See "Netherlands," Karin Vaneker, *EAFT*, pp. 454–62.)

⁓

New Zealand (Oceania), New Zealander American Food

New Zealand food culture is not well known in the United States, though the country itself is perhaps familiar to many Americans as the site for the filming of *The Lord of the Rings* and *The Hobbit* trilogies.

One iconic dish that has spread outside New Zealand and is found among New Zealanders living in the United States is the Pavlova. A meringue-like dessert dressed with cream topping and fruit, the dish was named for the Russian ballerina, Anna Pavlova, who toured Australia and New Zealand in the 1920s. Although a popular Kiwi dish, Pavlova's origin story is in longstanding contention, with Australia and New Zealand both claiming ownership. Along with plum puddings and mince pies, Pavlova is often served as dessert at Christmas dinners, which may be comprised of traditional UK fare such as meats, potatoes, and vegetables, or a barbecue or *hangi* (traditional Maori dug-out earth ovens heated by hot stones).

Pavlova (Meringue dessert)
Makes 1 large Pavlova

4 egg whites
1 cup sugar
Pinch salt
1 teaspoon vanilla
1 teaspoon white vinegar
2 teaspoons cornstarch

Whipped cream and fresh kiwi (or other fresh fruit or berries) for topping
Set the oven to 275°F. Line a baking sheet with parchment paper. To the bowl of an electric stand mixer, add the egg whites and beat on low, gradually increasing the speed to medium. When the whites have reached soft-peak consistency, add the sugar one tablespoon at a time while gradually increasing the speed. Continue to beat until the whites hold very stiff peaks. Add the salt, vanilla, vinegar, and cornstarch, beating for a few more seconds to incorporate. Pour the meringue into a pile in the middle of the lined baking sheet. Using a spatula, spread the meringue into a flat circle, about 8 or 9 inches in diameter, so that it resembles a single cake layer. Place the baking sheet into the oven and turn down the temperature to 250°F. Bake the Pavlova for about one hour or until the outside edges are dry and sound hollow when tapped. Turn off the heat, crack the oven door, and let the Pavlova sit

inside the oven until it is completely cooled. The top will sink slightly and cracks may form. Serve immediately, topped with whipped cream and fresh sliced kiwi.

Emily J. H. Contois and Katherine Hysmith
(See "New Zealand," Emily J. H. Contois, *EAFT*, pp. 462–64.)

⁓

Nicaragua (Central America), Nicaraguan American Food

Tamales are found throughout Central America, but each region has its own style of making them. Traditionally, this Nicaraguan tamale is filled with pork, pork fat, and more pork fat, wrapped in a banana leaf and steamed to perfection. It is a festive food, distributed to neighbors during Saint's Day celebrations and offered to city folk for weekend brunch. My mother-in-law, Rosa Herrera Castillo (*Mamita*), was a master cook, who worked to adapt this national dish to a North American palate. She wanted to make it healthier by substituting milk for rendered pork fat. She also added some nontraditional elements such as prunes and olives to the standard recipe. When she found herself visiting family in Miami or Delaware, where banana leaves were scarce, she adapted by wrapping the cornmeal packets in tin foil. Her friends remarked of her tamales: They're not traditional, they're delicious!

A note of caution: As a festival food, *nacatamales* are meant to be made in bulk and eaten by many. Invite some friends to cook with you and the whole neighborhood to partake of the results.

Also, you will need a large pot to steam the nacatamales over a low flame. (Nicaraguans often use an old oil drum.) You can find frozen packets of banana leaves in Latin groceries. You should also be able to find *naranja agria* in bottle form and the colorant paste, *achiote*, there.

Nacatamales (Festival tamales)

3 pounds pork shoulder and ribs, cut in 2-ounce pieces
1 cup *naranja agria* (juice of bitter orange, but can be substituted with a combination of lemon juice, vinegar, and wine)
1½ ounces *achiote* (paprika can be substituted)
5 large garlic cloves, mashed
½ tablespoon dried oregano
1 tablespoon salt

Dough:
  1½ pounds onions, sliced thin
  2½ large green peppers, sliced thin
  6 large plum tomatoes, sliced thin
  ¼ cup vegetable oil
  6 cups *Maseca* instant corn flour
  1–2 cups milk
  1–2 cups *naranja agria* (or a mixture of vinegar, lemon, and wine)
  1 cup vegetable oil
  1 bunch cilantro, chopped fine
  ½ cup *hierba buena* (mint), chopped fine

Prepare the meat. Best to marinate overnight.

Saute the onions in ¼ cup oil until translucent; add the peppers and to-matoes and cover, cooking 10 minutes until soft. Blend these ingredients to make a fine paste. Add the *Maseca*; add 1 cup oil, 1 cup *naranja agria*, and 1 cup milk, the cilantro, and mint. Mix with your hands. Add more milk, *naranja agria*, and water to achieve a porridge-like consistency. Heat slowly and stir constantly for about 30 minutes. When it starts sticking to the bottom of the pot, it's done. Take the mixture off the flame.

Filling:
  20–30 prunes
  1 cup raisins
  1 cup rice (rinsed in cold water) uncooked
  1 cup chopped cilantro
  2 cups finely chopped onions, tomatoes, and green pepper
  Potatoes sliced thin (about 3)
  ½ cup sliced *serrano* peppers (as substitute for chile *congo*)
  ½ cup olives
  ½ cup capers
  ½ cup *hierba buena* (mint leaves)

Place two banana leaves about 8×10 inches crosswise on a slightly larger piece of tin foil. Put a fistful of masa in the middle. Place one or two pieces of pork (one with bone) in the masa. Sprinkle about a tablespoon of rice, a tablespoon chopped onions, green pepper, tomato, and cilantro. Tuck in a prune, a few raisins, a few olives, and one or two hot pepper slices. Place 2–4 mint leaves on top. Put a slice of potato at each end of your mound. Bring two corners of the banana leaves together and roll tightly; tuck the remaining two ends up to make a compact packet. The potatoes should help keep the masa from squeezing out. Repeat the same process with tin foil. Tie firmly with string at both ends. One way to do this is to start at one end and cross your string widthwise, turn and cross lengthwise, turn and cross widthwise at the other end, and knot off.

Line a steamer insert with banana leaves and pack in the nacatamales, starting at the edge and moving in a circular direction toward the center. Cover with banana leaves. Fill the steamer bottom with water. Cover with a lid or tin foil and steam at low heat for 4 or 5 hours.

Katherine Borland
(See "Nicaragua," Katherine Borland, *EAFT*, pp. 465–68.)

⌒

Niger (West Africa), Niger American or Tuareg American Food

Located in the Sahara region of West Africa with rivers and irrigated land only in the south, Niger was historically inhabited primarily by the nomadic Tuareg people, who took their food culture to the bordering countries of Algeria and Libya in the north. Niger was colonized by the French from 1896 to 1960 but is now under military rule and experiences extreme poverty. Immigration to the United States is minuscule.

Poulet aux Arachides (Chicken in peanut sauce)

    1 chicken, cut into pieces
    2 large onions, chopped
    4 tomatoes, peeled and diced
    1 large eggplant, sliced
    4 large potatoes, peeled and sliced
    1 stock cube
    2½ tablespoons peanut butter
    Peanut oil
    Salt
    Pepper
    Pili pili (chili pepper)

Heat the oil in a Dutch oven and brown the chicken pieces on all sides. Add the onions and sauté until golden brown on moderate heat. Stir frequently and add the tomatoes, eggplants, and potatoes. Pour about 1½ cups of water in the pot, crumble the stock cube over the pot, stir and taste. Add salt, pepper, and chili pepper to taste. Cover the pot and simmer until the chicken is tender. Just before serving, add in the peanut butter, simmer, and stir for about 3 minutes. Serve hot over prepared rice, macaroni, or couscous.

Cecena (Cesena) (Black-eyed beans and onion fritters)

2 cups black-eyed beans
1 small onion, finely chopped
1 hot chili pepper, minced
1 egg
2 cups cooking oil
Salt
1 cup oil for frying

Wash the beans, place in a saucepan, and cover with cold water. Bring to a boil and simmer for 2 minutes. Remove the pan from the heat, and let the beans soak for 1 hour. Drain and remove the skins of the beans by hand by rubbing a few of them together at a time. Use a mortar and pestle or blender to grind the beans into a smooth paste. Add the onion and chili pepper and blend the mixture for about 5 minutes. Add salt and mix for another 5 minutes. Beat the egg in a cup and mix the beaten egg into the mixture. Heat the oil. Dip 2 tablespoons of the mixture into the hot oil, and use one to scoop out a tablespoon of the mixture and the other to drop it into the hot oil. Fry one tablespoon of mixture at a time until golden brown. Drain on a plate covered with paper towels. Eat hot.

Karin Vaneker and Lucy M. Long
(See "Niger," *EAFT*, pp. 468–69.)

⁓

Nigeria (Western Africa), Nigerian American Food

Traditional Nigerian meals are built on a starch with stews of various vegetables and meats. The staple starch is rice, but cassava, yam, sweet potato, plantain, *cocoyam*, millet, and corn are also used, frequently pounded into a paste called "swallow." Nigerian Americans tend to eat mostly rice, with other starches as they are available. They make stews from tomatoes, onions, peppers, okra, and greens, such as bitter leaf, water leaf, and baby eggplant leaves, as well as legumes such as cow peas and peanuts. Apart from bitter leaf, most of these ingredients are available in the United States, as are the favored proteins: beef, chicken, and fish. Goat is also traditional but not as available. Substitutions from "American" supermarkets are easily made: pumpkin seeds for *egusi* melon seeds; spinach for bitter leaf; potatoes for yams; and mashed potatoes mixed with a thicker cereal grain or Bisquik pancake mix as a replacement for "pounded" foods.

Obe (Nigerian chicken stew)

2 15-ounce cans whole tomatoes
2 medium onions
2 red bell peppers
1 habanero pepper
⅛ teaspoon thyme
⅛ teaspoon curry
1 cup oil
1 cup water
Salt to taste
4 bouillon cubes
1 roasted chicken

Pour 1 cup of oil in a pot on medium heat. Blend tomatoes, onions, peppers, and half a cup of water. Add the blended ingredients to the pot and cover; let cook for 20 minutes on medium. Add seasonings and the remaining water; let cook for another 10 minutes. Cut up the roasted chicken to desired size and add to pot. Let cook for another 10 minutes and turn off heat. Let it cool, and serve over your rice of choice.

Esther Spencer
(See "Nigeria," Esther Spencer, *EAFT*, pp. 469–71.)

～

Northern Ireland (Northern Europe), Northern Irish American Food

Soda farls are soda bread cooked on a griddle, similar to large buttermilk biscuits, then cut or broken into 4 quarters (*farl* means "quarter" in Scots

Gaelic). They are a distinctive and essential part of the food culture in Northern Ireland (but not the Republic of Ireland), where they are eaten any time of day and for both sweet and savory dishes. For breakfast, soda farls are usually served toasted with fried egg, streaky bacon, pudding (white and black), beans, broiled tomato, and fried potato bread. They also appear as a sandwich in an "Ulster Fry," sometimes referred to as "heart attack on a plate," with fried egg and bacon.

The following recipe can also be baked in an oven. Form the dough into a smooth round shape and bake at 375°F on a greased sheet. Bakers usually mark the top with lines across, some say as a blessing, others that it helps the bread to bake evenly.

Soda Farls (Soda bread quarters)

2 cups flour (all-purpose) (can use 1 cup whole wheat and 1 cup all-purpose or 2 cups whole wheat to make a "wholemeal" or "brown" soda bread. Wheat germ or other grains can also be added to make up the 2 cups. The flour in Ireland is different from American brands, so you might need to vary the amount.)

½ teaspoon salt

1 teaspoon baking soda

1 cup buttermilk (can use regular milk with 1 teaspoon vinegar or lemon juice mixed in and set for 5 minutes)

(1 tablespoon brown sugar can be added for a slightly sweet bread)

Stir together flour and salt. Sift in baking soda. Make a well in the middle and pour in buttermilk. Mix lightly and knead by hand on a floured surface.

Flatten the dough into a round circle about 1-inch thick. Score the bread with a knife into 4 quarters.

Cook over a preheated, floured heavy griddle (or a nonstick pan, not preheated) on medium heat about 6 minutes on each side until golden brown.

Remove from pan and break or cut into quarters.

Split each quarter and serve immediately with butter and jam or whatever toppings desired. They also are delicious toasted with cheese or can be made into a sandwich.

Hannah M. Santino and Lucy M. Long
(See "Ireland," Arthur Lizie, *EAFT*, pp. 305–9.)

~

Norway (Northern Europe), Norwegian American Food

Lefse, a pancake-like food popular among Norwegian communities on both sides of the Atlantic, is a good example of how foods have been changed in the United States. In Norway, *lefse* is a broad term encompassing all kinds of pancakes made with potatoes, wheat, or other starches and grains, and may be either very thin and tortilla-like, or thick, as in the case of the more cakelike *tjukklefse* ("fat lefse"), also known as *svele*. In the United States, however, *lefse* is narrowly defined as the tortilla-like, potato-based version. In both countries, *lefse* is enjoyed both as a savory and a dessert food. For dessert, butter and white sugar is a popular topping. For a savory meal, sausage (*pølse*) is often wrapped in *lefse*. This dish is known as *pølse i lompe* (*lompe* is another word for *lefse*).

Potetlefse (Potato pancakes)

    5 large potatoes
    ½ cup sweet cream
    3 tablespoons butter
    1 teaspoon salt
    Flour (½ cup per cup of mashed potatoes)

Boil and mash potatoes. Add cream, butter, and salt. Beat until well mixed, then place in refrigerator to chill. Add flour and knead until smooth. Cut into smaller balls, each about the size of an egg. Roll each ball into a thin circle, like a pie crust. Bake on a large griddle set to moderate heat until lightly tanned. Place each finished *lefse* between wax paper to prevent sticking and drying. Cut each *lefse* into halves or quarters to serve. Serve with butter and cinnamon sugar, jam, *gjetost* (brown goat cheese), wrap around *pølse* (sausage), or use another topping of your choice!

Sallie Anna Steiner
(See "Norway," Sallie Steiner, *EAFT*, pp. 471–78.)

O

Oman (Omani American Food), Western Asia

Situated on the Arabian Peninsula, Oman enjoys a strong economy and provides well for its citizens, making emigration relatively low. Omanis come to the United States primarily as students or professionals. Traditional Omani food is a mixture of Arabian and Indian, with a heavy reliance on rice as the basic staple, and spices being significant in flavoring meals—cardamom, cinnamon, cumin, ginger, pepper, turmeric, and saffron. Chickpeas are also a popular and traditional protein source, and meat (beef, mutton, goat, chicken, or fish) is usually marinated in spices, then roasted, grilled, or baked.

A favorite Omani dish is *halwa*, a sweet common across this area of the world and the Indian subcontinent but with a distinctive version in Oman, different than other highly sugar-based versions elsewhere in Arabia. Its taste is beautifully complex and delicately full bodied, and its effect is delightfully satisfying.

Halwa (Dessert)

2 cups corn starch (tapioca starch or corn flour also work)
1½ cups water
4 cups sugar
4 cups water
Few strands saffron

½ cup ghee (butter or oil can substitute)
1 teaspoon rose essence or 2 tablespoons rose water
½ teaspoon cardamom powder
½ teaspoon nutmeg powder
1 tablespoon toasted sesame seeds
20 cashew nuts
20 pistachio flakes
20 almonds

Preparation:

Add 1½ cups of water to the tapioca starch. Add the saffron. Mix well so that there are no lumps.

Blanch and sliver the almonds.

Heat 2 tablespoons of ghee in a nonstick pan. Add the cashew nuts and slivered almonds and roast for a few seconds. Remove from pan and keep aside.

Make sugar syrup by mixing sugar with 4 cups of water. Boil the mixture until the sugar is completely dissolved. Keep the sugar syrup on the stove and heat it. Add the tapioca starch; then stir and cook on reduced flame. Add the nutmeg powder, cardamom powder, and saffron.

Keep on stirring the *halwa* until it starts leaving the sides of the pan. Continue stirring and keep adding little by little as you keep stirring until you use all the ghee. Stirring will become difficult and your hand will pain, but don't stop. (You will certainly forget the pain and difficulty when the *halwa* is made and you taste it.)

When the *halwa* forms into a lump, add the rose essence/rose water and sesame seeds and mix well. Continue to cook and stir for 2 minutes.

Add the roasted cashew nuts and almond strips and mix well.

Switch off the flame and garnish with pistachio flakes.

Enjoy the *halwa* hot in a bowl if you don't have patience to wait for it to cool. Or—better—enjoy it cooled with family and friends. When cooled, cut it into pieces. For this, grease a tray with 2 tablespoons of ghee (or butter). Spread the *halwa* evenly on the tray using a spatula. Now garnish with pistachio flakes.

Either hot or cool, the *halwa*'s taste and fragrance will transport you momentarily to Oman, wherever you are. *Bil Afia!*

Barbara Toth
(See "Oman," Lucy M. Long and Nailam Elkhechen, *EAFT*, pp. 479–80.)

P

Pakistan (Southern Asia), Pakistani American Food

Pakistan is a new country, created during the partition of India at the end of British rule in 1947. Its culture, however, is ancient. Pakistan was originally comprised of those states in the northwestern provinces of British India that had a Muslim majority, plus the eastern sections of Bengal. In 1971, a volatile civil war broke out in the province of East Pakistan that led to the creation of the country of Bangladesh. Even though the Indian subcontinent is now divided into Pakistan, Bangladesh, and India, given the shared socioeconomic and political histories, there is a strong cultural connection between its people. Since matrimonial alliances between Pakistani, Indian, and Bangladeshi Muslims continue to take place, brides from the three countries continue to enrich local food traditions through their regional cuisine.

The Pakistani diaspora into the United States has brought these culinary traditions, and even though they follow Muslim dietary restrictions (particularly, no pork), they oftentimes intermingle and are confused with Indian cuisine (which forbids beef) in restaurants and groceries. Among Pakistani Americans, a majority prefers to cook and eat traditional cuisine from their native land. These foods include dishes unique to their family and their regions. As with many ethnic groups, Pakistani Americans celebrate specific food traditions during holidays. One of the most important occasions is *Eid-ul-Fitr*, also known as "Sweet *Eid*" because of the number of desserts served on this day, which marks the end of the month of Ramadan. One of the sweet dishes is *sevayyan* or *sevai*, a vermicelli and milk-based dish with lots of nuts and popularly served for breakfast.

Sevai (Sweet vermicelli)

50 grams (16 ounce) pack of vermicelli noodles (*sevayan*)
2 tablespoons raisins (optional)
2 tablespoons crushed cashews, almonds, and pistachios (optional)
2 freshly powdered seeds from green cardamom pods (*chhoti ilaichi*)
½ can condensed milk
3 cups whole milk
1 tablespoon ghee or clarified butter

Heat clarified butter in a pan and fry vermicelli until it turns light brown (if you are calorie conscious, you may use less butter). Boil approximately 3 cups of milk in a separate pot. Add condensed milk, vermicelli, and cardamom powder. Cook for 2 to 3 minutes, or until vermicelli is soft. Top with raisins and nuts. Serve hot with warm milk.

Deeksha Nagar
(See "Pakistan," Deeksha Nagar, *EAFT*, pp. 481–84.)

Palestine (Western Asia), Palestinian American Food

Palestinian American food shares much with other food cultures of the Levant, the area between Egypt, Syria, and the Arabian Peninsula. The ground chickpea dish, falafel, is claimed as a national food, and rice is a staple grain. A circular, flat, wheat bread, *khoubiz*, is also a basic part of the diet and is frequently used to dip into *hummous* or topped with other items. In the United States, pita bread is often substituted; topped with *za'atar* or sesame seeds or cheese, it is sometimes sold as "Middle Eastern pizza." A traditional holiday dish among Palestinians that is also referred to as their national dish is *Maklouba*. The dish is time-consuming to prepare and is usually found in the United States as a special-order item from Middle Eastern restaurants and caterers.

Maklouba (Upside-down rice)
Makes 6 servings

7 cups water
2 onions, chopped
1 tablespoon garlic, chopped
1 teaspoon ground cinnamon
1 teaspoon ground turmeric
2 teaspoons allspice

1 teaspoon cloves
3 bay leaves
Pinch salt and ground black pepper, to taste
2 cups cooking oil
2 cups lamb meat, cut into small pieces
1 large eggplant, cut into ¾-inch slices
1½ cups jasmine rice or basmati rice
Plain yogurt

In a large pot, bring the water, onion, garlic, cinnamon, turmeric, bay leaves, cloves, allspice, salt, and pepper to a boil. Add the lamb; reduce the heat to low and simmer 15 to 20 minutes. Separate the lamb from the liquid and set aside. Transfer the liquid to a bowl. While the lamb mixture simmers, heat the oil in a large, deep skillet over medium heat. Fry the eggplant slices in the hot oil, assuring the pieces do not touch, until brown on both sides; remove to a plate lined with paper towels to drain. Layer the lamb into the bottom of the large pot. Arrange the eggplant on top of the lamb in layers. Pour the rice over the lamb, and shake the pot gently to allow the rice to settle into the dish. Pour the reserved liquid from the lamb over the mixture until it is completely covered. Add water if needed. Cover the pot and simmer over low heat until the rice is soft and the liquid is absorbed, 30 to 45 minutes. Remove the lid from the pot. Place a large platter over the pot and flip the pot so the dish is "upside down" on the platter. Serve with plain yogurt on the side.

Nailam Elkhechen
(See "Palestine," by Nailam Elkhechen and Lucy M. Long, *EAFT*, pp. 484–87.)

Panama (Central America), Panamanian American Food

Although potatoes are not actually a staple starch in Panama when compared to plantains, yucca, or rice, they are quite popular for *ensalada de papas* that are featured at social gatherings. A festive version with beets is popular in the United States among Panamanian Americans, particularly during the Christmas season.

Panamanian Potato and Beet Salad
Serves 4–5
4 large potatoes
2 carrots, diced
1 beet

1 egg
1 stalk celery, diced
1 onion
1 cup fresh chopped parsley
1 clove garlic
½ cup mayonnaise
1 teaspoon of mustard
Salt and pepper to taste

Boil the potatoes, peeled, for about 10 minutes, adding the carrots and beet, both unpeeled (canned beets will do if a fresh one isn't available). Add one egg to hard boil to the mixture. Next add chopped celery, onion, garlic, parsley, and anything else you want to include. Boil about another 10 minutes.

Remove the carrots, beet, and egg, then drain, retaining the celery, onion, garlic, and parsley. Peel the carrots and beet, then chop them up. Do the same with the egg. Mix the egg with the celery, onion, garlic, and parsley in a deep bowl, adding mayonnaise and mustard. Add the chopped carrots and beet, mixing enough to coat everything with the mayonnaise. Season to taste with salt and pepper. The final product can be served hot or cold.

Holly Howard and Anthony Howard
(See "Panama," Holly Howard and Anthony Howard, *EAFT*, pp. 487–90.)

～

Papua New Guinea (Oceania, Melanesia), Papuan, Pacific Islander, Melanesian American Food

There are only a small number of people from Papau New Guinea in the United States (mostly professionals and students). Historically, the inhabitants of Papua New Guinea migrate from one village to another. Therefore, there are few social networks with developed countries. In addition, many people from Papau New Guinea lack formal education skills and cannot meet the high standard of skills in the United States.

People from Papua New Guinea eat the leaves of many wild and cultivated plants. The young tips, shoots, or leaves of pumpkins are among the most popular edible greens (*kumu*), and they are always cooked, as are other vegetables. Sweet potato (*kaukau*) is a staple, and traditionally people from the coastal regions use coconut milk or cream as a cooking liquid.

Chicken Pot

2 tablespoons vegetable oil
1 chicken (3½ pounds) cut into pieces
2 sweet potatoes
1 bunch of green (spring) onions, about 1 cup, cut into pieces
2 cups young pumpkin tips, sliced into 2-inch pieces
2 cups corn kernels (or 2 fresh corn cobs cut into 2-inch pieces)
3 cups coconut milk
1 teaspoon curry powder
Salt

Heat the oil in a pot over medium heat and brown the chicken pieces, about 5 minutes on each side. Meanwhile, peel the sweet potatoes, cut into pieces, and put on top of the chicken. Add the spring onions, the pumpkin tips, and corn kernels. Pour the coconut milk over the chicken and vegetables and mix. Bring to a boil, cover, and simmer gently for 30 to 40 minutes. Add curry powder and salt to taste. Serve with rice (optional).

Karin Vaneker
(See "Melanesia," Karin Vaneker, *EAFT*, pp. 407–11.)

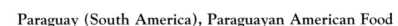

Paraguay (South America), Paraguayan American Food

Paraguayan dishes often include some combinations of corn, meat, milk, and cheese, and grains, in particular maize (corn, sometimes processed into hominy) and manioc (cassava), are widely used. These types of dishes reflect the cuisine of the Guarani indigenous Paraguayans and have continued to be prepared in the United States. *Sopa Paraguaya*, one of the most recognized dishes, literally translates as a Paraguayan soup. However, this *sopa* is in the Latin American tradition of the *sopa seca*—that is, dry side dishes such as Mexican rices or pastas. It is also similar to a traditional Guaraní dish, a cake made of corn or manioc flour, wrapped in banana leaves, and cooked amid hot ashes. For Paraguayans, sipping *mate* through a *bombilla* (metal straw) from a gourd marks cultural and national identity. Distinctively Paraguayan but also popular in Argentina, *mate* tea is made from the leaves of a tree native to South America. The actual name, *mate*, is a Guaraní word for the gourd that traditionally serves as the container for the drink. Other popular drinks include *terere*, an infusion of mate, mint or lemongrass, and cold water, and alcoholic beverages made from sugarcane.

Sopa Paraguaya (Cornbread cake)
Serves 8 as side dish

½ cup butter
1 large sweet onion, finely chopped
16 ounces frozen white shoepeg corn
½ pound farmer cheese (Whole milk fresh cheese, often available in Mexican food sections in the supermarket, is an excellent substitute. Small-curd cottage cheese, drained and pressed, may be substituted.)
½ pound Muenster cheese, grated
¾ cup evaporated milk
2 cups cornmeal
1 teaspoon sea salt
6 eggs, separated

Preheat oven to 350°F. Grease a 13 × 8 inch baking dish with butter; sprinkle with cornmeal. Melt butter in a large skillet. Add chopped onion and sauté until soft and golden, 3–4 minutes. Add frozen corn and evaporated milk. Cook at a simmer for 3 to 5 minutes. Place ingredients in large bowl. Stir in cornmeal and shredded cheeses. Mix well. Stir in egg yolks. Taste; season to taste with salt and pepper.

In a separate (preferably chilled) bowl, beat the egg whites until stiff peaks form. Gently fold egg whites into the batter, until just barely mixed. Spoon batter into loaf pan. Bake for 30 to 40 minutes. Check. Bake until cornbread is golden brown and gives back slightly when you press on the top. Remove from oven and cool in the pan.

Lois Stanford
(See "Paraguay," Lois Stanford, *EAFT*, pp. 490–92.)

⌣

Pennsylvania Dutch or Pennsylvania German (USA, North America), Pennsylvania Dutch Food

The Pennsylvania Germans, also known as Pennsylvania Dutch, are a diverse group comprised primarily of different Protestant groups (Anabaptists including

Mennonites, Amish, and the Church of the Brethren; Moravians; and Lutherans), but include some Catholic and Jewish immigrant groups as well. Their food and culture resulted from several generations of immigration to Pennsylvania in the seventeenth and eighteenth centuries by ethnic Germans from various regions of Europe, including Swabia, Alsace, Pfalz, and Switzerland. The term *Pennsylvania Dutch* is often regarded as a misnomer. *Dutch* is actually *Deutsch* or the older *Dietsc*, and it refers to German culture, language, and ancestry.

The food practices now attributed to the Pennsylvania Dutch are a hybridization of the foodways of several distinctive regions of Germany, France, and Switzerland combined with the foods available in central and eastern Pennsylvania in the seventeenth and eighteenth centuries. Of these, the Swiss contribution to Pennsylvania Dutch food culture has probably been the most significant.

A dish that has recently experienced a renaissance as a popular bar snack and appetizer in urban restaurants is the red beet egg. Originally devised as a way to preserve eggs through the winter (as chickens do not lay eggs year round in northern climates), these eggs use beets as coloring, which makes them an interesting and unusual treat.

Pickled Red Beet Eggs

> 12 eggs, hard-boiled
> For syrup:
> 1¼ cup apple cider vinegar
> 1¼ cups beet juice*
> ½ cup sugar
> 1 teaspoon salt
> 5 whole cloves
> 1 cinnamon stick

Combine all of the ingredients for the syrup in a medium saucepan. Bring to a boil and let simmer for 10 minutes. Strain spices and let cool.

Place peeled eggs in a quart jar. Cover with cooled liquid. Allow to brine at least overnight (the longer the more flavorful—after 3 days these eggs are excellent).

* Beet juice can be obtained by either draining a 16-ounce can of beets or boiling a bunch of beets (in enough water to cover) for 20 minutes.

Amy Reddinger
(See "Pennsylvania German," Amy Reddinger, *EAFT*, pp. 492–95.)

⌒

Peru (South America), Peruvian American

Two staple foods of the United States are indigenous to Peru—potatoes (both white and sweet) and corn—and many Peruvian American meals feature those as ingredients. The country's culinary culture, however, includes much more, including *limón peruano*, which is similar to Persian limes and were brought to Peru with Spanish settlers. *Limones* are central in the preparation of *ceviche*, Peru's iconic dish that is attributed to the coastal Moche civilization, which predated Inca culture by 683 years. Peruvian ceviche does not contain tomatoes (as does the better-known Mexican version) and is prepared minutes before consumption. Ceviche is customarily consumed for lunch, a practice that predates refrigeration.

Ceviche is considered the national dish of Peru, and it is customarily consumed only for lunch. More than a recipe, ceviche is a gastronomic paradigm whose culinary procedure allows for the substitution of regional white fish and/or shellfish. Moreover, the denaturation of fish protein may be achieved through the use of many acidic juices (e.g., blood orange, Seville orange, pineapple, tamarind), making ceviche the most accessible dish in Peruvian cuisine.

Limones are also featured in pisco sours, Peru's iconic drink. Peruvian Americans often substitute key limes for limones. The classic pisco sour, which is typically consumed in conjunction with ceviche, is prepared with *limón peruano*—limes indigenous to Peru that have a distinct flavor—however, Key lime juice is substituted in the United States. The pisco sour was created by an American émigré in Lima, and it emerges from the North American sour culture. Pisco bars specializing in infused piscos (i.e., litchi-raspberry-rose, cacao, blackberry) have become highly popular in Peruvian and North American urban centers.

Ceviche Mixto con Chicharrones de Calamar (Mixed ceviche with fried squid)
Serves 6

½ pound squid, ½-inch rings and tentacles
All-purpose flour for dredging
Oil for frying
½ pound sea bass, or similar, ¼-inch cubes
½ pound snapper, or similar, ¼-inch cubes
½ pound bay scallops

1 cup fresh-squeezed Key lime juice
Salt to taste
1 small red onion, halved and julienned
1–2 fresh ají amarillo, seeded and finely sliced (or substitute habanero)
2 teaspoon chopped cilantro
2 ears boiled corn, cut into 2-inch pieces
1 boiled sweet potato, cut into rounds

Combine flour and salt in a small bowl. Add squid and toss with seasoned flour. Heat oil in a large skillet over medium heat. Add squid, a few pieces at time, and fry, turning for 3–4 minutes. Remove and drain on paper towels. Set aside. Combine sea bass, snapper, bay scallops, ají, red onion, cilantro, salt, and lime juice in a nonreactive bowl. Set aside until fish and scallops just turn opaque. On a platter lined with Bibb lettuce, place strained fish. Add fried squid. Garnish with corn and sweet potato. Serve with reserved marinade (*leche de tigre*).

Maracuyá Sour (Passion fruit sour)
Serves 2

6 ounces pisco
3 ounces palm sugar syrup, or simple syrup
3 ounces passion fruit juice
2 egg whites
Angostura bitter (2–3 dashes per glass)
Ice cubes

Mix pisco, sugar syrup, passion fruit juice, and egg whites in a cocktail shaker. Add ice to fill; shake vigorously. Strain into old-fashioned glasses and sprinkle Angostura bitter on top of foam.

W. Gabriel Mitchell
(See "Perú," W. Gabriel Mitchell, *EAFT*, pp. 495–500.)

⁓

Philippines (Southeast Asia), Filipino American Food

Filipinos are the second largest Asian American group in the United States, but their cuisine is not widely known. The most popular—and iconic—dish is *adobo*, in which meats are simmered in vinegar, garlic, bay leaves, and peppercorns. Thought to come originally from Spain or Mexico, it reflects the colonial history of the Philippines as well as the fusion of culinary cultures that became traditional there. Adobo dishes can now be found at many pan-Asian restaurants, and packets of adobo seasonings are available at mainstream supermarkets.

Chicken *Adobo*
Pork may be used instead of chicken.

One whole chicken, cut into pieces (thighs or drumsticks can also be used)
1 cup coconut vinegar (or apple cider vinegar, or a blend of both)
½ cup soy sauce (or more to taste)
1 bulb garlic, crushed
1 teaspoon peppercorns
Several bay leaves

Place chicken in a big pot and add all the ingredients. Simmer for at least half an hour, with all pieces covered by the sauce, then increase to a boil until the chicken is cooked, about 30 minutes. Remove chicken and reduce sauce to a thick consistency. Serve chicken with sauce over rice. The amount of vinegar can be increased if more sour taste is wanted, and the soy sauce can also be adjusted or lessened. If desired, chicken can be marinated overnight in its sauce before being cooked.

Margaret Magat
(See "Philippines," Margaret Magat, *EAFT*, pp. 500–7.)

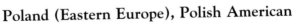

Poland (Eastern Europe), Polish American

Significant numbers of Poles came to the United States in the mid- to late 1800s and settled in urban areas with heavy industry, oftentimes living in tight-knit, self-contained neighborhoods where they maintained their food traditions. Many of these were based on the peasant fare of the old country and featured cabbage, potatoes, beets, ham, onions, diary products, and rye. *Kielbasa* sausages (distinctively flavored with marjoram), *pierogi* (dumplings), *golabki* (cabbage leaves stuffed with rice and meat mixture, and oftentimes called "pigs in a blanket"), and *kapusta kiszona* (sauerkraut) have continued as mainstays of Polish American food culture.

Grandma Nowak's *Pierogi* (Filled dumplings)

2 eggs
½ cup of water
2½ to 3 cups flour

In a large bowl, crack 2 eggs. Add water. Beat together well. Add flour. Mix together thoroughly.

Place dough on a clean board and work it for 10 minutes with the palm of hand. Always keep adding flour under dough as you roll. Don't let it get sticky. Put back in the large bowl and cover it with plate.

Fillings:

For cottage cheese filling: Cook and mash 3 to 4 potatoes with butter. Mix together into the potatoes 1 to 1½ cups cottage cheese. Melt some butter in a frying pan. Cut finely one large onion and cook until golden. Mix the sautéed onions into the cottage cheese and potatoes, adding salt and pepper as needed.

For meat filling: Cut up 2 to 3 onions finely and sauté in butter in a large pan. When they are golden, mix in 1 pound of ground beef and brown thoroughly. Rinse 1 cup of sauerkraut, squeeze out, and mix in the meat.

Roll out dough, cut into 4-inch-wide strips. Cut these strips into circles, using a large drinking glass. Put a little filling on the circle. Fold the circle together to make a half-moon shape. Close tightly by pressing with fingertips around edges. Drop into boiling water to cook. They are done when they float to the top.

After they've cooked in the boiling water, sauté lightly with green peppers and onion. Serve with sour cream. Though cheese and mashed potato fillings were very popular, Poles have always experimented with fillings. Today this evolution continues, as pierogis are often made with fruit inside, or cheeses that were never made before in Poland (feta).

Bonnie's *Mazurek* (Polish wedding cake)

Apricot filling (see below) or jam
1¼ cup flour
¼ teaspoon salt
1 cup packed brown sugar
¾ cup cold butter, cut in pieces
½ cup coconut
¾ cup old-fashioned (quick-cooking, not instant) oats
½ cup chopped walnuts

If desired, make filling*; proceed when cool.
Stir flour, salt, and brown sugar together.
Blend in butter with fork. Stir in coconut, oats, and walnuts.
Put ½ the mixture in 8 inch × 8 inch pan and press down with wax paper.
Spread apricot jam (or filling) to within ½ inch of the edge of crumbs.
Put remaining crumb mixture on top. Press with wax paper.
Bake at 325°F for 60 minutes.
When cool, sprinkle with confectioner's sugar.

*For homemade filling: In a small, heavy saucepan over high heat, bring to boil ¾ cup dried apricots and ½ cup water. Reduce heat to low, cover, and simmer 30 minutes or until apricots are very soft. Mash well and stir on 2 tablespoons sugar until dissolved. Cool.

Zachary Nowak
(See "Poland," Zachary Nowak, *EAFT*, pp. 507–12.)

~

Polynesia (Polynesia, Oceania), Polynesian American

See entries for Samoa, Tonga, French Polynesia (includes Tahiti), Cook Islands.
  The over one thousand islands that make up Polynesia share a culinary culture that features taro, breadfruit, yams, cassava, and sweet potato as the primary starches; seafood, pork, and chicken for protein; and coconut, bananas, mango, and papaya as staples. Popular methods of preparation involve cooking over an open fire, raw food marination, and baking, smoking, or steaming food in an underground oven. Trade, immigration, and tourism introduced other food traditions to Polynesia, and then Polynesians have brought those to the United States.

(See "Polynesia," Dillon Tautunu Smith and Eric César Morales, *EAFT*, pp. 512–19.)

~

Portugal (Southern Europe), Portuguese American

Portuguese American cuisine centers on potatoes, beans, sausage, kale, cabbage, squash, carrots, fish and seafood (especially cod, clams, and mussels), chicken, and pork, often combined in soups or stews.

Portuguese food is usually found in the United States only in Portuguese American enclaves. This may be due in part to the Portuguese American tradition of assimilation as well as to a history of confusing definitions about how Portuguese immigrants and their descendants (not to mention Cape Verdeans and Brazilians) should be classified in terms of ethnicity. Be that as it may, family recipes are treasured and passed down over generations, oftentimes being brought out for holiday celebrations.

My *vovoa* (grandmother) made this bread any time we visited her in New Bedford or during the several times she came to live with us to help with new babies. Both my Aunt Mary and I would desperately try to get her to tell us exact measurements, but she would always just grab cups, load them with flour and sugar, and start mixing. This recipe is one Mary gave me based on bread made by neighbors but tastes just like *Vovoa*'s. The kale soup was another family favorite, especially in winter.

Portuguese Sweet Bread
From Mary Louise Pimental Eleuterio Stephenson

5 to 6 cups flour
3 eggs
1 cup sugar
1½ teaspoon salt
1 cup butter (melted)
2 cakes or envelopes of yeast
¾ cup milk
½ cup water
1 egg for glaze

Have all ingredients at room temperature. Scald milk and cool to lukewarm. Dissolve yeast in lukewarm water. Let stand 5 minutes. Add 2 cups flour; beat for 5 minutes with milk, sugar, and yeast. Add salt and eggs; beat well again. Add melted butter and beat well again. Add remaining flour; now knead until smooth and satiny. Put into an oiled bowl and let rise until double in bulk (about 2½ hours). Cover and keep in a warm place while rising. Punch dough down and let rise again (for about 1½ hours). Knead the dough and shape into rolls or loaves. Before baking, brush dough with beaten egg.

Bake at 350°F. Loaves should bake about 30 to 40 minutes, rolls about 20 to 25 minutes. Makes about 3 dozen small rolls.

For Easter Sunday breakfast, make a round loaf (use an 8- or 9-inch cake pan) and put one or more whole eggs (shell and all, raw) in the bread by making a hole in the dough with your finger. As the bread bakes, the egg will cook. You end up with a hard-boiled egg. At breakfast on Easter Sunday you have the bread and the egg. If you had four people in the family, you would divide the bread in four and put four eggs in.

Kale Soup
Adapted from Donatila Pimental de Sousa Eleuterio

> 1 beef bone with meat on it
> 2 to 3 cans split pea soup
> 1 pound kale
> 1 pound potatoes
> 1 head of cabbage
> 1 can white northern beans
> 1 can chickpeas
> 1 can kidney beans
> 1 pound *linguiça* sausage

Note: Remove the liquid from all the beans.

Cook the beef bone (which will be given to the family dog) in 1 gallon of water for 1½ hours. Remove the meat, and then add the split pea soup, the potatoes, kidney beans, white northern beans, and chickpeas and cook for 30 minutes. Then add the kale and cabbage and linguiça* and heat until the vegetables are cooked.

*Heat the linguiça in a small pot of boiling water for about 15 or 20 minutes until the fat comes off, then drain the water and add the linguiça to the soup.

Susan Eleuterio
(See "Portugal," Susan Eleuterio, *EAFT*, pp. 519–25.)

⌣

Puerto Rico (America—Caribbean), Puerto Rican American Food

Puerto Rican cuisine, and its counterpart on the mainland, share many qualities with food cultures from other Caribbean islands, Spanish-speaking or otherwise. The foundation of Puerto Rican cuisine is *sofrito*, which is used as a base flavoring for many dishes and stews, but it is particularly associated with beans. It is made by combining *recao* or *culantro* (herbs in the coriander family similar to cilantro), garlic, onions, peppers, *ají dulces* (sweet chili peppers), and tomato paste (or tomato sauce depending on the individual), then sautéing and pureeing the ingredients. Many people store sofrito in the freezer in ice cube trays, making an ideal size of cube that can be taken out when needed and added to beans or other dishes. Salted, dried cod also features in Puerto Rican American cooking, and reflects the Spanish and Portuguese history of trade and colonization. The *bacalao* salad recipe below is adapted with permission from Stephanie Rivera, a Puerto Rican chef, who learned it from her mother-in-law.

Bacalao (Codfish salad)
Adapted from Stephanie Rivera

 1 pound codfish fillets, dried and salted
 1 large red onion, peeled and sliced into rings
 Romaine lettuce
 2 hard-boiled eggs
 Sliced olives (green)
 1 cup olive oil

First, soak codfish in water for 4 hours and then drain. Boil codfish in enough water to cover for 15 minutes. Rinse and discard skin and bones. Shred the meat of the fish. To construct the salad, place codfish on a platter on top of romaine lettuce; layer onion rings on the lettuce. Add eggs, onions, and olives. Drizzle with olive oil.

Elena Martinez
(See "Puerto Rico," Elena Martinez, *EAFT*, pp. 525–30.)

R

Roma American. See Gypsy.

Romania (Eastern Europe), Romanian American

Traditional Romanian foodways are an amalgam of influences from Turkey, Hungary, France, Slavic cultures, and Italy. These traditions continue to be found in Romanian American households but have been modified to fit with the predominant American culture.

Ingredients used by Romanian Americans include a variety of vegetables including root vegetables, cabbage, and eggplant. Grains include potatoes, rice, and a form of corn mush similar to polenta. Proteins consist of chicken, beef, pork, and a variety of meats, as well as eggs, cheeses, and dairy products. Romanian Americans are fond of a broad spectrum of cured meats. In certain cases, adaptation of the traditional diet has included Romanian dishes in popular festive, American meals. Cabbage rolls, for example, might be offered at Thanksgiving.

Chicken with Garlic Sauce

4 chicken thighs
4 tablespoons butter
Salt to taste

White pepper to taste
Paprika to taste
¼ cup minced garlic
2 cups low-sodium chicken broth

Melt butter and brush onto chicken. Lightly sauté chicken in a medium-size oven-safe skillet until slightly brown. Place skillet into an oven preheated to 375°F. When chicken is nearly done, deglaze the pan with the broth and add salt, pepper, and paprika. Taste and adjust seasoning. Add garlic and stir.

Charles Baker-Clark
(See "Romania," Charles Baker-Clark, *EAFT*, pp. 533–35.)

⁓

Russia (Eastern Europe), Russian American Food

As diverse as the American pancake, Russian *blini* come in numerous flavors and sizes, and are often discussed with a variety of terms such as *blin* (singular), *bliny*, *blinchiki*, and *blintz*. Traditional Russian blini are small 3-inch risen pancakes made with buckwheat flour and yeast. Influence from French cuisine turned the blini into a lighter, crepelike pancake made with white flour and liberal amounts of butter. The recipe below is an example of this particular kind of blini, which is often served alongside Russian tea or as part of *zakuski* (snacks).

Blini (Pancake)
(Makes about 9 6-inch blini)

1 egg
1 cup milk
½ tablespoon sugar
¼ teaspoon salt
¾ cup flour
2 tablespoons melted butter
Additional butter for the pan

Toppings: sour cream, caviar, smoked fish, raspberry preserves, melted butter, sweetened condensed milk

In a large bowl, whisk together the egg, milk, sugar, and salt. Continue to whisk while adding the flour, until a thin batter forms. Stir in butter, cover with a tea towel, and let the batter rest for about 15 minutes. Set a medium-sized skillet (preferably nonstick) over medium-low heat. Grease the bottom and sides of the pan with melted butter. Using a spoon or a ladle, pour about ¼ cup of batter into the middle of the pan. Quickly tilt the pan in a circular motion until the batter coats the entire bottom of the pan. Cook until the edges of the pancake curl slightly and the bottom is lightly golden, about 45 seconds. Flip and continue to cook on the other side for about 30 seconds. Transfer to a plate greased with melted butter. Repeat with remaining batter. Serve with traditional toppings and hot tea.

Katherine Hysmith
(See "Russia," Katherine Hysmith, *EAFT*, pp. 535–41.)

～

Rwanda (East Africa), Rwandan American Food

Immigrants from this former Belgian colony began coming to the United States in the 1960s to escape violence between the Hutu and Tutsi. Their food traditions are similar to other East Africans with a heavy reliance on a starch (*ugali* from white cornmeal, or mush from bananas or plantains) flavored with sauces. Bitter-tasting vegetables, apart from *dodo* (amaranth leaf), however, had almost disappeared from the menu before they arrived in America. The food is generally not spicy, and flavor usually comes from ingredients such as palm oil, peanut butter, onions, tomato, and celery leaves. Traditionally, goat was the most popular meat, but chicken tends to be substituted in the United States. Fish is also a mainstay of meals. Spinach is frequently substituted for the cassava leaves, which are widely used throughout Sub-Saharan Africa.

Imboga or *Isombe* (Cassava leaf "sauce")
Serves 4

> 1 pound cassava leaves (spinach can substitute but cut cooking time in half)
> 1 eggplant, cut into chunks
> 1 onion, chopped
> 1 green pepper, cut into pieces
> 2 tablespoons palm oil
> 2 tablespoons peanut butter (creamy)
> Salt, pepper

Wash the cassava leaves, remove from stalks, and pound or chop until broken down in a mortar or food processor. Cook the cassava leaves in boiling water with salt; drain. Sauté onion, pepper, and eggplant for a few minutes in a bit of oil in a large pot. Add the drained cassava leaves, a little water, salt, and pepper. Cover and simmer for 15 to 20 minutes, until the eggplant is done. Add palm oil and peanut butter; stir well until the "sauce" thickens.

Igisafuliya (Chicken stew with plantain and spinach)

1 chicken
2 onions, chopped
4 green (bell) peppers, seeded and chopped
4 tomatoes, peeled and cut in pieces
3 ounces tomato paste
1 bunch celery leaves, chopped
4 plantains, peeled, cut in half lengthwise and half width (substitution: unripe bananas or sweet potatoes)
⅔ cup fresh or frozen spinach
4 tablespoons oil

Divide the chicken into 4 to 6 pieces, heat oil in a pot, and sauté the chicken until brown on all sides. Add onions and pepper, stir and simmer for 10 minutes. Add the celery, tomatoes, and tomato paste, stir well, and simmer over medium heat for 15 minutes. Cover with water, add salt and pepper, and bring to boil. Reduce heat and simmer for 10 to 15 minutes. Remove half of the chicken pieces, place the plantain pieces in the pot, cover with spinach, and put the chicken on top. Add water; the plantains should be completely covered. Cover the pot and simmer on low heat for 25 to 30 minutes. Add water if necessary.

Karin Vaneker
(See "Rwanda," Karin Vaneker, *EAFT*, pp. 541–45.)

༺❦༻

S

Samoa (Polynesia, Oceania), Sāmoan American Food

The growth of agriculture industries in Polynesia coincided with the arrival of Europeans, resulting in the creation of plantations for copra, cacao, cotton, sugar, and rubber. Indentured laborers were brought in to work the fields through the Coolie Trade, which consisted of people of Asian descent, primarily from Southern China, the Philippines, and Indonesia. In Sāmoa, the Chinese arrived under German rule, when the first governor, Wilhelm Solf, lifted the 1880 ban set by Malietoa Laupepa's government prohibiting Chinese immigration. Perhaps one of the most notable Polynesian recipes inspired by European and Asian influence from this time period is the Sāmoan dish *Koko Alaisa*. It uses cacao introduced to Sāmoa by the Germans, mixes it with rice brought in by the Chinese laborers, and adds native coconut cream. Unlike other European plantations in Polynesia that are largely no longer in use, the cacao industry is still thriving in Sāmoa, and the presence of *Koko Alaisa* attests to it.

Koko Alaisa (Chocolate rice pudding)

3 cups medium grain rice
6 cups water
1 can coconut cream
1 block Koko Sāmoa or 1 cup cocoa powder
Sugar to taste
Lemon leaf or orange leaf

Put three cups of rice and six cups of water together in a large saucepan on medium heat. In a bowl, mix the Koko Sāmoa or cocoa powder with a little boiling water, stirring until a smooth consistency is reached. Add this mixture to the large saucepan and cover with a lid until boiling. Add sugar to taste, then add coconut cream and lemon or orange leaf; simmer until desired consistency.

Eric César Morales
(See "Polynesia," Eric César Morales and Dillon Tautunu Smith, *EAFT*, pp. 512–19.)

San Marino (Southern Europe), Sanmarinese American Food

San Marino, the third-smallest country in Europe, is ethnically northern Italian, and Sanmarinese Americans frequently are associated with Italian immigrants. A community developed in the 1930s in the Detroit, Michigan, area that was large enough to establish a social and cultural organization. Now housed in a castlelike building in Troy, the San Marino Club is open to membership only for individuals born in San Marino (and their descendants), but it also offers a venue for banquets and events, such as weddings. In 2008 it established a restaurant open to the public, the Tre Monti Ristorante. The menu identifies its food as "classic northern Italian," but it does offer one dish that is uniquely Sanmarinese—*Lasagna Verdi al Forno*, described as "a 15-layer creation of fresh spinach pasta, Parmigiano Reggiano, and Bolognese sauce." The dish involves numerous steps, and uses ground pork, ground beef, minced ham, and chicken livers in the filling. Layers of spinach lasagna are sandwiched around the filling and sauces (tomato ragu and béchamel). Ricotta and Parmesan cheeses are also used. It is then baked.

(The recipe is proprietary, so cannot be reproduced, but the description gives an idea of it.) Lucy M. Long
(See "San Marino," Lucy M. Long, *EAFT*, p. 548.)

Saudi Arabia (Western Asia), Saudi or Arabian American

Even though Saudi Arabia has many famous dishes, the most famous one has to be the *Kabsa*. It is served at any time, either for guests, for lunch, or special events. It is hard to find a house in Saudi Arabia that does not make *kabsa*! It is basically a large, round dish of rice, with lamb or chicken on top of it. The meat is seasoned with special spices, made for that dish especially, and cooked for about an hour or more depending on how much meat is served. Then the rice is soaked in the chicken or lamb broth and spices mix for about fifteen minutes or until it comes all together and all the broth dries out in the rice. Once the process is done, we start by putting the rice on a main large dish, then add the chicken or lamb on top of the rice. *Kabsa* is a very tasty dish, but what makes it even more interesting is the gathering around it: Everyone sits down in a circle with the dish in the middle, each person eats from his side, and conversations spark while eating, which creates a unique experience.

Kabsa (Rice and chicken)

> 1 whole chicken, cut into 8 pieces
> ¼ cup butter or ghee (palm oil)
> 1 onion, finely chopped
> 6 cloves garlic, minced (3 teaspoons)
> ¼ cup tomato paste
> 1 can (14.5 ounce) of diced tomatoes (do not drain)
> 2 carrots, peeled and grated
> *kabsa* spice mix (see below)
> 2 whole cloves
> ⅛ teaspoon grated nutmeg
> ⅛ teaspoon ground cumin
> ⅛ teaspoon ground coriander
> ⅛ teaspoon salt
> ⅛ teaspoon black pepper
> 3½ cups water, hot
> 1 cube (1 tablespoon) chicken bouillon
> 2¼ cups rice (basmati is preferred), unwashed
> ¼ cup raisins (golden can be used)
> ¼ cup almonds, toasted and slivered

Melt ghee in a large pot. Cook onion and garlic on medium heat until onion is soft. Add chicken pieces and brown. Add tomato paste and stir.

Add diced tomatoes, carrots, spices, bouillon, and the *kabsa* spice mix. Bring to a boil, then simmer about 30 minutes until chicken is lightly cooked.

Stir in rice (unwashed). Cover pot and let simmer about 25 minutes until rice is tender.

Add raisins. Add more water if needed. Cook another 5–10 minutes until rice is dry.

Transfer rice to a platter. Arrange chicken pieces on top and sprinkle almond slivers.

First make *kabsa* spice mix by mixing:

½ teaspoon saffron
¼ teaspoon cardamom
½ teaspoon ground cinnamon
½ teaspoon allspice
¼ teaspoon ground white pepper
¼ cup dried whole lime powder (sold in Middle Eastern groceries, made from Persian limes)

Suleiman Almulhem
(See "Saudi Arabia," Lucy M. Long and Nailam Elkhechen, with Suleiman Almulhem, *EAFT*, pp. 549–52.)

～

Scotland (Northern Europe), Scots or Scottish American (Scotch-Irish; Ulster Scots)

Scotland is one of the ancestral homes for numerous Americans whose families date to colonial times. The culture has been highly romanticized, and icons of bagpipes and thistles tend to be found in areas, such as the parts of the southern Appalachia, celebrating that heritage. Scottish food was also one of the foundational culinary cultures of the United States, but it has generally not been carried over as an ethnic symbol. Consuming oatmeal or whiskey, for example, does not mark anyone as Scottish. Haggis, on the other hand, a sort of sausage made of sheep's "pluck" (liver, lungs, heart) and oatmeal and cooked in a sheep's stomach, is generally treated as a joke and tends to appear only at Burn's Day celebrations. Another food that is an iconic Scottish one in the American imagination is Scotch shortbread. These rich cookies are usually sold in tins with Scottish designs and are frequent accompaniments to tea. They also tend to appear at any event celebrating Scottish heritage or culture.

Scotch Shortbread (Cookies)

4 cups flour (all-purpose)
1 cup sugar (can substitute 1 cup packed brown sugar)
1 pound butter (cold and cut into cubes)

Preheat oven to 325 degrees. Combine flour and sugar in large bowl. (Some cooks cream the sugar and butter first; then add the flour.) Cut in the butter with a fork. Dough should look crumbly. Knead dough on a floured surface until smooth. Add more flour if the dough is too sticky. Pat the dough into an ungreased pan; 15×10×1 is best to get even baking. Use a fork to pierce the dough, making a design. Bake at 325 for 25–30 minutes until lightly browned. Cut while still warm into 4 dozen squares. Let cool.

Tavia Rowan
(See "Scotland," Hannah M. Santino, *EAFT*, pp. 552–55.)

⌣

Senegal (West Africa), Senegalese American Food

Thiebou-dienne (pronounced "cheb-boo-jen"), considered the national dish of Senegal, is often a midday meal typically eaten around a common bowl by family and invited friends. *Thiebou-dienne* has traveled with Senegalese immigrants to cities around the United States in the last forty years, but the dish, created in the northwestern coastal town of St. Louis by families from the Wolof ethnic group, may also be the ancestor of Louisiana red rice.

A good Senegalese cook is judged by the *Thiebou-dienne* that she prepares, and although women are the primary cooks, many Senegalese American men learn to make this comfort food. Gorgui N'Diaye remembers as a youngster in Senegal, on the rare occasions when his family served a different dish for the midday meal, he would find the house of a playmate where *thieb* was on the menu. In the 1960s before moving to Paris and New York for college, he learned how to cook the dish from his mother and older sisters.

Poulet Yassa, a Diola dish from the south of Senegal, has become standard fare in African restaurants in the United States as well as for festive occasions in Senegalese immigrant homes.

Thiebou-dienne (Stewed fish with rice)
Serves 10–12

Preparation and seasoning of fish:
1 large bunch of parsley, coarsely chopped
1 or 2 large cloves of garlic
1 large onion, chopped

2 fish or beef bouillon cubes
2–3 small hot peppers
Salt and pepper to taste
5 pounds of whole fish cut into thick crosswise slices (grouper is preferred
by many Senegalese)

Grind seasonings, parsley, and onion with a mortar and pestle. Stuff the fish with the seasoning mixture. Set aside.

Stew:
2 or 3 large onions
1 large eggplant
1 head cauliflower
6 large carrots
1 medium cabbage
1 pound fresh okra
4 large sweet potatoes
1 to 2 cups peanut oil (the traditional recipe calls for more oil than is
generally used in American cooking)
2 6-ounce cans of tomato paste
3 quarts of water
1 4-inch piece of dried fish (available at Spanish or African markets)
5 cups of rice
Salt and pepper to taste
Cayenne or red pepper flakes to taste
Dried and preserved conch (called *yett* in Senegal), optional

Chop all vegetables, except one onion and the okra, and set aside. Chop the last onion and set aside separately.

In a large pot (8- or 9-quart capacity), heat peanut oil until hot. Carefully, to prevent splashing, add tomato paste and single chopped onion. Sauté for 10 to 15 minutes.

Add chopped vegetables to pot with 3 quarts of water. Bring to boil and cook for about 10 minutes. Add okra and cook another 5 to 7 minutes.

Add dried fish and stuffed fresh fish pieces and cook for another 35 to 45 minutes.

Take fish and vegetables out with a slotted spoon and keep warm.

Wash rice three times and measure liquid in the pot to make sure you have 10 cups of liquid to the 5 cups of rice. Add rice and simmer with the lid on until done, about 20 to 25 minutes.

To serve, put cooked rice in a large bowl or platter and top with fish and vegetables.

Poulet Yassa (Chicken with onions and lemon)
Serves 10 to 12

Marinade for chicken:
  Juice of 12 lemons
  Dijon mustard to taste
  Cayenne pepper to taste or 2 or 3 whole red peppers
  Salt and pepper
  2 beef bouillon cubes dissolved in ½ cup of warm water

Stew:
  12 to 15 chicken breasts, thighs and legs (about 5 pounds)
  8 to 10 chopped onions
  5 cups rice
  ¾ cup vegetable oil
  ¾ cup lemon juice
  1 small jar Dijon mustard
  6 beef bouillon cubes (dissolved in 1 cup hot water)
  2 to 3 bay leaves
  Garlic powder to taste
  Black and red pepper to taste
  Salt to taste
  2 6-ounce jars of pitted green olives

In a large bowl, mix together the marinade ingredients and marinate the chicken overnight (or at least 6 hours).

Remove chicken from marinade and prebake in oven at 325°F Fahrenheit. Instead of prebaking, the chicken can be sautéd in a little oil.

Heat oil in a large, heavy pot. Sauté onions until soft. Add chicken, lemon juice, mustard, spices, and bouillon cubes. Cook on medium heat for about 1 hour. Add olives when chicken is almost done. Serve over rice.

To serve and eat Senegalese style, pile the rice in a large, wide serving bowl and arrange the meat and sauce in the center with chicken pieces evenly distributed around the center.

Spread a large cloth on the floor and place the bowl in the middle. After guests have washed their hands and removed their shoes, invite them to sit around the bowl. Each guest should eat the portion directly in front of them, and a good host or hostess makes sure there is enough food in front of each guest and will be sure to invite guests to eat to satisfaction.

Food is eaten only with the right hand. (In Senegal it is considered very bad manners to use the left hand, which is used to wash the body.) To eat, keep fingers together and scoop a mouthful of rice, chicken, and sauce, squeezing it into a compact ball against the side of the bowl directly in front of you. Then, you should be able to pop it neatly into your mouth. When you have finished eating, and only then, you are allowed to lick the sauce off of your fingers and wash your hands with soap and water. Often, the host or hostess will provide a bowl of warm, soapy water and towels for this purpose. A polite guest will eat well, compliment the host or hostess, and say *surnaa* ("I'm satisfied") when finished eating.

Diana Baird N'Diaye
(See "Senegal," Hannah M. Santino, *EAFT*, pp. 555–57.)

～

Serbia and Montenegro (Southern Europe), Serbian American; Montenegrin American

Serbians and Montenegrins share a similar Slavic background, but Montenegro declared its independence from Serbia in 2006. Both food traditions have roots in Mediterranean, Turkish, and Austrian/Hungarian cuisines, featuring potatoes, chili peppers, onions, cabbage, fish, various fresh and cured meats, and an array of cheeses. Serbian and Montenegrin immigrants to the United States have settled predominantly in urban areas, and their food habits mirror, to an extent, those of contemporary mainstream Americans as well as other ethnic groups with Slavic heritage. An example is *Sarma*, a stuffed cabbage dish found in many eastern and southern European American households.

Sarma (Stuffed cabbage rolls)
Yield: 6 servings

    1 large cabbage head
    1 pound lean ground beef
    1 pound ground pork
    1 cup uncooked long-grain rice
    1 medium onion, finely diced
    1 large egg, lightly beaten

2 garlic cloves, minced
1 teaspoon salt
1 teaspoon coarse ground black pepper
½ teaspoon ground paprika
1 16-ounce jar of sauerkraut, rinsed and drained
1 8-ounce can of tomato sauce
Water as needed

Steam cabbage until outer leaves are soft. Remove leaves. Reserve tough outer leaves. With a paring knife, remove ribs from the tender leaves. Mix ground beef, ground pork, rice, egg, onion, garlic, salt, black pepper, and paprika. Place 2 tablespoons of the mixture on each leaf and wrap the leaf to encase it. Line the bottom of a casserole dish with the sauerkraut. Place cabbage rolls seam-side-down onto the sauerkraut. Cover cabbage rolls with tomato sauce, adding water as needed to cover. Bring the sauce to a boil and reduce to a simmer. Cover and simmer for 3 hours, adding water as needed.

Charles Baker-Clark
(See "Serbia and Montegro," Charles Baker-Clark, *EAFT*, pp. 557–60.)

Seychelles (Eastern Africa), Seychellois American Food

An archipelago in the Indian Ocean consisting of 155 islands, Seychelles is the smallest African nation. The British and French colonized it, and languages spoken there today are primarily French and Creole. Few citizens immigrate to the United States.

Daube de Banane Plantain (Braised plantains)

4 large plantains
Cinnamon leaves or 1 cinnamon stick
1 vanilla pod
4 tablespoons cane sugar
½ teaspoon salt
1 pinch ground nutmeg
1 can (14 ounces) coconut milk

Peel the plantains, cut in half, and slice lengthwise. Put the cinnamon leaves or stick in a wide pot and the plantain pieces on top. Add the vanilla, sprinkle with sugar, salt, and nutmeg, and cover with coconut milk. Bring to a boil and cook for 10 minutes on high heat and simmer for 25 minutes.

Karin Vaneker
(See "Seychelles," *EAFT*, p. 560.)

～

Sicily (Southern Europe), Sicilian American, Italian American

Sicily, a region on the southern coast of Italy, has a distinct food culture separate from Italian. It has incorporated Greek, Spanish, French, and Arabic influences, and features seafood, semolina (as *cuscusu*) and rice, heavy breads, and tomato sauces. Sicilians began immigrating to the United States in the second half of the 1800s, and their food traditions became representative for Americans of all Italian cuisines. Although many Sicilians have assimilated into American society, there are still pockets of Sicilian culture in the United States. The Sicilian community in Gloucester, Massachusetts, is singular. Almost all of the families are from two villages in Sicily, and their cuisine is a reflection of those towns. Food names, like *Mudiga* and *Pasta Gazoots*, Italian words that translated into something new when spoken in the Gloucester streets, are unique to this culture.

St. Joseph's Day, March 19, is a significant celebration, and a pasta created specifically for that day is made in homes throughout the city. Since St. Joseph's Day comes during Lent, the grand luncheon served on March 19, after nine days of evening novenas, is always meatless. The flour used to make the special St. Joseph's Day bread and the *fettucini* for the St. Joseph's Day pasta is blessed the night before by a priest. The pasta is handmade that morning, with a *goranza*— a Gloucester Sicilian word for "sauce"—of chickpeas, favas, cauliflower, and fennel fronds, clearly a dish to be eaten on the cusp of winter and spring.

Each Gloucester family has its own variation on St. Joseph's Pasta. This recipe comes from the Tarantino family; generations and branches of them all come together early in the morning to begin making the St. Joseph's Day feast.

Gloucester, Massachusetts, St. Joseph's Pasta (*Fettucini* with cauliflower, fennel, and dried beans)
Serves 6–8

1¼ cups dried fava beans
1 can fava beans

⅔ cups dried lentils
⅔ cups yellow split peas
Salt and pepper to taste
1 tablespoon + ¼ cup olive oil, divided
1 can chickpeas, rinsed
1 small cauliflower
1 can black-eyed peas, rinsed
1 fennel bulb, stems and fronds, sliced thinly
Salt and pepper to taste

Wash dried fava beans and let soak over night. Rinse canned *fava* beans and peel. Drain soaked fava beans. Cover in fresh water and simmer in a very large pot until tender. (This pot will hold all the sauce.)
Wash the lentils and yellow peas and pick out any small stones. Place in a medium-sized pan with water to cover, and cook until slightly tender. Add salt, pepper, and 1 tablespoon olive oil while cooking.

Wash and cut up cauliflower and place in a medium to large pan covered with salted water, and cook until slightly tender.
Add lentils with their liquid, peeled fava beans, chickpeas, cauliflower with its liquid, black-eyed peas, and chopped fennel to the large pot with the now cooked, dried fava beans, and mix everything together. Pour in ¼ cup oil, and taste for salt and pepper. Simmer ½ hour or until the fennel is tender and the flavors mingled. Cook the pasta as directed. Follow directions below for finishing the pasta.

4 cups sifted all-purpose flour
½ teaspoon salt
4 eggs
6–8 tablespoons cold water

Sift flour and salt into a large bowl. Make a well in the center of flour. Add eggs one at a time, mixing slightly after each addition. Use hands for this. Gradually add 6 to 8 tablespoons of cold water. Still using your hands, mix well to make a stiff dough. Turn dough onto a lightly floured surface, and knead dough into a ball. Knead for approximately 20 minutes. Allow dough to rest. Then cut off small portions, the size of a small egg, and shape them between your hands into a football shape. Roll each of these shapes through a pasta machine first set on #3 to slightly flatten, and then set on #6 to flatten more. Allow to rest again on clean dish towels. Then cut a final time into *fettucini* shapes. Spread pasta ribbons out again on a clean surface so that they can dry slightly and not stick together. Bring a large pot of salted water to boil. Add pasta, and cook for 8 minutes. Drain. Ladle pasta into the prepared sauce, which will still have a lot of liquid. Allow pasta and sauce to "marry," letting it sit on a low temperature for 15 minutes before serving. When serving, stir up from the bottom to make sure you get all the *goranza*.

Heather Atwood
(See "Italy," Anthony Buccini, *EAFT*, pp. 314–23.)

～

Sierra Leone (Western Africa), Sierra Leonean Food

Sorrel is a popular herb in Sierra Leone, but is generally thought of as a weed in the United States. It is not usually available in grocery stores, but it grows in most yards that have not been treated with chemical herbicides. This sauce can be used on any meat, although fish is a staple in Sierra Leone. It is then eaten with *fufu*, made originally from fermented cassava pounded into a paste. The process for making *fufu* is time consuming, so in the States, people use Bisquik pancake flour mix as an alternative. Traditionally, the *fufu* would be used to scoop up the sauce by hand, but spoons are more common in the United States. Rice traditionally is also a basic starch and frequently is used instead of *fufu*.

Fufu is made from Bisquick: 2 cups Bisquick to 1 cup of water. Mix into a thick paste.

Sorrel Sauce with Fish on *Fufu*
Serves 4

> ½ pound sorrel leaves
> Fish, tilapia (1 whole fish, cleaned and descaled or 2 filets)
> Water—enough to cover
> Salt
> Pepper

Clean the sorrel leaves and remove the stems. Cook in water and change the water two to three times to reduce the sour taste of the leaves. Drain and squeeze the remaining water from the leaves. Pound the sorrel into a paste. Put fish in pot, and cover with water, and add the sorrel paste, salt, and pepper, and any other desired seasoning. Cook for 5 to 10 minutes. Let it cool, and serve with *fufu*.

Esther Spencer
(See "Sierra Leone," Esther Spencer, *EAFT*, pp. 560–62.)

～

Singapore (Southeastern Asia), Singaporean American

Singapore "cuisine" frequently means hawker food, the food served at open-air food courts and street vendors. An amalgam of Singapore's multicultural society—Chinese, Malay, Indian, and Eurasian—hawker fare is enjoyed by everyone. In the United States, many Singaporean Americans attempt to make these dishes at home, though not on an everyday basis. Ready-made spice pastes (Prima Foods is a popular brand) and spice packets make prep for favorite dishes like beef *rendang* and *laksa*, and *bak kut teh*, easier, but they lack the pungency and flavor of freshly made, from-scratch pastes.

Other everyday meals in the United States reflect the various ethnicities of Singapore. Chinese ones include soy-braised pork belly, *congee*, stir-fries, simple soups, *hor fun* (wide rice noodles in gravy), steamed fish, fried noodles, and fried rice. Malay meals include *mee rebus* (egg noodles with sweet potato gravy), beef *rendang*, *mee goreng* (fried noodles); Indian: *dals*, meat and egg curries, *rasam* (tamarind soup), vegetable *pulav* (vegetables and rice). Eurasian ones might include curry devil/*debal* (meat curry) and pork chops. Snacks, meanwhile, mix these traditions with cream puffs, curry puffs, fried bananas, sausage rolls, chicken pies, and fried spring rolls. The recipe included here is a popular one among Singapore Americans, and is named after the province in China where it originated.

Hainanese Chicken Rice
Makes 6 to 8 servings

Chicken:
    1 (3 to 3½ pounds) chicken
    1 thumb-sized piece of ginger, bruised
    4 cloves garlic, smashed
    6 green onions
    3 quarts water
    3 teaspoons salt
    1 tablespoon sesame oil

Rice:
    3 cups jasmine rice
    Vegetable oil
    4 cloves garlic, minced

4 Asian shallots, minced
3 cups chicken broth
4 (1/8-inch thick) slices ginger
1 teaspoon salt

Garnish:
1 large cucumber, sliced
Fresh cilantro leaves or sprigs
Bottled chili-garlic sauce
Thick black soy sauce

Prepare the chicken. Trim chicken of excess fat and reserve for rice. Rub chicken inside and out with 1 teaspoon salt. Stuff the cavity with ginger, garlic, and green onions. Bring water and remaining 2 teaspoons salt to a boil in a 6- to 8-quart pot large enough to hold chicken. Put chicken, breast down, in water. If chicken isn't fully submerged, add more water. Cover and return to a boil. Reduce heat to a simmer and cook chicken for about 35 to 45 minutes. Test by poking a chopstick into its thigh; if the juices run clear, the chicken is cooked. Let broth drain from chicken cavity, then plunge bird into a large bowl filled with ice and cold water. Reserve broth for rice and soup. Cool chicken completely and discard ginger, garlic, and green onions. Drain and pat dry with paper towels. Rub sesame oil into the chicken skin. Cut into serving pieces. Make the rice. Render reserved chicken fat in a wok over moderate heat. Discard solids and add enough vegetable oil to make 4 tablespoons fat. Add garlic and shallots and stir and cook over moderate heat, until golden brown and fragrant. Add rice and cook, stirring gently, 1 minute. Transfer rice mixture to a rice cooker. Add chicken broth, ginger, and salt and cook according to manufacturer's directions. Assemble. Arrange chicken pieces and cucumber on a large serving plate. Garnish with cilantro and serve with individual bowls of rice and soup, and little dishes of chili-garlic sauce and black soy sauce.

Pat Tanumihardja
(See "Singapore," Pat Tanumihardja, *EAFT*, pp. 562–65.)

⁓

Slovakia (Eastern Europe), Slovak American Food

Over four hundred thousand Americans reported Slovak ancestry in the American Community Survey from 2008 to 2012. Slovaks settled primarily in the Midwest and Mid-Atlantic states (particularly Pennsylvania, Ohio, Illinois,

New Jersey, and New York) beginning in colonial times and throughout the 1900s. As political boundaries shifted in the homeland, cultural identity and food practices altered as well. As was the case with other Eastern European immigrant communities, some food practices and dishes were maintained in the United States but vanished in the area of origin, and others became "pan" Eastern European (such as *pierogis*, nut rolls, and cabbage rolls) due to intermarriage and assimilation. At the same time, there are specific fillings and ways of making some traditional dishes that remain Slovak. Basic ingredients include cabbage, potatoes, rice, cheese, wheat flour, beef, fish, sausage, pork, and onions.

Stuffed cabbage (*halupki*) is one of the most popular and well-known dishes made by Slovak Americans. Interestingly, some Slovak immigrants first learned about it when they came to America, perhaps because some Slovak foods came from specific regions of Czechoslovakia. Known in some families as "pigs in a blanket," the cabbage is rolled around ground beef, rice, and onion and baked with tomato sauce. Another popular dish also made by other European Americans (typically called *piergoi*) are *pirohy* (dough stuffed with cheese, sauerkraut, prune, or potatoes) and boiled, fried, or steamed.

Desserts, typically thought of as treats for holidays, include cookies and *kolache* or *kolachi* (sweet yeast pastries). Kolache is made with a variety of fillings: walnut (sometimes called "Hungarian Nut Roll"), poppy seed, and fruit.

Kolache (Hungarian nut cookies)
With permission from Helen "Sandy" Sourlis

Dough:
  2 cups flour
  2 3-ounce packages cream cheese
  ½ pound oleo (margarine)

Filling:
  1 6-ounce bag walnuts (finely chopped)
  2 tablespoons sugar
  ¼ cup milk

Mix together flour, cream cheese, and margarine. Refrigerate dough. Divide the dough into balls and roll out about ¼ thick, then cut into 2 inch × 2 inch squares (or a bit smaller). Mix walnuts, sugar, and milk together. (You want enough milk to hold the sugar and walnuts together.) Place a teaspoon or so of filling in a corner of the square and roll up. Sprinkle a little sugar over each cookie before baking.

Bake at 375°F for about 10 minutes.

Cindy Sourlis Mooney notes: "Mom would make the dough ahead of time, separate the dough enough for each batch and cover with wax paper and put into the refrigerator to use when she was ready to bake. It kept well for a few days, so when she was ready to do all the baking the dough was already prepared."

Susan Eleuterio
(See "Slovakia," Susan Eleuterio, *EAFT*, pp. 565–67.)

~

Slovenia (Southern Europe), Slovene American Food

Potica (pronounced "poh-teet-suh") is a very traditional nut roll in both Slovenian and Slovene American homes. It is typically served along with coffee or tea, and is decidedly old world in flavor profile, as it is only mildly sweet and relies on nuts as a filling, as do many central European desserts and sweets. The following is a recipe based on one Marylynne Offredo serves for holidays and other special occasions in Massillon, Ohio.

Potica (Nut roll)

> 1 cup butter, melted (about two 4-ounce sticks)
> 2½ cups flour
> ½ cup milk
> ¼ teaspoon salt
> 2 packages (¼ ounce each) dry active yeast
> 2 tablespoons sugar
> ¼ cup lukewarm water (approximately 90°F)
> 3 egg yolks (Keep the egg whites, once separated; you will need them for the filling.)

Mix melted butter and milk and allow to cool. (One can do this in the microwave or on the stove in a saucepot.) Mix yeast in lukewarm water (this activates the yeast). Place in the bowl of a 5-quart mixer, and allow to sit several minutes. While waiting, sift together flour, salt, and sugar. Whisk the egg yolks into the milk and butter mixture. Add to the base mixture of water and activated yeast. Add sifted dry ingredients to the mixing bowl and knead on medium for approximately 3–4 minutes, ensuring all butter is thoroughly mixed in. The dough will be very tacky. Put dough in a floured bowl and cover with plastic wrap (to ensure a skin will not form). Refrigerate overnight.

Filling:
½ cup ground nuts (walnuts are traditional)
1 teaspoon cinnamon
3 tablespoons sugar
3 egg whites, stiffly beaten
2 tablespoons milk
1 cup sugar

In a small saucepan, mix ground nuts, sugar, cinnamon, and milk over medium heat. Let cool. Beat the egg whites until stiff peaks develop, gradually adding one cup of sugar. Fold in the previously made filling. Roll out half of the dough into a 20-inch square on a well-floured cloth. Spread ½ of the filling over dough and roll up as a jelly roll. Put into a greased loaf pan. Roll other half and proceed in the same method as above. Bake 1 hour and 5 minutes at 350°F (internal temperature should reach 190°F). If desired, glaze with a mixture of confectioners' sugar and milk (see glaze recipe below). Allow to cool. Slice and dust with powered sugar if desired (unnecessary if you used the glaze). Serve with whipped butter.

Glaze recipe:
3 tablespoons confectioner's sugar
2 teaspoons milk

Mix until smooth, brush onto hot potica, and allow to cool before service as directed above.

Nicholas Eaton
(See "Slovenia," Nicholas Eaton, *EAFT*, pp. 567–69.)

Solomon Islands (Oceania, Melanesia), Pacific Islander American, Melanesian American, Soloman Islander Food

Slippery Cabbage Soup

1 bunch of slippery cabbage (edible hibiscus)
½ quart coconut milk
1 onion, chopped
3 shallots, small pieces

2 tomatoes, chopped
2 medium sweet chili peppers
Salt

Slice the hibiscus very fine. Put the coconut milk in a pot, bring to a boil, and add the onions. Stir in the hibiscus and tomato pieces; bring to a boil. Add the shallots and chili peppers, and continue to simmer until the ingredients are well cooked. Add salt to taste.

Karin Vaneker
(See "Melanesia," Karin Vaneker, *EAFT*, pp. 407–11.)

⌒

Somalia (Eastern Africa), Somali American Food

Somali refugees began coming to the United States following the outbreak of the Somali Civil War in 1991. As of August 2012, approximately eighty-five thousand Somalis have immigrated, and most live in close-knit ethnic communities across the country, particularly Columbus, Ohio; Minneapolis, Minnesota; and Maine. The vast majority practice Sunni and Sufi Islam. Thousands of years of trade with India and the Arabian Peninsula, as well as a history of colonial rule by Italy and Great Britain, have influenced the foodways of the Somali people. Those traditions are being replicated and adapted in the United States to new circumstances.

The little fried triangles, called *sambuus*, are a very popular dish among Somali Americans. Some even call it their national dish, although it probably originated in Indian *samosas* introduced through ancient trade routes. The treats are eaten not for regular meals but are snacks, brought to parties, and are typically used to break the Ramadan fast each evening. *Sambuus* are a very adaptable and flexible food and are frequently sold in Somali American groceries and shops, where they are popular with Somalis and non-Somalis alike. They can be prepared quickly and easily with spring roll wrappers found in the frozen section, as in the recipe below, demonstrating the fusion of different ethnic traditions that frequently happens in American food culture.

Sambuus (Samosas or stuffed savory pastries)
Adapted from Abdi Sharif, proprietor of the Community Halal Store in Burlington, Vermont.

Pack of spring roll wraps
2 boiled potatoes (cooked but still firm), diced into small cubes
1 pound ground beef
1 large onion, finely diced
1–2 jalapeño peppers (to taste)
2 tablespoons to ½ cup chopped cilantro (to taste)
¼ cup flour
¼ cup water, or as needed
Oil for frying
Salt to taste
Optional extra flavorings: pepper, coriander, cumin, curry, and cardamom powder, minced garlic

Heat a small amount of oil into a large pan. Add the ground beef, onion, potatoes, and chopped cilantro to pan and cook until meat is cooked and the liquid has been absorbed, making sure to break up any clumps that form. Set aside the beef to allow it to cool. The beef must be dry and completely cooled for the *sambuus* not to be soggy. Mix water and flour together to form glue. Cut the spring rolls into 3 rectangular strips. Fold the bottom over and again to create a cone, spoon in about 2 tablespoons of filling, fold the top flap over, continue folding until only a small flap overhangs the triangle, and use more flour/water glue to seal the *sambuus* shut. See online for how to fold *sambuus*. Heat a generous amount of oil in large pan over medium-high heat. Cook small batches of *sambuus* at a time until golden brown (about 1–2 minutes). Be careful—it's easy to burn them. Drain on paper towels.

Katrina Wynn
(See "Somalia," Alyce Ornella with Shamsa Ahmed, *EAFT*, pp. 569–73.)

⌢

South Africa (Southern Africa), South African American Food

South African cuisine is as varied as the many ethnic groups making up its citizenry. The main influences on the national cuisine of the country are Dutch, German, French, Portuguese, Xhosa, Zulu, Indian, and Malaysian. One treat South Africans continue to make in the United States: the deep-fried, doughnut-type pastries called *Makoenya*. These are often served as a snack, especially for children and for parties, and frequently appear at holiday celebrations. They are served with any meat dish, such as chicken curry or beef stew. These might also be accompanied by *rooibos* (red bush), a popular South African herbal tea, which has also gained favor among American herbal tea drinkers for its bold taste and health benefits.

Makoenya (Pastry)

> 6 cups white flour
> 3 teaspoons yeast
> 1 cup sugar
> ½ teaspoon salt
> 1 spoon margarine
> 1 cup lukewarm water
> 10 cups cooking oil
> 2 cups shortening (In South Africa, cooking oil and Holsum—similar to Crisco—would be used.)

In a bowl, mix flour, sugar, salt, and margarine; set aside. Mix yeast in a cup of lukewarm water and let it stand for 10 minutes. Mix in all dry ingredients, and knead for 20 minutes. Dough should rise fully. In an hour your dough should be ready. Using a large spoon, scoop the dough and drop on a lightly floured surface. In a large, deep pan or deep fryer, heat cooking oil. Add shortening, mix, and heat until almost boiling.

Drop several makoenya into the cooking oil. Fry until golden brown and drain on paper towels.

Nomvula Mashoai-Cook
(See "South Africa," Betty Belanus with Nomvula Mashoai, *EAFT*, pp. 573–76.)

⌣

South Sudan (Northern Africa), Sudanese American

A decades-long civil war in Sudan has displaced thousands of individuals from the more than five hundred ethnic groups living in the area. Thousands of refugees from what is now South Sudan, which is largely animist and Christian, have come to the United States, and they represent diverse tribal cultures—primarily Didinga, Acholi, and Madi, but also Dinka, Murle, Nuer, and other tribes.

Culinary practices among South Sudanese groups are quite similar and share ingredients and dishes with neighboring nations to the south, but they are very distinct from the spicier cuisine of Sudan. A staple is a type of flat bread, usually called by its Arabic name, *kisra*. This large, thin pancake is prepared from sorghum flour, often mixed with a bit of wheat or millet flour so that it will not crack during cooking. In South Sudan, *kisra* is prepared on a large, hot, flat cooking stone over a fire, but in the United States a greased frying pan is commonly used. Frequently vegetable oil in lieu of the traditional sesame oil is used. At main meals, *ugali* (porridge) and *kisra* are served with vegetable stews and sometimes with minced meat such as goat or beef. Okra or *molokhia* (also called *otego* in Acholi) is added to give the stew a slimy consistency.

In the United States, many of these traditional foods are not prepared on a daily basis by South Sudanese immigrants, and American frozen and fast foods are frequently consumed. All meals are traditionally prepared and served by women; however, unmarried South Sudanese men in the United States, such as the "Lost Boys of Sudan" (men who were forced to flee their homes as children and survived arduous journeys to safety), have out of necessity learned to cook their own meals. The recipe below comes from one of these "Lost Boys" and demonstrates how modern ingredients are being incorporated into traditional recipes to make dishes that are still meaningful carriers of identity and culture. The author, Dominic Raimondo, now resides in Salt Lake City, Utah, and says this is his favorite food and he eats it with rice and bread during lunch and dinner. He also observes: "*Kabab* is a number one favourite food you will never miss to find in South Sudanese communities around the world and in South Sudan. It is very delicious and breath-taking dish! In a big occasion and all holidays, you will never miss [seeing] it."

Kabab (Beef and vegetable skillet fry)

2 pounds boneless beef meat
5 pounds potatoes
3 large onions
2 teaspoons of "beef magic" (prepared spice)
Ready-cut carrot mix with peas
4 cloves of garlic
½ teaspoon black pepper
3 green peppers
1 small (6 ounce) can of tomato paste
Oil
Salt

Clean the potatoes, and peel and cut them into small slices. Put the oil into the cooking pan and fry the potatoes. Cut onions into small pieces and fry until they turn brown. Cut meat into small pieces; put the meat into the cooking pan with the onions. Once the meat is well cooked, add salt, "beef magic," black pepper, and tomato paste. Mix in the garlic in the meat, boil carrots into the meat, and let it warm for 3 minutes. South Sudanese *kabab*! You can eat this South Sudanese kabab with rice and bread.

Recipe by *Dominic Raimondo*. Introduction adapted and expanded by Lucy M. Long
(See "South Sudan," Felicia McMahon, *EAFT*, pp. 576–79.)

Spain (Southern Europe), Spanish American Food

Gazpacho originated in Andalusia and has become a dish widely known outside its home region as an excellent summer soup. Many versions exist in the United States, and can be found in non-Spanish restaurants, at farmers' market produce demonstrations (always during tomato season), and in private homes. The Spanish recipes usually include stale bread blended into the soup, but American versions frequently leave it out, and some incorporate novelties such as figs and watermelon. Tomatoes and peppers are some of Spain's most popular vegetables, and eggs are a staple as well. The three ingredients are combined for a dish similar to an American omelet, but it is more likely to be eaten at dinnertime rather than for breakfast.

Gazpacho (Chilled tomato soup)
Serves 4

2 pounds ripe red tomatoes
1 small cucumber, cut into pieces
1 small onion, cut into pieces
½ medium-sized green bell pepper, cut into pieces
1 garlic clove, peeled and chopped
1 tablespoon sherry vinegar
¾ cup Spanish extra-virgin olive oil
Salt to taste

Combine vegetables in a blender with sherry vinegar and blend until the mixture becomes a thick liquid. Start with 1 tablespoon of vinegar, but add more to taste depending on the character of the tomatoes. Add the olive oil, season with salt, and blend again. Strain the gazpacho and refrigerate for at least an hour. Garnish with rustic white bread, cubed and fried in olive oil on the stovetop, or with some combination of diced vegetables from the recipe above. Drizzle with additional olive oil if desired.

Piparrada (Eggs scrambled with tomato and pepper)
Serves 1

> 2 tablespoons olive oil
> 3 tablespoons finely chopped onion
> 1 clove garlic, minced
> 3 tablespoons green pepper, finely chopped
> 3 tablespoons red pepper, finely chopped
> 2 tablespoons cured ham, finely chopped
> 1 small tomato, chopped
> Salt
> Freshly ground pepper
> 2 eggs

Heat 1 tablespoon of the oil in a medium skillet and sauté the onion, garlic, green pepper, and red pepper slowly until the peppers are tender. Add the ham and cook another minute. Mix in the tomato, salt, and pepper. Cover and cook another 10 minutes.

In the bowl, lightly beat the eggs with a fork. Stir the vegetable and ham mixture into the eggs. Wipe out the skillet and heat the remaining oil. Add the contents of the bowl, and stir constantly with a fork until the eggs are set but not dry.

Whitney E. Brown
(See "Spain," Whitney E. Brown, *EAFT*, pp. 579–87.)

⁓

Sri Lanka (South Asia), Sri Lankan American Food

Sri Lankan American foodways are a conglomeration of long-held culinary practices, past colonialisms, and present diversities. Dutch, Portuguese, and British colonizers brought new foods to Sri Lanka, which were fused with Sinhalese, Tamil, Arab, and Veddah (indigenous peoples) cuisines. Religious infusions of Islam, Buddhism, Hinduism, and Christianity added even more layers to an already labyrinthine culinary heritage. Sri Lankan Americans introduced these gastronomic complexities to the U.S. food landscape. The journey from one continent to another called for ingredients such as fresh coconut, coconut milk, and treacle (a sweetener extracted from kitul palm trees) to be substituted for canned coconut products and honey; and tamarind for *goraka*, also known as *gamboge*. A less successful example is basil for curry leaves. A reliance on coconut milk distinguishes Sri Lankan American cooking from other South Asian American cuisines.

The word *curry* is a British invention referring to both a type of dish and to a spice mixture. The British simplified and standardized a very complex culinary practice that entailed household cooks adding distinct blends of freshly ground spices to each dish. The freshness and individuality of these spice blends helped guarantee unique flavors for each dish. "Curry powder" allowed the British to easily imitate the taste of Indian and Sri Lankan dishes. Cinnamon, however, distinguishes Sri Lankan curries, and Sri Lankan Americans freely add this spice to already packaged curry blends.

Brinjal (Eggplant curry)

    1 large eggplant
    1 small red onion, chopped
    2 green chilies, chopped
    ⅓ cup coconut milk
    2 teaspoon turmeric
    1 teaspoon salt
    2 teaspoons chili powder
    2 teaspoons roasted curry powder
    1 cinnamon stick, approximately 2 inches
    3 cloves
    1 sprig of curry leaves
    2 tablespoons vegetable oil
Sauce (mix together and set aside):
    4 cloves garlic
    2-inch piece of ginger, grated
    1 teaspoon sugar (or sugar substitute)
    ½ cup water
    1 tablespoon apple cider vinegar

Slice eggplant into thin 3-inch strips (like French fries) and mix with 1 teaspoon turmeric and salt; let marinate for 45 minutes. Heat oil and brown eggplant strips until crisp, then drain on paper towels. Add more oil to pan and sauté onions and chilies; as they cook, add cinnamon, cloves, and curry leaves to the pan. When the onions are translucent and begin to brown, add 1 teaspoon turmeric and roasted curry powder to pan, mix well, and continue to cook until onions are brown. Add eggplant to the pan, mix well, and then add coconut milk; mix well and then let rest for 2 minutes. Add sauce mixture to the pan, stir well, and continue to cook for 5 to 10 minutes.

Pol Sambol (Coconut sambol)

1 large coconut, grated
3 tablespoons chopped red onion
1 tablespoon maldive fish (dried tuna fish—dried shrimp is used in Malay sambols, but gives a different taste)
1 lime, juiced
1 tablespoon chili powder or crushed red chilies
1 teaspoon salt (optional)

Use a food processor or coconut scraper to chop the coconut; pour into a large mixing bowl. Using the food processor, blend the red chilies, onion, and maldive fish for 30 seconds until fairly smooth. Add mixture to coconut, add lime juice and salt if desired, and mix well.

Use as a sauce or condiment.

Jane Dusselier
(See "Sri Lanka," Jane Dusselier, *EAFT*, pp. 587–93.)

⁓

Sudan. See South Sudan.

⁓

Suriname (South America), Surinamese American Food

Surinamese food is similar to other cuisines in the Greater Caribbean and reflects the ethnic diversity of the smallest South American country, drawing ingredients, cooking techniques, and dishes from native Indians, colonial powers, African slaves, and Asian immigrants. This variety was then brought by immigrants to the United States and adapted to available ingredients. Clipfish is dried, salted cod, and salted beef is beef in brine, a simple version of American corned beef. Sweet potatoes can be substituted for cassava, one of the basic starches throughout Africa and the Caribbean. *Telo*, fried *cassava* strips, is the Surinamese equivalent of French fries and is eaten with and without clipfish.

Telo met Bakkeljauw (Deep-fried cassava strips with stewed clipfish)

1 pound dried and salted clipfish (dried, salted cod)
5 tablespoons sunflower oil
1 onion, chopped
5 tomatoes, chopped
½ teaspoon black pepper
2 pounds *cassava* (frozen or precooked), cut into finger-thick pieces
8 cups sunflower oil (for deep-frying)

Desalting the clipfish:
Wash the clipfish under cold running water and pull off the skin of the fish. This can be done with the aid of a knife. Put the fish in a pan with about 2 quarts of cold water. Bring to a boil on high heat; simmer the fish for 10 minutes. Remove the fish from the water with a slotted spoon and rinse with cold water. Use a paper towel to clean the edges of the pan. Put approximately 8 cups of cold water into the pan and add the fish. Bring to a boil and simmer for 10 minutes. Remove the fish from the pan with a slotted spoon and allow to cool. Remove the bones and divide into small pieces with clean fingers.

Preparation of *bakkeljauw*:
Heat 5 tablespoons oil in a deep frying pan and add the onion. Braise 5 minutes, until soft. Stir occasionally. Add the tomatoes and add the small pieces of clipfish. Stew for 5 minutes, stirring occasionally, on medium heat. Reduce the heat to low.

Deep-frying cassava:
Heat the oil to 375°F in a wok or deep pan (about 10 inches).
Fry a few pieces (about 5) of cassava at a time, until golden brown. Remove with a slotted spoon and place on paper towels. Sprinkle with salt or serve with *bakkeljauw*.

Surinamese Sauerkraut with Salted Beef and Potato

4 ounces salted beef
1 pound potato
3 ounces butter

1 large onion, chopped
2 tomatoes, finely chopped
2 tablespoons tomato paste
2 tablespoons sugar
1 pound sauerkraut
1 Madame Jeanette pepper

Rinse the salted meat under cold running water. Put 8 cups of cold water in a pan, bring to a boil over high heat, and add the salted meat. Simmer on low heat for 20 minutes and remove with a slotted spoon. Allow to cool, remove the fat and hard pieces, and cut the meat into thin slices. Peel the potatoes and cut into chunks. Heat the butter in a skillet and add the onion and meat pieces. Braise for about 5 minutes, until the onion is soft; stir occasionally. Add the chopped tomatoes and potatoes and cook about 5 minutes. Add the tomato paste, sugar, and 1¼ cups of water. Bring to a boil and simmer for about 10 minutes. Stir in the sauerkraut and put the Madame Jeanette pepper on the sauerkraut. Put a lid on the pan and simmer for about 20 minutes (until the potatoes are done). Remove the Madame Jeanette pepper after 5 to 10 minutes.

Karen Vaneker
(See "Suriname," Karin Vaneker, *EAFT*, pp. 593–96.)

⁓

Sweden (Northern Europe), Swedish American Food

Christmas is the season for extensive baking for Swedish American families. Home bakers turn out a variety of Christmas cookies, especially *pepparkakor*, ginger cookies; as well as the deep-fried *fattigmann*, spritz butter cookies made with a cookie press; *sandbakkels*, shortbread cookies pressed into small tart molds; and the delicate *krumkake*, made with a special iron and rolled into cylinders. Another traditional treat is *julkaka*, a sweet, rich Christmas bread flavored with cardamom and studded with fruits and raisins. Julkaka may be purchased in Scandinavian bakeries during the Christmas season, or it is easy to make at home.

Julkaka (Yule cakes)

1 package dry yeast
¼ cup warm water

1 cup milk
¼ cup butter
¼ cup sugar
1 teaspoon salt
1–1½ teaspoons ground cardamom, to taste
1 egg, beaten
3½–4 cups flour
1 cup raisins, or a mix of raisins and fruits (glacé fruit or small pieces of dried fruit)

Glaze:
1 egg, beaten
Pearl sugar or granulated sugar for sprinkling on top

Preheat the oven to 375 °F. Scald the milk and melt the butter in it. Let cool to lukewarm. In a mixing bowl, dissolve the yeast in the warm water and let stand a few minutes until bubbles appear. Add all ingredients except flour and raisins/fruit and mix well. Add flour a cup at a time, beating thoroughly after each addition, until the dough forms a soft ball. Turn dough out onto a floured board and knead for about 10 minutes. Knead in the raisins or fruits, form the dough into a ball, and let rise in a greased bowl covered with a clean kitchen towel until doubled in size. Punch down the dough, form it into a round loaf for baking, and let rise again on a greased baking sheet until doubled in size. Brush the beaten egg over the loaf to glaze, then sprinkle the loaf with sugar. Bake 30 minutes or until the loaf sounds hollow when tapped on the bottom.

Amy Dahlstrom
(See "Sweden," Amy Dahlstrom, *EAFT*, pp. 597–602.)

Switzerland (Northern Europe), Swiss American Food

Swiss American food is frequently stereotyped as cheese-based, notably fondue, in which bread is dipped into melted cheese, although fondue in Switzerland is more varied. That has been adapted to melted chocolate. The food culture is more varied, of course. One traditional dish considered representative of heritage is *kuttle* (tripe) and is eaten in winter. Also, the season surrounding Lent includes food traditions that have been passed down through generations and frequently differ according to region. Immigrants from the canton of Glarus have a pastry, *Fashnacht Kuekli,* which some cantons refer to as "Knee Caps" or "Big Nothings."

Cheese Fondue

1 pound Swiss cheese, coarsely grated (about 4 cups)
3 tablespoons cornstarch
¼ teaspoon white pepper
½ teaspoon salt
¼ teaspoon nutmeg
1 clove garlic
2 cups buttermilk

Toss cheese with cornstarch, salt, pepper, and nutmeg. Heat buttermilk with garlic over low heat. When hot, remove garlic. Add cheese mixture. Stir constantly until the cheese is melted. Serve from pan by having individuals dip cubes of bread or bagels or cut fruits such as apple.

Chocolate Fondue

3 milk chocolate bars (3 ounces each, or 2 chocolate bars and 1 3-ounce bittersweet chocolate bar)
⅓ cup heavy cream
2 tablespoons brandy (kirsch or an orange-flavored brandy)

Melt slowly to a smooth consistency while stirring. Dip fruit or angel food cake cubes.

Fashnacht Kuekli (Deep fried pancakes)

Pour 2 cups of hot milk over ½ pounds of butter and let cool. Beat 4 eggs until foamy, and add ½ teaspoon salt. Add to cooled milk mixture and then add about 8 cups of flour to make stiff dough. Roll very thin, dinner-plate-sized pieces (or stretch over the knee cap). Deep fry in fat. When cooked, sprinkle with sugar.

Kuttle (Tripe)

Place 2 pounds of tripe into an enamel pan, cover half with water. Simmer for 1½ hours until soft and tender. Cool and drain. Then slice very thin.

Brown 4 tablespoons butter and 2 tablespoons flour in a heavy skillet. Add 3 cups of cold water and a cube of bouillon. Add the tripe, salt, pepper, and caraway seeds and a dash of white wine. Let set ½ hour before serving with rye bread.

Linda E. Schiesser
(See "Switzerland," Linda E. Schiesser, *EAFT*, pp. 602–7.)

~

Syria (Western Asia), Syrian American Food

Syrians first started immigrating to the United States in the late nineteenth century due to turmoil within the Ottoman Empire. These immigrants were mostly Christian, but a second wave in the latter half of the twentieth century were mostly Muslim. Most Syrians have integrated fully into American society, holding professional positions and degrees in higher education. Syrian American food is part of the larger categories of Mediterranean and Middle Eastern cuisines that have recently become popular in the United States, particularly among vegetarian and health-conscious eaters as they use a large amount of nonanimal fats such as olive oil, nuts, and seeds. Most of the ingredients for Syrian food are available in mainstream supermarkets as well as in ethnic groceries, and many of the dishes have been adopted into American food culture. The two dishes included here, for example, can easily be purchased throughout the country as packaged mixes as well as prepared in restaurants and groceries. They are frequently not associated specifically with Syria, even though they are staples in that cuisine.

Syrian Hummus (Chickpea dip)

> 1 15-ounce can garbanzo beans (also called chickpeas), rinsed (reserve a few beans for garnish, if desired)
> 2 cloves of garlic, pressed
> 1 lemon, juiced
> 2 tablespoons tahini
> Salt, to taste
> Olive oil, for garnish
> Paprika or cumin, for garnish

In a food processor or blender, combine the tahini and lemon juice until well incorporated. Add the garbanzo beans, garlic, and salt and blend, stopping periodically to scrape down the sides of the food processor to ensure complete integration of all ingredients. The mixture might be chunky or thick; add water or ice a little at a time, and blend, to achieve the desired consistency. To serve, spread in a relatively shallow bowl, creating a dough-nut-like divot with the round end of a spoon; this will act as a moat for the olive oil garnish. Generously fill the moat with olive oil and sprinkle paprika on as garnish. Reserve a few whole beans for garnish, placing them in the center, or use pickles or parsley for décor.

Syrian Tabbouleh (Parsley-bulgur salad)

1 tablespoon bulgur (bulgur #1), finely ground (dry bulgur, do not soak in water)
1 tomato, finely diced
1 lemon, more or less, juiced
2 green onions, finely chopped
2 bunches parsley, finely chopped
2 teaspoons fresh and/or dried spearmint, to taste (Every cook prepares her tabbouleh differently, depending on whether she has fresh spearmint or her preference for the taste of dried spearmint.)
Olive oil, to taste
Salt, to taste

Wash the parsley and lay out to dry. Place the bulgur in a large bowl (the bowl you will make the entire salad in). Dice the tomato very finely and pour it and all of its juice over the bulgur to soak. Meanwhile, "pick" the parsley, that is, arrange all of the parsley so that the bottom of the leaves are aligned and the stalks are in a bundle; when this is done, cut off the stalks and dis-card, and finely chop the parsley (traditionally this is done with a *mezzaluna* knife). Add parsley and onion to bulgur/tomato mix. Toss with olive oil, lemon juice, salt, and mint.

Note: Syrian tabbouleh is made dry—not having a "sauce"—versus Leba-nese tabbouleh, which isn't considered made well unless it has a "zoom"—the extra liquid that the tabbouleh sits soaking in.

Sally M. Baho
(See "Syria," Sally M. Baho, *EAFT*, pp. 607–11.)

T

Taiwan (East Asia), Taiwanese American Food

Taiwanese cooking is luscious and rich. Bold, assertive seasonings like five-spice powder, basil, sesame oil, and fried shallots bring character to the food of this island. These flavors linger in your palate and memory long after they've been consumed. The Taiwanese are also fond of texture, celebrating "mouthfeel" in embracing chewiness, fattiness, and slipperiness. *Lu rou fan* (Mandarin) or *Loh bah bun* (Hokkien), braised aromatic pork on rice, represents the Taiwanese predilection for assertive seasonings and sumptuous textures.

Lu rou fan is a staple of Taiwanese cuisine. Served in homes and in restaurants, it is easy to prepare but is impactful in its taste. During poorer times of the past, this dish would have been made with scrap cuts of meat, simmered slowly to tenderize and stretch out limited protein among many diners. The star of this dish is the resulting sauce, which coats and elevates humble white rice into a sumptuous delicacy. This rich, soy sauce–based braise is fragrant and deeply savory. In America, Taiwanese American versions feature rich cuts like pork belly. Or they incorporate store-ground fatty pork, a convenient time saver for the home cook with no time to grind their own. This version acknowledges the acculturation of this dish to American lifestyles in its use of pork belly and ground pork.

Lu rou fan or Loh bah bun (Braised aromatic pork on rice)

2 tablespoons vegetable or peanut oil
3 garlic cloves, finely minced
1½ pounds pork belly (skin removed), cut into bite-sized pieces
½ pound fatty ground pork (preferably a 60/40 mixture)
1 shallot, finely minced
1 tablespoon sugar
2 teaspoons five-spice powder
1 cup Shaoxing rice wine
2 cups chicken stock (low-sodium stock preferred)
¼ to ½ cup regular soy sauce
3 to 4 tablespoons dark soy sauce
1 star anise
1 bay leaf
3 or 4 eggs (optional)
2 scallions, sliced into rings

Heat the oil in a large saucepan, Dutch oven, or wok over medium heat. Once hot, add garlic and shallots. Let gently cook until pleasantly fragrant and just golden, about one minute. Add the pork, breaking it up into pieces with a spatula as you stir. Continue to cook, stirring occasionally, until browned. Sprinkle sugar and five-spice powder on the meat, and toss until sugar is dissolved. Pour in rice wine, raise the temperature to high, and bring to a boil. Let the alcohol cook off for about 1 minute. Add chicken stock, regular soy, dark soy, star anise, and bay leaf. Stir to incorporate and bring to a boil. Lower heat to medium low or low. Cover and simmer for at least one hour. Two hours ensures a really luscious dish. Optional: While the dish is cooking, hard-boil the eggs in a separate saucepan. Cool, peel, and set aside.

When the pork is done, add the eggs, and bring the pot to a gentle simmer. Turn off the heat. Let the mixture sit, uncovered, for fifteen minutes to let the flavors meld. This dish can be refrigerated for several days. Reheat before serving.

Right before serving, bring to a boil and let reduce to thicken the sauce. Serve with steamed rice, sliced eggs, and sliced scallions as garnish. A fragrant long-grain variety like jasmine rice pairs nicely. Feel free to drizzle the meat and its sauces directly over a bowl of rice. As with many braises, the leftovers are even better the next day, if there are any left.

Willa Zhen
(See "Taiwan," Willa Zhen, *EAFT*, pp. 613–15.)

⌣

Tajikistan. See Central Asia.

⌣

Tanzania (East Africa), Tanzanian American

The relatively small population of Tanzanian Americans in the United States tend to be well-educated professionals who maintain close ties among themselves and make efforts to celebrate their cultural heritage with food.

Tanzanian cooking combines African ingredients with spices that originated on the Indian peninsula. Staples include *ugali* (cornmeal porridge), *chapati* (Indian-style unleavened flat bread), and *wali* (rice). These are served with accompaniments, which might include: meat stews (beef, goat, lamb, chicken, fish), ground nut stews, eggplant, beans, amaranth greens, kale, and both the flesh and the leaves of sweet potatoes, cassavas, and pumpkins. Coconut milk is important for flavoring and thickening, and common spices include turmeric, black pepper, garlic, ginger, chili peppers, and curry blends. Tomatoes are frequently added to these dishes, making them different from similar ones in Eritrea and Ethiopia. *Pilau* is rice dish infused with spices, meat, and potatoes and usually served with *kachumbari*, a tangy tomato sauce. It is often featured at holidays and, to be more festive, can include nuts, raisins, and vegetables. A special spice mix called *pilau-masala* can be made or purchased for pilau, and consists of cumin, cardamom, black pepper, cinnamon, and cloves.

Pilau (Rice dish)

  1 cup basmati rice
  2 potatoes, cut into quarters
  2 tablespoons oil (olive or coconut)
  1 cup cubed meat, beef or chicken (Optional for a vegetarian dish; but traditionally a piece of meat with the bone would be preferred.)
  ½ cup onions, minced
  1½ cups garlic ginger paste (equal parts ginger and garlic, minced or crushed)
  1½ tablespoons *pilau-masala* (see above)
  1 teaspoon ground flax seeds
  2 to 3 cups water or broth (chicken or beef)

½ cup coconut milk (canned)
Cilantro
Salt
Black pepper

Brown beef in 1 tablespoon oil at high temperature. Remove from pan. Sauté onions, garlic, ginger, and rice in same pan with oil until translucent. Add spices (whole cardamom, cinnamon, ground flax seeds) and mix thoroughly. Mix coconut milk with water or broth. Add to rice. Add potatoes. Add meat (optional). Cover pot, sealing lid with a paper towel, and turn to lowest heat. Simmer until liquid is absorbed, about 30 minutes.

Serve with *kachamburi* (mixture of onions, tomato, cilantro, and lemon/lime juice).

Kale (or other greens)
Enough to make 4 cups

Kale greens
1 onion, minced
4 garlic cloves, crushed
2 tomatoes, skinned and chopped
1 teaspoon salt
3–4 tablespoons oil (coconut is preferred)

Wash and slice kale (or other greens). Do not dry. Put in pot. Place onions, garlic, tomatoes, and salt and oil on top of greens. Cook on high until kale is softened.

Samaki Wa Nazi (Coconut fish curry)

2 pounds firm, white-fleshed fish (whole fish with head is preferred, but fillets are acceptable)
3 tablespoons oil (coconut is preferred, but olive or vegetable is acceptable)
1 onion, chopped
4 cloves garlic, crushed
1½ teaspoons curry powder
4 tablespoons tomato paste
1 red chili pepper (or 1 teaspoon chili paste)—adjust for spiciness
1 lemon (or 2 tablespoons lemon juice)
2 cups coconut milk

Rinse fish. Season with salt. Brown it in oil over medium heat. Remove from pan. Using the same pan, add more oil if needed, then sauté onion until brown. Add garlic and sauté for 1 minute. Add curry powder, tomato paste, pepper, and lemon juice. Stir together until blended. Stir in the coconut milk. Bring to a boil, then decrease heat to simmer. Add fried fish. (Can also skip the frying.) Simmer until fish is done and sauce has turned creamy (about 10 minutes). Serve with *ugali* and kale.

Sarah Tekle
(See "Tanzania," Alan Deutschman with Sarah Tekle, *EAFT*, pp. 615–17.)

Thailand (Southeast Asia), Thai American Food

One of the most popular Thai dishes in the United States is *Pad Thai* (also spelled *Phat Thai*). Originally a street food in Thailand, it is a standard on menus at Thai restaurants as well as pan-Asian and fusion cuisine establishments. Packaged mixes as well as the separate ingredients are also sold in many American supermarkets. We recommend you visit a Southeast Asian market if at all possible.

Pad Thai (Stir fry rice noodles)

10 ounces thin rice noodles
1 cup raw chicken meat, sliced
4 cloves garlic, minced
2 teaspoons cornstarch
2 tablespoons soy sauce
3 cups bean sprouts
2 eggs
⅓ cup chopped peanuts
½ cup chicken stock
¼ teaspoon black pepper
Oil

Toppings:
1 cup chopped scallions or spring onions
⅓ cup chopped peanuts
1 cup chopped cilantro leaves (coriander plant) for garnish

Pad Thai Sauce:
  ¾ tablespoon tamarind paste OR substitute 1 tablespoon rice vinegar OR
    white vinegar
  1 tablespoon lime juice
  2 tablespoons brown sugar (in addition to brown sugar below)
  2 tablespoons fish sauce (use either Vietnamese *nuoc mam* or Thai *nam pla*)
  2 teaspoons Thai sweet chili sauce or ¼ to 1½ teaspoons chili flakes
  2 tablespoons brown sugar

First marinate the chicken with soy sauce and cornstarch. Next, make Pad Thai sauce by combining tamarind paste and ¼ cup of water. Then add fish sauce, red chili sauce, and brown sugar. After that, crack eggs in a bowl and stir to break yolks.
Soak noodles until opaque (roughly 20 minutes). Drain and run through cold water. In a large frying pan on medium high heat, stir-fry 2 tablespoons of oil with the garlic. Stir for one minute and add the marinated chicken. Begin adding small amounts of chicken stock until the stock is used up and all the chicken is cooked. Push chicken into the edge of pan and pour eggs into center. Scramble the eggs. Add the noodles to the chicken/egg mixture. Pour Pad Thai sauce over the noodles. Lift and turn the noodles to fry them for 2 minutes. Add bean sprouts and black pepper. Continue turning noodles until they are finished cooking. Add lime juice. Add fish sauce or chili sauce to taste, if desired. Serve immediately. Top with chopped cilantro leaves, spring onion, and peanuts.

Rachelle H. Saltzman and Emily Ridout
(See "Thailand," Rachelle H Saltzman with Emily Ridout, *EAFT*, pp. 617–23.)

~

Tibet (Southern Asia), Tibetan American Food

Every culture has some sort of filled dumpling or turnover. The Tibetan version, *momos*, has become very popular in urban centers in the United States and can be easily adapted to fit American tastes. Beef, chicken, or pork can be substituted for the traditional yak or goat meat, and the vegetables traditional for the filling—potatoes, onion, and cabbage—are already part of mainstream tastes. Variations of ingredients and textures (how finely chopped or blended, or how chunky, the ingredients are) can lead to a range of flavor and palate experiences. Regional varieties have developed among the Tibetan and Nepalese diaspora in other countries, as can be seen in the appearance of momos on menus in a range of "ethnic" restaurants in the United States. As for recipes, a Nepalese individual stated that she does not have a recipe and that most South Asians never follow a recipe. Below are basic guidelines for homemade momos to adapt to your taste.

Momos (Filled dumplings)

Recipes for *momos* vary widely but include basic elements. The following makes four servings.

> 2 cups flour (white or whole wheat, or a wheat-free and gluten-free alternative flour)
> ¾ to 1 cup water (depends on the flour you use—test for consistency)

Mix flour and water and knead by hand until you make a ball of dough. Continue kneading until dough is flexible. Put ball of dough in pot and cover while preparing other ingredients.

Prepare fillings with meat or vegetables. Yak meat is traditional, but other meat can be substituted. Experiment with meats, or substitutions, of your choice.

For vegetable *momos*, chop the following ingredients finely:
> 2 onions
> 2 inches fresh ginger
> 2 or 3 cloves of garlic
> Cilantro to taste
> 1 pound cabbage
> 1 pound of tofu
> Quarter pound of brown mushrooms
> 2 tablespoons soy sauce
> 1 teaspoon of bouillon (your choice)

For meat *momos*, try the following:
> 1 pound ground beef or beef chopped into small pieces
> Put all ingredients in pot and mix.

Roll out dough thinly. Cut circles out of dough for each *momo*. For uniform-sized circles, you can use a small glass to cut out the circles, turning the glass onto the dough and pressing.

One tablespoon of filling goes into each circle of dough.

Pinch filled circles of dough closed. Boil water in a large steamer. Steam the completed *momos* for ten minutes. Serve with chili sauce, Tibetan hot sauce, or soy sauce.

Momos can also be boiled or fried.

Zilia C. Estrada
(See "Tibet," Zilia C. Estrada, *EAFT*, pp. 623–25.)

⁓

Togo (West Africa), Togolese American

Togo's food culture is similar to other nations in West Africa but shows the legacy of its colonial history with both German (beer) and French (bread) influences. *Fufu* from yams and cassava and a cornmeal cake are the basis of meals and are eaten with sauces of various kinds, usually made from some combination of tomatoes, eggplant, and spinach. Fish is also frequently used in sauces along with other types of seafood, particularly oysters and prawns, and chicken in peanut sauce is a favorite dish.

Like other immigrants, Togolese Americans adapt available ingredients to their traditional recipes. Since cassava or plantain flour is difficult to find in the United States, they find substitutions, such as mashed potato flakes or cream of wheat cereal. Also, while they traditionally would not season the *fufu*, in the United States they might add salt and pepper and even butter to the basic recipe below, giving more texture to the *fufu* but also adapting it to American tastes.

Fufu (Dough ball)

4 cups of water
2 cups plantain flour or cassava flour (sometimes called *fufu* flour) (or 2 cups of potato flakes and 1 cup of cream of wheat)

Bring water to a boil. Turn heat to low. Stir flour into water, stirring constantly to prevent sticking or lumps. Optional: Add 2 tablespoons of butter and salt and pepper. Stir in a little additional water if needed for desired consistency. Serve with soup or sauce.

Eat by taking a small ball of *fufu* and rolling it in your right hand with your fingers. Make a small indentation. Use the *fufu* to dip into the soup or sauce.

Anne Pryor
(See "Togo," Anne Pryor, *EAFT*, pp. 626–27.)

⁓

Tonga (Polynesia, Oceania), Tongan American Food

Immigration of Europeans and Asians into Polynesia resulted in a number of changes to the regional cuisine, one of the most significant of them being the introduction of canned goods such as tuna, Spam, or corned beef. Due to the insufficient land for cattle grazing and the expense of fresh beef as an import, canned goods allowed Polynesians to actively integrate foreign meats into their traditional recipes, liking the taste and its function as a symbol of the West. Additionally, new, fresh produce items also started to be imported or grown locally, such as brown and shallot onions, cabbages, peppers, carrots, eggplants, lettuce, pumpkins, tomatoes, and zucchini. One of the most popular recipes using many of these new ingredients is a salad dish of marinated raw fish with lime. In Tonga, it is known by the name of *'ota 'ika*, but variations of it can be found throughout Polynesia.

Lupulu (Corned beef in coconut milk)

> Taro leaves (washed, without stems. See entry on French Polynesia for more instructions on cooking these leaves.)
> Onions
> Tomatoes
> Unsweetened coconut milk
> 1 can New Zealand corned beef

Chop onion and tomatoes, while preheating oven to 350°F. Place several layers of taro leaves on the table and drop a tablespoon of onion and tomatoes in the middle along with two tablespoons of corned beef. Add ¼ cup of coconut milk on top and then fold the taro leaves to make a bundle. Wrap again with banana leaves or aluminum foil. Place in pan and bake for 2 to 3 hours or more, ensuring that the taro leaves are thoroughly cooked as it can irritate the throat and mouth if underprepared. Serve with rice or baked sweet potatoes or baked yams.

Margaret Magat

'Ota 'Ika (Fish salad)

> 1 tilapia (or any fresh, firm, white fish with no bones)
> 5 lemons
> 1 can coconut milk
> 1 tomato (diced)
> 1 carrot (grated)
> ½ white onion (finely chopped)
> ½ green bell pepper (sliced into strips)
> ½ red bell pepper (sliced into strips)

1 cup of spinach or lettuce (shredded)
1 red chili pepper (finely chopped)
1 tablespoon salt

Cut the fish into small cubes, then place the cubes in a regular-sized bowl. Squeeze the lemon juice onto the fish and add salt. Let it marinate for roughly 8–10 hours or overnight. With freshly caught fish, the time marinating can be cut considerably shorter. The citric acid will "cook" the fish in a process called acidification. Remove the fish from the marinade and squeeze any excess liquid off of it. Discard the marinade. Mix the diced tomato, grated carrot, finely chopped onion, sliced peppers, and shredded spinach in a large mixing bowl. Add the fish and the whole can of coconut milk. Season with finely chopped chili pepper and additional salt according to your preference.

Eric César Morales
(See "Tonga," Margaret Magat, *EAFT*, pp. 627–30.)
(See "Polynesia," Eric César Morales, *EAFT*, pp. 512–19.)

⁓

Trinidad and Tobago (America-Caribbean), Trinidadian American and Tobagonian American

Trinidad and Tobago cuisine is a study in multiculturalism. The population of the Republic of Trinidad and Tobago, a two-island nation united under one government, is a reflection of its tumultuous history of years of colonization, conquest, and immigration. The islands are primarily comprised of two major ethnic groups: Afro-Trinidadians and Indo-Trinidadians, who account for approximately 78 percent of the population. The remaining 22 percent are largely comprised of European, Chinese, Syrian, Lebanese, and mixed-race inhabitants. Much of the local food in Trinidad and Tobago, and consequently the food that is exported to places like the United States, has been influenced by the cultures of the former colonizers as well as by the confluence of other local cultures there. East Indian foodways were adapted in Trinidad and then also adapted to life in the United States. Curry dishes, along with a kind of flat bread locally referred to as *roti*, *dhall* (boiled, seasoned split peas served with *roti* or rice), and *kachori* (fried, seasoned split peas or chickpeas) show these influences. East Indian food is consumed all year round in Trinidad and in Trinidadian and Tobagonian households in the United States, but people particularly enjoy dishes such as curry chicken during Hindu holidays like Diwali.

Curry Chicken

1½ pounds chicken (boneless thighs are best, but you can use breasts or a
  mixture of both cut into small pieces)
3–4 cloves of garlic, minced
2 tablespoons green seasoning*
1 teaspoon salt, to taste
1 scotch bonnet or habanero pepper, thinly sliced (this is optional)
2 tablespoons vegetable oil, coconut oil, or olive oil
2–3 tablespoons yellow curry powder (try Trinidad brand Chief curry
  powder found in local Caribbean, African, or Mexican food stores or
  in the Mexican or ethnic food aisle in most grocery stores)
½ cup chopped onion (reserve about a tablespoon of onion)
¼ cup hot water

* In a food processor blend 3–4 springs of cilantro (stems and leaves), 2–3
sprigs of green onions or scallions, remainder of the chopped onion, and 3–4
cloves of garlic to make green seasoning. If using a whole scotch bonnet or
habanero pepper, add it to this mixture as well.

Cut chicken into small pieces and season with green seasoning and a pinch
of salt. Marinate for 30 minutes or more. Heat oil in an iron pot or skillet.
Throw in a tablespoon of onion and cook until translucent. Mix curry powder
with ¼ cup of water until smooth; add to hot oil and onions and cook for 1–2
minutes. Add chicken and stir to coat in curry; cook until curry coating chicken
is golden in color; stir well (about 5–10 minutes). Lower heat to medium and
add 2–3 cups of water and cover pot. Cook until meat is tender and sauce has
slightly thickened; add more water if more sauce is necessary. Adjust salt to
taste. Enjoy over jasmine rice or regular white rice or with roti.

Tricia Ferdinand
(See "Trinidad and Tobago," Tricia Ferdinand, *EAFT*, pp. 630–32.)

～

Tunisia (North Africa), Tunisian American Food

Tunisian food culture shares flavors and dishes with other cuisines from the
Maghreb region in northern Africa but also reflects the colonial French
legacy. Tunisian Americans brought this culture with them, and it is usually associated now with other Middle Eastern and Mediterranean culinary
traditions. *Couscous* is considered the national dish of Tunisia. Extremely

versatile, it can be made with beef, lamb, fish, spicy sausage (*merguez*), or just vegetables. Dishes are usually served with *harissa*, a chili paste that originated in Tunisia but is found throughout North Africa. Along with tomato sauce, it gives Tunisian food a distinctive red color. Made from peppers and tomatoes, *harissa* contains chilies, cumin, garlic, coriander, caraway seeds, cinnamon, and olive oil. It is used as a meat rub when mixed with oil or water and is also a popular condiment.

Tunisian Americans oftentimes use packaged couscous available in most supermarkets rather than go through the lengthy and laborious process of rinsing, cooking, and stirring that is required for traditional couscous. The recipe below calls for a traditional pot, but can also be made in standard saucepans.

Tunisian *Couscous* (Crushed wheat) with Chicken
Makes 4 to 6 servings

> 2 cups *couscous*
> 4 medium potatoes, cubed
> 2 cups baby carrots
> 1 large turnip
> 2 to 3 green peppers, cored and quartered
> 1 (10-ounce) can tomato paste
> ½ cup olive oil, to cover pot bottom
> 1 large onion, chopped
> 2 whole boneless chicken breasts
> 2 tablespoons *ras el hanout* spice mix*
> 1 tablespoon turmeric
> 1 pinch saffron, ground
> ½ teaspoon chili powder
> ½ teaspoon *harissa*, if desired (or more)
> 1 (15-ounce) can chickpeas, drained (optional)
> ¼ cup salted butter
> Salt and pepper
> Water

Pour couscous into a large bowl and cover with water until water is absorbed. Set aside. In the pot part of the *couscousiere* (special cooking pot), pour a generous amount of olive oil, maybe ½ inch deep, and the chopped onion. Add a little salt and sauté until onion is translucent. Add chicken, more salt, and brown until not pink but not overcooked. If the temperature gets too hot, add warm water to cover and continue to cook.

Add dry spices, including about ½ teaspoon salt and a generous sprinkling of pepper. Before adding the saffron, dilute in hot water. Mix thoroughly, cover, and bring to a boil. Add tomato paste and mix thoroughly. Add carrots, turnip, and green peppers. Mix thoroughly, adding enough water to cover vegetables. Add potatoes and give the stew a good stir, making sure nothing is stuck to the bottom of the pot. Add about ½ cup of water to wet the couscous. Place the "steamer" part of the couscousiere atop the stew pot. Pour in the wetted couscous; don't worry—it won't fall through the holes! Spread evenly. Make a little opening so steam can escape through a hole or two. Now, put the lid on the top and turn down the heat to a simmer.

(Note: When stirring occasionally, have a plate ready to put the steamer part on while you stir the stew. Be sure to wear oven mitts because the steam can easily burn.)

From the time you put the top on, it takes about 20 to 30 minutes to cook. The couscous will become very fluffy. If it looks too dry, pour some hot water over. Make sure the carrots are done, but turn off heat before potatoes turn to mush. Just before removing from heat, add *harissa* and drained chickpeas and mix thoroughly. (Some people ladle out some broth and add more *harissa* as an optional topping for those who like it extra hot!)

Taste-test for salt at the end. It should be slightly on the salty side to compensate for the bland couscous. Remove the couscous and pour into a large bowl. Stick a fork in a butter stick and coat thoroughly. Then ladle out some broth and coat thoroughly for very wet consistency.

Option #1: Place couscous in large bowl or platter and make a well in the center for a mixture of chicken and vegetables.

Option #2: Mix chicken pieces and vegetables throughout the couscous.

Option #3: Place the couscous and stew portions in separate bowls for assembly at the table.

(Note: Because of the amount of water you need to cover everything, you'll no doubt end up with more broth than needed. Once cool, freeze in freezer bags. It makes an ideal sauce for a quick pasta meal. Just be sure to coat with butter first; it's a crucial step to make the sauce stick.)

Ras el hanout Spice Mix

3 teaspoons ground cinnamon
3 teaspoons ground cumin
3 teaspoons ground turmeric
2 teaspoons ground coriander
2 teaspoons ground ginger

2 teaspoons ground cardamom
1 teaspoon ground nutmeg
1 teaspoon ground cloves
1 teaspoon mace
1 teaspoon cayenne pepper
1 teaspoon garlic powder
1 teaspoon ground celery seed
1 teaspoon ground black pepper
2 teaspoons cornflour

Nailam Elkhechen and Lucy M. Long
(See "Tunisia," by Nailam Elkhechen and Lucy M. Long, *EAFT*, pp. 632–36.)

～

Turkey (Western Asia), Turkish American Food

Wheat is one of the main staples of Turkish cuisine, and many of the signature dishes for everyday meals contains it in some form, including bulgur. *Ezogelin* soup is an example, and it incorporates another staple item, red lentils. It is frequently made at home, but it is also a constant fixture of kebab restaurants in Turkey and abroad, including the United States. Ezogelin, which has now become a combined word, translates as "Ezo the Bride." Ezo was a real person whose life story made its way into the domain of Turkish legend and popular culture. Zöhre Bozgeyik, nicknamed "Ezo," was born in 1909 in a village of Gaziantep in Southeastern Anatolia. Ezo had captivating beauty, but was forced into two unfortunate marriages. The first one, arranged according to the custom of swapping siblings between two families (known as *berdel*), did not last very long. The second one was in 1936 with her first cousin, who lived in Syria. Though she managed to visit her family in Turkey from time to time, Ezo was famously homesick. She died in Syria in 1956 and was buried on a hill overlooking the Turkish border. Her body was repatriated in 1999. Ezo's story made its way to folk music, and eventually to the silver screen and the stage. Ezogelin soup has no actual connection to her life, though legend has it that Ezo made it in Syria to please her difficult mother-in-law, who was also her aunt.

Ezogelin Soup

½ cup bulgur (alternatively ¼ cup bulgur and ¼ cup rice or rice with other grains like quinoa), rinsed

⅓ cup red lentils, rinsed
1 large onion, finely chopped
2–3 cloves garlic, finely chopped or minced
1 tomato, peeled and chopped
1 carrot, finely chopped
1 celery stalk, finely chopped (optional)
1 small potato, finely chopped (optional)
1 tablespoon Turkish red pepper paste (rarely found in United States, so
    substitute tomato paste)
1 tablespoon tomato paste
2 tablespoons olive oil
2 tablespoons butter
1 tablespoon dried mint
Salt, black pepper, paprika, red pepper flakes, and cumin to taste
7–8 cups (1 ½ liters) of water
1 lemon, cut into wedges

Heat olive oil and butter in a large pot over medium heat. Lower heat and cook garlic and onions until lightly golden. Add carrot (and celery and potato) and cook until softened. Then add pepper and tomato paste, and stir until mixed well with the vegetables. Add tomatoes, mint, paprika, red pepper flakes, and cumin, and cook five minutes more. Add red lentils, bulgur, and rice and stir well. Pour in water; season with salt and black pepper. Cover and simmer for 30–35 minutes on low heat until bulgur, rice, and lentils soften, stirring occasionally. Add more water if it becomes too thick. Allow to cool for 10 minutes before serving. If desired, use a hand blender to smooth when cool. Serve with lemon wedges on the side to squeeze over.

Y. Ozan Say
(See "Turkey," Y. Ozan Say, *EAFT*, pp. 636–45.)

～

Turkmenistan. See Central Asia.

U

Uganda (Eastern Africa), Ugandan American Food

Uganda has some of the most fertile soil in the world, but the former British colony has experienced extreme political upheavals and now has widespread poverty and hunger. As in other East African cultures, meals are built around starches (sorghum, millet, maize, cassava, sweet potatoes, and yams) that are supplemented with sauce from a wide range of different vegetables, beans, and groundnuts. *Posho*, a porridge or polenta from corn flour, is eaten nationwide, and plantain consumption is the highest in the world. In rural areas meat is eaten on special occasions. All parts of animals are used: Apart from offal (brains, feet, head, heart, liver, kidney tail, tongue, and bones), tripe and sweetbreads (*byenda*) are used for a sauce with the same name and are considered a cheap alternative for beef.

Many Ugandans immigrating to the United States are well educated and hold professional positions. Ugandan food traditions are not always duplicated at home, partly because ingredients are difficult to find, but also because many individuals come from urban areas where they had a variety of foods, including European and American. Ugandan dishes are featured for community and family gatherings and for some holidays.

Katogo-byenda (Tripe and sweetbread casserole)

3 pounds tripe and sweetbreads (*byenda*)
2 pounds plantain, peeled

293

5 large tomatoes, ripe, grated
2 large onions, chopped
2 medium green peppers, chopped
2 large carrots, chopped
2 tablespoons tomato paste
1 stock cube (beef)
1 to 2 chili peppers, finely chopped (optional)
1 tablespoon oil
Salt

Soak the tripe and sweetbreads in cold water for an hour and change the water frequently. Use a sharp knife to remove the outer skin from the sweetbreads and excess fat and veins from the tripe. Rinse and cut into pieces. Boil the pieces in salted water for about 20 minutes. Reduce the heat and simmer until tender, for around 40 minutes. Use a slotted spoon to remove the *byenda* from the pot. Heat oil in a casserole dish, and add the onions, green pepper, and carrots; stir frequently, and add the tomato paste. Keep stirring until the color of the paste darkens. Use a cup of the boiling water to dissolve the stock cube (or crumble it above the water). Pour it into the casserole; add the grated tomatoes and chili pepper. Bring to a boil, cover the pan, and simmer until the tomatoes are done. Gradually add the rest of the boiling water and bring to a boil. Add salt to taste. Cut the peeled plantain in pieces, and simmer the casserole gently, until they are done, approximately 20 minutes.

Gnut Sauce (Groundnut sauce)

8½ ounces unsalted peanuts
2 to 3 cups water
1 tomato, chopped
1 onion, pieces
Salt

Use a food processor and a few tablespoons of water to blend the peanuts to a smooth paste. Put the tomato and onion pieces in a saucepan; add 2 cups of water and bring to a boil. Add the peanut paste and ½ teaspoon salt, stir well. Bring to a boil, lower the heat, and stir continuously until the sauce is thick and creamy. Pour the sauce over boiled plantains or *pocho*. Peanut sauce is also prepared with pieces of dried fish (soaked overnight in cold water), cayenne pepper, and curry powder.

Pocho (Corn flour porridge)

4 cups *pocho* (finely ground white corn flour)
8 cups water
Salt

Bring the water to a boil in a large saucepan and slowly pour the corn flour into the water. Stir continuously, until all lumps are gone and the porridge starts to pull away from the sides of the pot. Serve immediately.

Karin Vaneker
(See "Uganda," Karin Vaneker, *EAFT*, pp. 647–51.)

～

Ukraine (Eastern Europe), Ukrainian American Food

There is a saying that there are as many variations of *borshch* as there are Ukrainian cooks. This soup is generally made from meat or fish stock with beetroot as the main ingredient, and it often includes cabbage, potatoes, or beans, with sour cream as a garnish. The following simple vegetarian *borshch* recipe would be appropriate for the traditional meatless Christmas Eve supper.

Borshch (Beet soup)

Serves 2–4, depending on water amount and hunger of participants

2 tablespoons oil
1 cup chopped boletus mushrooms (can substitute chanterelle or hedgehog)
1 medium onion, diced
3 large beets, peeled and julienned
1 each carrot, parsnip, and potato, diced
2 tablespoons to ½ cup beet *kvas* or lemon juice
Salt and pepper to taste
Fresh chopped dill and sour cream to garnish

Sauté onion in oil until translucent; add mushrooms and continue to sauté until soft. Add vegetables and cover with water. Simmer until vegetables are tender but not falling apart, about 1 hour. Add *kvas* or lemon juice and salt and pepper to taste. Serve hot with sour cream and chopped dill.

Charlie McNabb
(See "Ukraine," Charlie McNabb, *EAFT*, pp. 651–54.)

～

Uruguay (South American), Uruguayan American Food

Uruguay's cuisine is more European than other South American neighbors, reflecting the influence of Spanish and Italian immigrants, as well as the influence of neighboring Argentina and Brazil. Spanish presence is witnessed in the common consumption of stews, such as the *puchero*, or beef stew, or *fabadas*, bean stews traditionally from the Spanish region of Asturias. Italian influence is measured in the great quantity and variety of pastas consumed in Uruguay, including all varieties of spaghetti, lasagna, ravioli, fettuccini, vermicelli, penne, and gnocchi. Characteristically Uruguayan, the traditional pasta sauce is the Caruso sauce, made of cream, meat extract, onions, ham, and mushrooms. Also popular in Uruguay are pizzas, empanadas, and tarts, such as this Easter tart, common as well in Argentina. Reflecting its name, the *Torta Pascualina* would also be common in the Lenten period before Easter, when practicing Catholics would abstain from consuming meat.

Torta Pascualina (Easter tart)
Serves 8

3 tablespoons butter
1 cup onion, chopped
2 cloves garlic, minced
1 cup mushrooms, chopped
1½ teaspoons salt
½ teaspoon nutmeg
1 pound fresh spinach, chopped
1 cup ricotta cheese
½ cup mozzarella cheese
½ cup Parmesan cheese, grated
2 eggs
4 hard-boiled eggs
1 package frozen puff pastry sheets or pastry dough equivalent
Egg wash:
1 egg mixed with 1 tablespoon water

Chef's note: If you prefer, you may use packaged, prepared pie dough crusts. This is definitely not as "authentic," but easier in a pinch.

Preheat oven to 400°F. Prepare 9-inch springform pan by greasing bottom and sides with butter. Sauté onion and garlic in butter until soft and slightly golden. Add salt and nutmeg. Add mushrooms and sauté for 3–5 minutes. Cook spinach in a little water for 5–8 minutes, press out water, and chop roughly. Add spinach to mushrooms and cook for one minute. Remove from heat and let cool. Mix ricotta, mozzarella, and Parmesan cheese. Beat eggs and add to cheese mixture. Mix cheese and egg mixture with spinach mixture. Season with salt and pepper to taste. Roll out one of pastry sheets in a circle. Drape over prepared springform pan. Press pastry sheets into pan. Fill with cheese/spinach mixture. Slice hard-boiled eggs in half, and press them face up into filling. Roll out the other piece of puff pastry and place on top of pie. Press edges and seal them by pressing with fork tines. Brush top of pie with egg wash. Use a sharp knife to poke a few slices in the pie to release steam. After placing the pie in the oven, reduce temperature to 350°F and bake for one hour. Cover with aluminum foil if pie browns too quickly.

Lois Stanford
(See "Uruguay," Lois Stanford, *EAFT*, pp. 656–59.)

～

Uzbekistan. See Central Asia.

V

Vanuatu (Oceania, Melanesia), Vanuatuan, Pacific Islander, Melanesian American

Also see entries for Melanesia and other islands: Fiji, Papua New Guinea, Solomon Islands, and Vanuatu

The population of the over eighty islands of the Republic of Vanuatu comes to around 267,000 inhabitants. In recent years, due to natural disasters, climate change, and adverse economic conditions, Fiji, New Zealand, and the United States have become popular destinations for Vanuatuans.

Lap Lap is a staple of Vanuatuan diet and is considered the national dish. It is commonly made from a paste of (grated) taro roots, but variations also include cassava, sweet potato, and plantains. The slippery cabbage (*L. Abelmoschus manihot*) Vanuatuans use can be substituted with spinach or Chinese cabbage. The root paste is wrapped in a banana leaf and cooked in coconut milk. It can also be cooked in coconut stews such as chicken pot.

Lap Lap (Taro, cabbage, coconut milk pudding)

2 large (green) banana leaf squares
5 cups grated taro (or cassava, sweet potatoes, or plantain)
2 cups coconut milk
2 cups slippery cabbage, shredded
Salt and pepper to taste

Steam or boil the slippery cabbage for a few minutes. Spread the banana leaves on a flat surface and sprinkle with a bit of coconut milk. Add a layer of the cabbage, sprinkle it with coconut milk, and put grated taro on cabbage. Pour some coconut milk over the grated taro, season with salt and pepper, and mix. Wrap the banana leaves around the paste. Put in a pot, pour the remaining coconut milk over the parcels, and simmer for 30 minutes.

Karin Vaneker
(See "Melanesia," Karin Vaneker, *EAFT*, pp. 407–11.)

～

Venezuela (South America), Venezuelan American Food

La Reina Pepiada is a variation of a popular dish, the *arepa*, which can be served for any meal depending what you stuff it with. Traditionally the *arepa* is a breakfast food or a late-night treat, filled with savory foods. It is interesting to know that to add flair, *Areperas* (places where arepas are sold) have baptized the most popular fillings with distinctive names for immediate recognition. There is *La Reina Pepiada* (the good-looking beauty queen), an *arepa* with chicken salad, avocado, and green peas; *Domino*, like the game tiles, an arepa with black beans and Venezuelan white cheese; and *La Rumbera* (the raver), an arepa with pork shoulder and gouda cheese. More conservative *arepas* are filled with the traditional *perico* (scrambled egg with onion, garlic, and tomato).

Arepas are becoming popular in the United States and can be found in many South American– and Latin-inspired restaurants. They also are a popular street food, especially in urban areas with large Colombian and Venezuelan American populations.

La Reina Pepiada (Filled pie)
Serves 4–6, makes 4 large *arepas* or 6 small

Harina Pan flour, 2 cups (purchased in Latino groceries or carried in international sections of supermarkets)
Water, 2 cups (lukewarm)
2 tablespoons vegetable oil
Salt, pinch

Preheat oven to 350°F. Knead flour with water, and add 1 tablespoon of oil and salt until it reaches a homogenous consistency. Form round patties. With remaining oil, grease a griddle and cook patties on high on each side until a hard shell forms. Then transfer to oven. Bake for 15 minutes, or until the arepas have risen, then flip them and bake for another 10 minutes.

Salad

> ¾ pound (350 grams) chicken breast (poached or roasted, shredded)
> Mayonnaise, 4 tablespoons
> Red onion, 1½ tablespoons (minced)
> Green peas, ½ cup (steamed)
> Avocado, 1 whole (sliced)
> Salt and pepper to taste
> Mix the salad ingredients together, slice avocado, and stuff the arepa.

Andrea M. Lubrano
(See "Venezuela," Andrea Lubrano, *EAFT*, pp. 661–64.)

Vietnam (Southeast Asia), Vietnamese American

Vietnamese dishes have become trendy in American food culture since the mid-1990s. *Pho*, a rice noodle soup originally from the North, is made from a rich broth of slow-steeped bones and marrow (usually beef). Thin slices of raw or cooked beef are usually added, and the soup is garnished with fresh Thai basil, cilantro and mint leaves, bean sprouts, spring onions, sliced chili peppers, and lime wedges, that the eater adds according to taste. Variations include pork, chicken, meatballs, and tofu. *Pho* was originally a street food in Vietnam, and in the United States it is usually served at lunchtime at smaller cafes that specialize solely in the soup. These are advertised as *pho* restaurants and tend to be found in areas with a large Vietnamese population. After 2010, *pho* became popular enough to be included on menus of pan-Asian and more adventurous and trendy American restaurants. Packaged mixes for it can now be found in some mainstream supermarkets.

Pho (Meat broth noodle soup)

> Beef bones, 4 pounds (shanks, knuckles are best)
> Onion, 1, cut in half
> Fresh ginger, 5 slices
> Star anise, 2 pods
> Coriander, 1 tablespoon (optional)
> Cinnamon stick, ½ (optional)

Salt, 1 tablespoon
Fish sauce (*nuoc mam* in Vietnamese), 2½ tablespoons
Water, 4 quarts
Rice noodles, dried, 1 8-ounce package (sometimes sold as "rice sticks")
Beef—top sirloin or beef flank, 1½ pounds, thinly sliced, can be raw or precooked (other types of meat, sausages, fish, or tofu can be substituted. Tripe is traditional also.)
Green onion, 1 tablespoon, chopped
Cilantro, ½ cup, chopped
Bean sprouts, 1½ cup
Thai basil, 1 bunch
Cilantro, 1 bunch
Mint, 1 bunch
Lime, 1, cut into 4 wedges
Chili peppers, 2, cut into slices or rings
Hoisin sauce, ¼ to ½ cup
Chili sauce, ¼ to ½ cup

Pho derives its rich flavor from the beef bone broth, which is simmered for an extensive time (6–10 hours), although some cooks claim that only 3 hours is enough. A crockpot or slow cooker can be useful for making the broth. This broth is difficult to replicate without beef bones, making it difficult to offer a vegetarian option.

If desired, roast beef bones for one hour until browned. Or parboil the bones for 10 minutes. Discard the water and rinse the bones. (This helps remove some of the fat.)

Roast until charred the onion and ginger.

Bring to a boil the bones, onion, ginger, anise, cinnamon stick, coriander, salt, and fish sauce in 4 quarts of water. Let simmer for approximately 8 hours. (Some cookbooks claim that 3 hours is enough.) Strain into a saucepan, so that the broth can be brought to a simmer again once the noodles are ready.

Prepare rice noodles by soaking for 1 hour in room-temperature water. Then plunge them into boiling water for 1 minute. Remove and drain the noodles.

Separate noodles and place into 4 large soup bowls. Cover with cilantro, green onions, and choice of meat or other protein. Pour hot broth into each bowl, covering the noodles, stir and let sit 1–2 minutes. The meat will cook partially in the hot broth.

Serve with bean sprouts, basil, additional cilantro, mint, chili peppers, lime, and sauces. These are added to the soup by each eater according to taste.

Lucy M. Long
(See "Vietnam," Lucy M. Long, *EAFT*, pp. 665–71.)

W

Wales (Northern Europe), Welsh American Food

Welsh Americans share a common food culture with other immigrant groups from the British Isles, and for the most part they have assimilated thoroughly into American life. They have retained some traditions of baked goods, particularly at Welsh American gatherings. The "Welsh Cake" is a rich, small, round cake made with butter, flour, currants, and spices baked on a griddle. Usually served with tea, it has become an iconic food. Each family has their own recipe variation, and each claims theirs is the best! Other cakes, such as *bara brith*, a dark, sweet loaf cake studded with raisins, are also baked but are not nearly as ubiquitous.

Mary's Welsh Cake

2 sticks good margarine (or butter)
1 cup sugar
3 eggs
1 teaspoon or less vanilla
3 cups flour
¾ teaspoon nutmeg and cinnamon (or spice mix of your choice)
1 heaping teaspoon baking powder
Salt (optional—leave out if using salted butter or margarine)
1 cup currants

Cream together margarine and sugar, then beat in eggs and vanilla. Add flour, spices, baking powder, salt, and currants. Chill in covered bowl overnight. Make into small balls, 1 or 1½ inch, and flatten. Cook like pancakes at 325°F on an electric griddle, six to eight minutes on either side or until medium brown. Sprinkle with cinnamon sugar if desired and serve immediately while still warm.

Betty Belanus
(See "Wales," Betty Belanus, *EAFT*, pp. 673–75.)

Yemen (Western Asia), Yemeni American Food

While many Yemeni foods resemble other Middle Eastern cuisines, Otto-man- and Mughlai-style Indian influences make for some unique flavors. *Saltah,* a stew served with fenugreek froth (*hulba*) and a spicy tomato-chili salsa (*zhug*), is considered by many to be the national dish of Yemen. *Hawaij,* a spice mixture of aniseed, fennel seeds, ginger, and cardamom, is used in many Yemeni dishes, lending a distinct flavor.

Substitution of ingredients in traditional recipes by Yemeni Americans is usually out of necessity, but occasionally it is an aesthetic choice. As example is *aseed,* a large, hollowed-out dumpling filled with tangy sauce. Some Yemeni Americans prefer to use processed flour instead of the more traditional organic variety due to its smoother texture. Other changes include typical American metal pots in place of stone cookware, and stirring the dough with a small wooden spoon rather than a thick wooden rod. While lunch is the preferred time of day for heavy meals in Yemen, Yemeni Americans would instead serve aseed at dinner.

Aseed (Meat pie)

Dough:
 3 cups white flour
 2 cups wheat flour
 3 tablespoons olive oil

3 tablespoons plain yogurt
5 cups water
1 cup water
Salt to taste
Sauce:
    One whole chicken, quartered
    2 tablespoons olive oil
    2 medium onions
    2 cloves garlic
    1 green jalapeño (optional, to taste)
    1½ teaspoons ground cumin
    1 teaspoon ground coriander
    ½ teaspoon ground cinnamon
    ½ bunch of fresh cilantro
    ½ cup water
    1 teaspoon concentrated tamarind
    2 cups water
    1 teaspoon tomato paste

Place a large pot on the stove and fill with 5 cups of water; bring to a boil. Once the water is boiling, salt well and reduce the heat to medium. In second, medium-sized pot, put 1 cup of water and bring to a boil. Remove from heat. Add the yogurt, then the flour. Begin to stir the flour into the mixture with a sturdy wooden spoon. As you stir, hold the pot steady with a potholder, as the pot will still be very hot. Begin adding small amounts of the hot salted water from the large pot into the dough, ¼ cup at a time. Continue to stir vigorously as you do so, or until the dough becomes manageable but thick. Place the medium pot containing the dough mixture back on the stove, on medium heat. Once the dough starts to bubble, continue to stir and add the hot, salted water in small, ¼-cup increments from the larger pot. Continue doing so with vigor for half an hour. If need be, remove the pot from the heat momentarily and steady it using the potholder(s) again so that you may mix everything well. After getting in a few good, strong stirs, return the pot to the stove, add more of the salted water, and repeat.

Once the half-hour passes, let the dough mixture cook undisturbed for roughly 15 minutes or until it has difficulty bubbling. When it is ready, the dough should be very thick, sticky, and smooth (no lumps), and will begin to pull away from the sides of the pot. Remove the pot from the stove and let cool to a manageable, yet still hot, temperature.

Grease a large serving plate. Apply oil or flour to your hands (or wear gloves, if the dough is still too hot to touch), remove the dough from the pot, and arrange it in a circular "bowl" shape: It should resemble a large, flattened ball with a deep indentation in the middle. You can make the indentation with your hands or with the back of a large ladle or small bowl. Once it is shaped, the sauce will be served from the indentation in the dough.

Next, prepare the sauce. Do so quickly before the *aseed* (dough) becomes cold. If need be, cover the *aseed* to keep it hot.

Add olive oil to a medium-sized pot. Add the chicken and let cook.

While the chicken is cooking, place all the vegetables and spices in a blender or food processor with ½ cup of water and liquefy. Pour the vegetable/spice mixture over the cooking chicken and bring to a boil. Allow the sauce to boil for five minutes. Add the concentrated tamarind and let boil for another five minutes. Add two cups of water and the tomato paste. Lower heat, cover, and let simmer for ten minutes. Add salt to taste.

Serve immediately in the center of the hot *aseed*, with *hulba* (fenugreek froth) spooned on top of the sauce if desired. For *hulba* recipes, check online. Fenugreek is a staple item kept in most Yemeni American homes, and *hulba* is simple to make. *Aseed* is served communally and eaten with the hands. To consume, tear off pieces of the dough and dip them in the sauce. Enjoy!

Dr. Lamya Almas
(See "Yemen," Shannon Davis, EAFT, pp. 677–81.)

C⊗כ

Z

Zambia (Middle Africa), Zambian American

Zambia is a landlocked country in central Sub-Saharan Africa. Although there are seventy-two tribes in Zambia, it is known in the region for being a very conservative and peaceful country. This is due in part to Zambia's first president after independence from the UK in 1964, Kenneth Kaunda, who established the concept of "tribal cousins," "a reconciliation mechanism in which certain ethnic groups are allowed to playfully insult others, providing a useful vent for ethnic rivalries."

Zambia's only major source of economy is copper mining, although tourism is very popular in the town of Livingstone because of its proximity to Victoria Falls, one of the seven wonders of the natural world. It has very fertile land, and most Zambians are subsistence farmers growing corn, cassava, pumpkins, sweet potatoes, white potatoes, okra, tomatoes, onions, cabbage, Chinese cabbage, rape leaves, peanuts, and beans.

All Zambians eat a starch called *nshima*, which is so culturally significant that no amount of food is considered a meal unless *nshima* is present. In fact, in most Zambian languages there are separate words for "cooking" and "cooking *nshima*." Children are generally fed a thinner version of *nshima* termed "porridge," which is sweetened with sugar. Porridge can be supplemented with peanut powder for added protein for the children. It is traditionally made out of maize (corn); however, different areas of the country vary the starch used. In Northwestern province, *nshima* is made from cassava flour. In order to process the cassava tuber into an edible form, Zambian women harvest the tubers from the field, soak them in the river for several days, remove the brown outer layer from the white flesh, pound the white flesh in a mortar and pestle, lay the white flesh in the sun to dry for several days, return the dried white flesh to the mortar and pestle and pound it into a powder, then sift the powder until it is a fine flour, which is then used to make *nshima*. Fortunately, cassava flour can be purchased in ethnic groceries in the United States.

A traditional meal in Zambia includes *nshima*, a boiled dark leafy vegetable with either beans, fish, or chicken, and *supu*, a tomato-based sauce used to dip *nshima* in when eating vegetables and/or meat. The only seasonings used are salt and oil, causing most Zambian food to be bland and oversalted.

Cassava nshima (Bread)

Cassava flour
Water

Uses the same general technique as described in the *nshima* recipe from Malawi. The major differences found in cassava *nshima* are the color and consistency. Cassava powder is very fine and white. Once it is combined with the water and begins to cook, it turns into a dark gray color. Cassava nshima gets very thick while cooking. Once it is finished, it has the texture/feel of a bouncy ball. Since cassava *nshima* is much more dense and sticky than its corn-based counterpart, it is not scooped into "lumps." It is simply in a giant lump that is put in the center (family style), and each person tears off one ball of *nshima* at a time. They then roll the piece in their hand to form an edible spoon used to pick up vegetables or sauce.

Supu (pronounced soup-ew, as in *flew*) (Tomato dipping sauce)

2 tablespoons oil
2 tomatoes, diced
¼ cup onion (optional)
2 tablespoon salt

Heat oil. Add tomatoes, stirring and mashing constantly. Cook about 5 minutes. Once it forms a sauce, add onion and salt. Continue cooking until onions are no longer raw. Enjoy with *nshima*.

Ariel Lyn Dodgson
(See "Zambia," Betty J. Belanus, *EAFT*, pp. 683–84.)

~

Zimbabwe (East Africa), Zimbabwean American Food

Zimbabwe's food culture is typical throughout Sub-Saharan Africa, with an emphasis on a starch (in this case, corn), peanuts, squash, and green leaves. The staple dish, called *sadza*, is made of cornmeal and eaten at least twice a day. It is so prevalent in the Zimbabwean diet that meals are named *sadza re masikati* (meal of the afternoon (lunch]) and *sadza re manheru* (meal of the evening). Corn (maize) is ground into a flour called *mealie-meal*, which is then used for a wide variety dishes including porridges and drinks. Zimbabwe was formerly a British colony known as Rhodesia, so that bread, sugar, and tea are prevalent. Zimbabwean Americans are able to find substitutes for many of their traditional foods, but the greens they use are frequently either not available or not considered edible by Americans. Young pumpkin leaves, for example, are prepared with and without peanut butter, and are a popular accompaniment to *sadza*.

Muboora (Pumpkin leaves sauce)

 1 bunch of pumpkin leaves (about ¼ pound) (can be substituted with spinach)
 2 tomatoes, chopped
 ½ cup water
 ½ teaspoon baking soda (used to tenderize older leaves)
 1–2 tablespoons peanut butter
 Salt to taste
 A pinch of chili or cayenne pepper (to taste)

Clean the pumpkin leaves by removing the fibers. Gently break off a small portion of the stem and drag it down to the leaf. When the fibers are peeled off, peel the fibers and "thorns" directly off the leaves. Cut or chop the leaves in strips. Bring the water to a boil in a small pot and add the baking soda and salt. Add the pumpkin leaves and tomato, cover and simmer for about 10 minutes. Stir occasionally. The texture should be like cooked spinach. Remove the vegetables and put aside. Add the peanut butter to the pot and stir to a paste. Add the pumpkin leaves when the mixture starts to boil, mix well, and heat through. Add the chili or cayenne pepper. Serve hot.

Sadza (Corn porridge)

2 cups white cornmeal
1 cup cold water
3 cups boiling water

Put around ½ cup of the cornmeal in a pot, add the cold water, and stir with a wooden spoon. Bring to a boil while stirring in the boiling water. Cover the pot, reduce the heat, and let the porridge gently cook for 15 minutes. Slowly stir in the rest of the cornmeal. Stir until the porridge pulls away from the sides of the pot and forms a ball. Cook for a few minutes more and transfer to a bowl. Serve hot with vegetables and meat.

Karin Vaneker
(See "Zimbabwe," Elinor Levy, *EAFT*, p. 684.)

Index

acorn flour, 205

allspice, ground, 109, 169, 179, 180, 226, 227, 248; allspice berries, 90, 91, 92

anise, star, 39, 48, 154, 188, 189, 191, 278, 301, 302; seeds, 169, 191, 305

aniseed, 305

apples, 21, 48, 72, 108, 153, 154, 162, 167, 191, 273; applesauce, 73, 106, 172

apple cider vinegar, 108, 153, 231, 233, 268

apricot, 2, 68, 235

arepas, 300, 301

avocado, 24, 25, 56, 75, 76, 300, 301

bacon, 3, 21, 22, 30, 31, 172, 174, 175, 209, 214, 221

baking soda, 6, 7, 31, 42, 64, 221; soda bread and soda farls, 220, 221

banana, 24, 25, 32, 35, 46, 56, 74, 85, 93, 94, 127, 128, 168, 192, 236, 243, 244, 257; leaves, 32, 42, 93, 94, 98, 99, 125, 216, 217, 218, 229, 285, 299, 300; pepper, 64; wine, 35

basil, 37, 120, 268, 277, 301

bat meat, 101

bay leaves, 9, 44, 62, 200, 209, 234

beans, 5, 22, 23, 34, 44, 60, 72, 119, 159, 167, 205, 208, 239, 254, 296; black, 44, 60, 83, 84, 300; butter, 44; chickpeas, 157, 170, 171, 223, 238, 274, 289 (*also see* garbanzo beans); fava, 44, 86, 157, 158, 254, 255; garbanzo, 80, 274, 275 (*also see* chickpeas); green, 39, 87; kidney, 35, 60, 151, 152, 238; lentils, 74, 79, 86, 90, 193, 210, 211 255, 290, 291; lima, 44, 209; long, 39; red, 60, 72, 180; runner, 34; sprouts, 165, 166, 281, 282, 301, 302; white, 238

beef, 3, 4, 5 9, 13, 21, 24, 28, 29, 30, 31, 32, 40, 41, 44, 47, 48, 51, 58, 61, 62, 66, 74, 75, 76, 96, 97, 101, 102, 119, 120, 121, 127, 128, 139, 160, 161, 162, 165, 168, 181, 188, 193, 197, 198, 206, 220, 223, 225, 241, 257, 259, 265, 266, 269, 279, 288, 293, 301, 302; bones, 113, 238, 301, 301; bouiloun, 24, 51, 250, 251; broth,

About the Author

Lucy M. Long, director of the nonprofit Center for Food and Culture, explores food's role in constructing, performing, and negotiating identity, community, and meaning. She grew up in North Carolina, the Washington D.C., area, and South Korea, all of which gave her a taste of the diversity and complexity of food cultures. After earning a PhD in folklore and folklife from the University of Pennsylvania, she taught as an adjunct assistant professor at Bowling Green State University in Ohio, including, starting in the mid-1990s, courses on food and culture. She has published numerous articles, researched and curated museum exhibits, produced video documentaries, and developed curriculum materials on a variety of topics around food as well as other cultural forms. Her books include *Culinary Tourism* (2004), *Regional American Food Culture* (2009), *Ethnic American Food Today: A Cultural Encyclopedia* (2015), and *Food and Folklore Reader* (2015).